An Anthology of
Scottish
Women Poets

Edited by
Catherine Kerrigan
with
Gaelic Translations by
Meg Bateman

for Kate,

with love

from

Rod

EDINBURGH UNIVERSITY PRESS

Nairn, Scotland · May 1992

© Edinburgh University Press, 1991
22 George Square, Edinburgh

Set in Linotron Palatino
by Koinonia Ltd, Bury, and
printed in Great Britain by
Redwood Press Limited
Melksham, Wiltshire

British Library Cataloguing in
    Publication Data
An anthology of Scottish women poets
    1. Poetry in English. Scottish
       women writers –
       Anthologies
    2. Poetry in Scottish Gaelic –
       Anthologies
    I. Kerrigan, Catherine
    821.00809287

ISBN 0 7486 0125 2 (cased)

The publisher acknowledges subsidy from the Scottish Arts Council towards the publication of this volume.

The royalties from this book will be donated to the Scottish Campaign for the Homeless (Shelter).

In memoriam

Geneviève Bergeron, Hélène Colgan, Nathalie Croteau, Barbara Daigneault, Anne-Marie Edward, Maud Haviernick, Barbara Maria Klueznick, Maryse Laganière, Maryse Leclair, Anne-Marie Lemay, Sonia Pelletier, Michèle Richard, Annie St-Arneault and Annie Turcotte

who died 6 December 1989 at L'Ecole Polytechnique, Montreal

Contents

iv

CONTENTS

CONTENTS

CONTENTS

Introduction

That was my mother's tale.
Seventy years had gone
Since she saw the living skein
Of which the world is woven,
And having seen, knew all;
Through long indifferent years
Treasuring the priceless pearl.

Kathleen Raine *from* 'Heirloom'

After many years of neglect, and sometimes outright derision, writing by women has begun to find its permanent place on the cultural map. There is now available more work by women writers – past and present-day – than ever before. Novels, poems, journals and diaries have not only given great reading pleasure, but also have opened to women a new consciousness of their place in the world. The recovery of the past has played a significant part in this process, for these tales of our mothers, these spiritual heirlooms, give us a sense of a positive formative influence. These works contain the trials and triumphs of women's experience and lead us to understand that women's drive to control their lives is not some kind of modern cultural aberration, but a long and continuing desire for self-determination.

In the recovery of women's writing, the novel (for obvious reasons) has played a more important part than poetry. Yet, as I believe this anthology will show, it is in poetry that we find the most sustained tradition of women's writing. The work presented here, while rooted in a distinct geographical location, records an enormous range of poetry by women – ballads, working songs, political verse, love songs, satire, historical narratives, and much more. Dating back to at least the eighth century, this work crosses the boundaries of class, place and time to form an extraordinary continuum. In fact, this anthology presents the most sustained literary performance by women yet recorded.

The scope and range of this poetry is, by any standards, impressive. But the question of how best to present this work is a vexed one. As most historians of women's literature have recognised, works by women do not fit neatly into traditional perceptions of the growth and development of literature. The real characteristics of women's literature are only now beginning to be discovered and, with so much historical reclamation to be done, it is likely to be some time before any coherent theories emerge.

The problem then is one of arrangement. Presenting the poems in terms of subject matter was not the solution because such an arrangement did not do justice to distinctive groups within the broader national picture. Natural divisions, however, did suggest themselves.

The most obvious division was linguistic. While Scotland has several linguistic traditions, Gaelic presents itself as a distinct entity. Furthermore, women's poetry in Gaelic has a long history and, unlike women's writing elsewhere, has been well-preserved and its achievements accorded a rare equality within Gaelic culture. Although translations of several poets' work are already in print, given the nature of this enterprise, I opted for new translations by a woman poet. Meg Bateman responded instantly to the challenge and has not only translated this work, but has provided an introduction which gives a guide to the various traditions and developments of women's poetry within the broader Gaelic cultural context.

The second division which emerged was the ballad/folk tradition.[1] While the ballad is unquestionably a communal tradition, the common perception is that it was a tradition handed down by men and women. In fact, when sources are examined, it emerges that women played such a significant role as tradition bearers and transmitters that it can be claimed that the ballad tradition is one of the most readily identifiable areas of literary performance by women.

Although unintended, this point comes across very strongly in George Lyman Kittredge's introduction to the 1904 edition of Child's *English and Scottish Popular Ballads*:

A great number of [ballads]...have been derived from women, – the most stationary part of the community... Take an example. 'The Cruel Brother' was furnished to Professor Child by Miss Margaret Reburn in a version current in Ireland about 1860. With this as a starting point, let us see how far back we can trace the ballad as actually in oral circulation. In 1855 Aytoun remarks that 'this is, perhaps, the most popular of all the Scottish ballads, being commonly sung and recited even at the present day'. In 1846 Dixon notes that it is still popular among the peasantry in the west of England. In 1827 Kinloch recorded it in his manuscript from the recitation of Mary Barr of Clydesdale. In 1800 Alexander Fraser Tytler obtained a copy from Mrs Brown of Falkland... In the last years of the eighteenth century Mrs Harris learned the piece, as a child, and she recited it to her daughter long afterward. In 1869 it was printed in Notes and Queries as 'sung in Cheshire amongst the people' in the preceding century. In 1776 David Herd recorded it in his manuscript as he had heard it sung. Thus we have a succession of *testimonia* for 'The Cruel Brother' from 1860 back to 1776. (p. xxiii)

While the writer set out to trace the antiquity of the ballad, what emerges is the way in which the ballad was almost exclusively preserved and transmitted by women. The same pattern can be seen in the major male collectors of the ballad – Burns, Scott, Hogg, Greig-Duncan – all of whom refer to women as a prime source of their material. Add to this the legion of male writers who cite their mother, housekeeper or nurse (Robert Louis Stevenson's 'Cummie' comes immediately to mind) as their first teachers of old songs and stories, and a very strong case can be made for saying that the ballad presents a vital and sustained women's tradition.

It is nevertheless essential to stress that the milieu of the ballad *was* communal and that proprietary rights – male or female – were never part of the folk tradition. However, versions of particular ballads were clearly associated with individual singers. Collectors in recording ballads recognised this and identified the source of the ballad with the singer. In doing so, they unconsciously provided evidence of the major part women played in the preservation and transmission of folk literature.

While many of the ballads in this anthology can be found in Child's *English and Scottish Popular Ballads*, the versions which have been selected are from a variety of sources. In general, selection has been made on the basis of authenticity; that is, versions which seemed closest to the work in performance have been chosen over those which seemed more 'literary'. The end result may seem less elegant – there are often gaps in the story or repeated lines and words – but this gives a more realistic sense of the delivery of a work to an audience.

Even so, what is missing from the versions of the ballads in this anthology is the music to which they were sung. Those familiar with these ballads will find it impossible to dissociate the works from their familiar tunes, and that is as it should be. Bell Robertson, whose ballads are presented here, always regretted her lack of voice and once said, 'I have heard many a ballad sung, but I never heard one recited without an apology for the absence of the singing'.[2] Ideally, the words and the music should not be separated, but to include the music would have made this anthology unmanageable. All that can be done in the circumstances is to refer readers to the excellent *Greig-Duncan Folk Song Collection*, where they will find a large number of traditional ballads presented together with their musical accompaniments.

One of the great appeals of the ballad tradition is its universality. The ballad transcends national and cultural boundaries, and thus it will be clear that many of the ballads presented here are not exclusively Scottish. While it is certainly not my intent to claim any kind of superior ranking for Scottish versions of certain ballads, at the same time, the Scottish ballad tradition is unquestionably one of the richest in the world and its presentation in this anthology is designed to give some sense of the cultural and thematic range in what is primarily, but not exclusively, a national context.

The universal attraction of the ballad lies in its narrative power. The ballad is a tale told in verse and, given the predominance of women in the tradition, it is not surprising to find that many of these works recount a whole range of women's experiences. There are ballads about love and courtship which celebrate relations between the sexes, but there are many which tell of the darker side of love. Tales of forced marriage, abandonment, murder, death in childbirth, physical cruelty, jealousy and revenge, abound in the ballad tradition and are told with that stark objectivity and graphic detail which are the hallmarks of the form. The recounting of intimate experiences is often direct and frank, but it has to be borne in

3

mind that a number of these works have been bowdlerised. Many ballads in performance were bawdy, but when they began to be written down and published they were modified in order to make them more acceptable to contemporary bourgeois tastes. Of course, there were class and gender barriers. At least one male collector is known to have found some of the women's ballads too racy to print.[3]

So many of these tales, with their emphasis on faery and folklore, suggest a primitive psychology. The picture is of minds which moved in a world of marvel and fantasy, elements which might have provided explanations for the otherwise unexplainable conditions of their lives. But works which deal with fantasy are counterbalanced by ballads which tell of political activism, of women who were vociferously fighting the kind of social injustice which affected both sexes.

This range of experience in the ballad provides an entry into the broad social and cultural life of women as it was told and heard throughout the centuries. To say that the ballads are an extraordinarily rich source of women's history is an understatement. The ballad tradition represents an experential and emotional range which has few equals, and therefore offers a whole social, cultural, political and psychological text to be studied, reinterpreted and reclaimed. In the ballad, women's joys and pleasures exist side by side with their fears and anger. The latter emotions in particular are a potent reminder that Scotland – the last country in Europe to stop burning witches – has some very dark chapters in its so-called romantic past.

In identifying the ballad as a unique area of literary performance by women, it is very tempting to present the body of works which are now available to us as an homogeneous tradition. Even a cursory study of the ballad, however, reveals that there are linguistic, regional and class divisions. On the linguistic side it is evident that the density of Scots varies considerably, ranging from phonetic spellings of Scottish pronunciations of common words in English to a distinctive Scots vocabulary. In certain cases linguistic density can be associated with region. The North-East has always been a rich source of ballads, and that dialect is evident in many of the works. In the transmission of the tradition from oral to written forms, class differences certainly played their part, and for several reasons. Firstly, most of the ballad collectors were educated (although there are some exceptions) and therefore a station above those they were recording. Secondly, collectors were invariably male and this might well have influenced their selection of material. Thirdly, among those women who were identified as the source of works there are clear social differences.

Anna Gordon (Mrs Brown of Falkland, 1747-1810) is a classic example.[4] She was the daughter of a Professor of Humanities at Aberdeen University and the wife of a minister of a prestigious Presbyterian parish. She is reputed to have learned her songs from family members and servants, but undoubtedly social conventions would prohibit her from including any material which would cast aspersions on her in her role as a lady and the

4

wife of a minister. Furthermore, Anna Gordon did not write the songs down. The material was recorded by male collectors who must have had at least some influence on what was and what was not recorded. One of the three manuscripts of her songs, the Tytler Brown manuscript, came into Walter Scott's possession in 1795, that is, immediately before the publication of the *Minstrelsy of the Scottish Border*. Obviously, the material from that manuscript which Scott used would be works which were suited to a literate and (generally) a genteel audience. Anna Brown's history gives a very clear picture of the process of collecting and recording ballads, but the very fact that so much is known about her is due to her social position. As will be seen from the biographical entries on other women balladeers, information on their lives is much more difficult to come by. Often all that is known is the name: their history is largely invisible.[5]

Of course, this lack of information about women and their history is both the plague and the challenge of any study of women's activities. Nevertheless, I hold that in reading the ballads with an open mind it is impossible to escape the fact that here is a chorus of voices, different in class and education, but which offers a broad and complex picture of the psyche of women.

While in the present anthology the ballad/folk tradition has been presented as a separate entry, it has to be noted that the influence of the ballad was – and is – the strongest continuing influence in Scottish poetry. As will be seen in the work of traditional singers like Jeannie Robertson and Lizzie Higgins, the ballad in performance continued to find a place in modern life. But even outside its traditional place, the influence of the ballad on women poets has been singular. In the third section of this anthology the presence of the ballad will be felt again and again. This is hardly surprising. In its power to tell a story, in providing a place for unrecorded experience, the ballad became for many women poets the home of their history.

The third and largest section of poetry is arranged chronologically. This body of works consists mainly of poetry in Scots and Anglo-Scots. The earliest poems are, significantly, by Mary, Queen of Scots, and are translations from French and Latin. This work is followed by 'Ane Godlie Dreame', a poem in the style of the mediaeval dream vision, and one sonnet, both written by Lady Culross. Dating from the Reformation, these poems are a response to Protestant persecution and consequently are vehemently anti-Catholic.

It is not until the eighteenth century, with the development of mass publication, that a larger body of poems by women began to appear. Among the most original voices of this period is that of Jean Adam. Her impassioned 'The Impartial Law of God in Nature' sets a tone of protest against the limitations of a woman's place in the world, a protest which will be repeated over and over again in many of the poems that follow. Similarly, the course of her life from that of a bright, ambitious woman

5

with far-sighted ideas to a vagrant who died destitute in the workhouse is a pattern which is repeated too often for comfort.

It was during the eighteenth century that many traditional ballads and songs found their way into print. This material ranged from the popular and sensational broadsheets or chapbooks to more elegant works like Allan Ramsay's *Tea-Table Miscellany* (1724). A classic example of what happened to a work when it moved from an oral to a written form is 'The Flowers of the Forest'. This is a very old song about the Battle of Flodden (1513) and two versions of it are presented here for comparison. While both poems are gentrified versions of the original, in Jean Elliott's poem the Scots vocabulary and rhythm preserve elements of the older tradition. On the other hand, the poem by Alison Rutherford (Mrs Cockburn) is an Anglicised and literary version which has reduced the force and vitality of the old ballad to a tinkling prettiness.

The leisure enjoyed by aristocratic women meant that they could play their part in collecting and preserving many of the traditional songs and ballads. For those of Jacobite families there was a particular impetus for preserving the songs of a way of life which, after the 1745 Rebellion, was rapidly passing into history. Of course, as a great deal of Scottish literature will attest, a romantic past is hardly a liability for aspiring writers. Later in the period, Joanna Baillie drew on both her own family history and national myths and legends as the subject of her poems. She went on to establish a considerable reputation as a dramatist in London, but her reworking of traditional ballads like 'Tam o' the Lin', works which preserve the language and structures of the original forms, are among the best poetry she produced.

While Joanna Baillie enjoyed a considerable public reputation in her lifetime, such was not the case with Carolina Oliphant (Lady Nairne). This nineteenth-century writer produced over eighty songs under the name of 'Mrs Bogan of Bogan' and it was only after her death that her authorship was revealed. Obviously, the reason her literary activities remained secret had a great deal to do with notions of respectability and social status.

While there is much to criticise in the poetry of some aristocratic women, at the same time many of their poems show a deep sensitivity towards the plight of the poor and the situation of women whose choices in life were even more limited than their own. Dorothea Ogilvy's 'The Weary Spinnin o't', records the monotonous labour that was the lot of many peasant women in Scotland. The tedious hours spent eking out a living by the spinning wheel and the hopelessness and despair about the future come across strongly in the refrain, 'I maun spin till I grow old'.

In nineteenth-century Calvinist Scotland a respectable literary activity for women was clearly the writing of hymns and religious poems. Some representative poems are given here, but these are a minute part of the mass of material which found its way into print in the period. Much of this was written (as would be expected) by the wives of ministers and a great deal of it was popular beyond the borders of Scotland. North America in particular seems to have provided a considerable (and lucrative) market for this work, and made the names of several of the writers well known.

In contrast to this large of body of hymnody, Janet Hamilton's work is fresh and energetic, mainly because its focus is more the material than the spiritual. Her 'Oor Location' is one of those rare poems in the Scottish tradition about life in industrial Scotland. The poem uses the resources of a dialect to recreate the noise, rush, smell and smoke of life in the factory:

A hunner funnels bleedin', reekin',
Coal an' ironstone, charrin', smeekin';
Navvies, miners, keepers, fillers,
Puddlers, rollers, iron millers;
Reestit, reekit, raggit laddies,
Firemen, enginemen, an' Paddies;

Such poetry is all the more remarkable when it is known that its working-class author was a self-educated woman who did not learn to write until she was fifty-four.

Despite the strictures of nineteenth-century Calvinism, traditional songs still found their way into print and are evidence that the vitality of the folk tradition continued to be largely unaffected by bourgeois morality. Towards the end of the nineteenth century, with the growth of the women's movement and the increasing educational opportunities for women, work by women intellectuals began to find a public. The poems of Mary Gray and Ella Burton are translations of major European writers and are an indication that the potential influence of the European tradition was anticipated long before Hugh MacDiarmid made it the cornerstone of his own work and theory.

In poems which date from early twentieth century, the striking factor is not so much the innovatory techniques of modernism as the emergence of a new – and often angry – self-consciousness about women's life and times. In Agnes Begbie's poem 'My Little World', it is clear that the 'world' is one of the poet's own making – 'I built me my own little world,/Not God' – but even in this self-created world, love turns bitter and is fated to fail. As many modern women poets made the discovery that love alone could not shape their lives, it is interesting to note that there is a turning to – or a rediscovery of – earlier women writers who had faced similar dilemmas. Floris Cortis-Stanford's 'To Emily Brontë' shows what she has learned from that writer, just as, in more recent times, Liz Lochhead's 'Dreaming Frankenstein' acknowledges the feminist voice of Mary Shelley's work. But while these poets rediscovered the work of women in the English tradition, others turned to an influence closer to home.

The evidence of an emerging women's consciousness in early twentieth century poetry is a phenomenon which is fairly common to early modern women writers the world over, but there is an additional movement in Scotland which strikes me as quite unique and of great significance because it represents the continuation of an older tradition. It is now

7

well-established that the modern Scottish literary movement spear-headed by Hugh MacDiarmid was preceded by the work of several vernacular poets. A number of these were women with roots in the north-east, that region which Greig and Duncan had found such a fertile source of ballad material. The most important of these writers were Violet Jacob, Marion Angus and, the youngest of the trio, Helen B. Cruickshank. All of these women wrote in the vernacular and developed distinctive styles.

Although critics (including myself) have tended to treat the work of these women as minor ripples in the modern literary revival, I now believe that this interpretation is based on a failure to look at their work in the appropriate context. When their poems are compared with the work of MacDiarmid, the arch-modernist, they are seen as deficient. The themes and ideas of their poems seem much more of a piece with what has gone before than does MacDiarmid's poetry. But – and this is the important distinction – their work is traditional within female, not male, writing. It is the failure by critics to perceive the difference which has led to the undervaluing of these women poets. To take an example: Roderick Watson (in what is otherwise a sensitive response to Jacob's work) feels that her choice of subject matter leads inevitably to the expression of the sentimental: 'her focus is on the pains of love, the fears of children, or the onset of old age'.[6] These themes are dismissed because, in Watson's eyes, they do not produce a high order of poetry. But these are recurrent themes in women's literature, and for very good reasons. These poems need to be read – not in contrast to MacDiarmid, or a traditional male canon – but in terms of women's work and women's experience.

These poems need to be read in terms of their own tradition, a tradition which is only now beginning to be reclaimed and recorded. Furthermore, it is time to recognise that the work of this group of women poets is distinctive because their vernacular poetry – a poetry which by this period had certainly deteriorated into repetitive sentimentality in the hands of male and female writers – shows a remarkable confidence. Their poetry has a directness and assuredness which assumes the presence of an understanding audience. This contrasts starkly with the writing of other women of the period, whose sense of isolation and need for self-determination in 'a room of one's own' is the recurring chord. Why is this not the case with these writers? Where did their confidence come from? Why do these women seem so completely at home in their métier? I believe the answer lies in the fact that they drew so heavily on the ballad tradition. If, as I have argued earlier, the ballad tradition is primarily a women's tradition, I would now claim that what these women were rediscovering (however unconsciously) was the female voice of the ballad tradition. That being so, it is little wonder that the themes they deal with – the failure of love, the care and burden of children, the fear of growing old – are also found in the traditional ballad. The voices of these women are confident in the subjects they handle because a whole chorus of similar voices preceded them.

8

But while these new vernacular poets drew on the ballad tradition, they also reshaped it. One feature of the traditional ballad is its impersonality. The speaker or singer relates events with little or no sense of personal involvement. The facts – the graphic representation of events – stand for themselves and, accordingly, direct the tale. In her 'Tam i' the Kirk', Violet Jacob adopts a male persona and the end result is a fine and rhythmically haunting poem about a young man's obsessive love. From Browning onwards, the use of a persona has been a major device of modern poetry, and Violet Jacob in using this device was clearly effecting a new synthesis of old and new. That Helen B. Cruickshank understood what Jacob was doing is evidenced by her 'Shy Geordie', again a poem which very successfully adopts a male persona. Many more examples of this bringing together of the old and new could be given, but the foregoing will serve to challenge the idea that all that these women were producing were simply well-crafted, but sentimental, works in the vernacular. In fact, they were very much pioneers in the use of the vernacular as a modern medium, and while they have begun to receive some of the acclaim their work deserves, their contribution needs to be seen as central, not peripheral.

In the period following these vernacular poets, the emergence of women writers in all spheres of literary activity has been quite remarkable. True, the situation is of a piece with the extraordinary (and continuing) growth of the modern Scottish literary revival. But, significantly, in any contemporary histories of the movement, the role of women writers has been consistently underplayed and undervalued. The signs are that this will be redressed in the future when women begin to write literary histories. In the meantime, bringing the work of women together in this kind of anthology serves to highlight both the very real achievements of well-established writers and to bring to notice writers whose work has not received the attention it deserves.

Among recently discovered voices, that of Olive Fraser is perhaps the most tragic. A poet of extraordinary talent in her youth (in 1935 she was awarded the Chancellor's Gold Medal at Cambridge), through misdiagnosis she spent many years in a mental institution before she received the treatment that restored her to health and freedom. The posthumous publication in 1981 by Aberdeen University Press of a collection of her poems, *The Pure Account*, was the first real public platform her very fine work received.

Others were more fortunate. Naomi Mitchison and Kathleen Raine have long enjoyed international reputations. While Naomi Mitchison is better known for her fiction than her poetry, Kathleen Raine's poetry – a poetry often located in a Highland landscape – has always won accolades. Similarly, Jessie Kesson's popularity has stemmed from her novels, but she is quickly gaining a reputation as a poet, mainly through her wonderful readings of her own work. It was at one of those readings I first heard Jessie Kesson read a work by her friend Nan Shepherd, whose long-neglected novels are now back in print.

In the work of younger women poets the range and diversity is both enormous and impressive. Scots continues to be a viable medium for many of these poets and Sheena Blackhall in her dialect poems proves herself a worthy descendent of those earlier women poets of the northeast. For many, Rhoda Bulter's poem will be the first introduction to work in the dialect of Shetland. Tessa Ransford, who as founder and director of the Scottish Poetry Library has done so much to encourage and promote the work of both men and women poets, in her recent collection, *Shadows from the Greater Hill*, shows the kind of engagement with the landscape which is so central to the Scottish tradition.

As would be expected, in poetry by younger women writers the single uniting factor is the growth of a feminist consciousness. In the work of Alison Fell (another novelist) and Liz Lochhead (now a flourishing dramatist), their mapping of the mind of modern women is combined with experiment in form and language. They are both particularly impressive in their creative use of colloquialisms and the exploitation of cliché.

The publication of Polygon's *Original Prints II* brought to attention a whole group of new poets, many of whom promise much for the future. Their wide-ranging subject matter – the holocaust, the plight of the third world, the persistence of poverty, the destruction of the environment – does not exclude the more traditional themes of child rearing, relationships between the sexes, and the right of women to freedom of choice. No longer prepared to play the quiescent serving-maid to their male counterparts, this work makes a forceful statement about the new place of women in the art and culture of modern Scotland.

There are many more women poets whose work could, and perhaps should, have been included here, but restraints of time and space, and obtaining the consent of living poets, meant that I had to be selective. The selection is personal and if there are omissions, then the fault is mine. My purpose in producing this work was to provide a starting, not a finishing, point for the very real challenge that awaits those who are committed to the reclamation of women's literature. As I hope this anthology will demonstrate, that literature is not only a strong and vital part of a national tradition, it also belongs to the universal past of women's history and, at last, to our more promising future.

Catherine Kerrigan,
University of Guelph, Ontario, 1990

NOTES

1   I have followed David Buchan in adopting the term 'ballad/folk' in preference to 'oral' tradition. Although the work presented here has strong roots in the oral tradition, as Buchan points out, the term 'oral' suggests a non-literate society and therefore can be a misleading description (see *The Ballad and the Folk*, pp. 3-4).

2   Quoted in Patrick Shuldham-Shaw's introduction to *The Greig-Duncan Folk Song Collection*, Vol. I, p. xi.

3   The collector James Bruce Duncan wrote in his notes that the material of some of the ballads was too coarse to record (see *The Greig-Duncan Folk Song Collection*, Vol. II, p. xiii).

4   For a fuller account of Anna Gordon and her ballads, see David Buchan's *The Ballad and the Folk*, pp. 62-73.

5   Emily Lyle (co-editor of *The Greig-Duncan Folk Song Collection*) is currently researching biographical material on a number of these women.

6   Roderick Watson, *The Literature of Scotland* (Macmillan, 1984), pp. 346-8.

Gaelic Women Poets

Hundreds of songs and poems, composed by women over the past five centuries, survive in Gaelic. They may be differentiated by the form of language and metre available to the poet as a result of her social status; they may also be unified by the vigour of emotion expressed in all of them. This ever-present buoyancy could not be further from the languishing, prone Muse, so often wished upon Gaeldom by others, projecting her nostalgia onto the grand and mist-enshrouded landscapes on the edge of the civilised world. Lament and loss certainly are considered by the Gaelic poets, but these are understood as the reflex of happiness and celebration; there is no addiction to regret *per se*. Whatever the emotion – joy or sadness, love or anger, pride or shame – its expression is tightly controlled by the poet, illustrated crisply and sharply through concrete imagery.

The poems' survival depended on their acceptance by the group, for they were orally composed and orally transmitted as song. Only a fraction were recorded in writing before the last century or so, when they were collected by individuals who feared their loss as Highland society broke up. All the songs share much in terms of expression and imagery, if not in whole passages. Many are anonymous, and, in the case of the work-songs, many have composite authorship. Thus, modern notions of the poet as an individual dissolve: the song becomes the possession and the utterance of the group. A single song may be a microcosm of the experience of many women of many generations. Again and again the songs strike an extraordinarily fresh note perhaps for the very reason that the forms and diction were so well established that the singer could give more or less spontaneous expression to a whole breadth of emotion.

Every anthologist complains of the frustrations involved in making a small selection of poems from a large corpus of good work. My feelings were no different. I have tried in my selection to give examples of work from the four main traditions and to indicate the major characteristics of each group.

In order to have some sense of where and how the work of women poets fits into the Gaelic tradition, it is necessary to understand the significance of poetry in ancient Gaelic society. From the earliest times, poetry played a vital role in Gaelic society, for it enshrined the values of a largely oral culture. The chief of the tribe depended upon the poet's skill, both to affirm the chief's genealogy and to define and enlarge the kind of qualities which would ensure that he maintained his position as chief. In turn, the poet was rewarded liberally for his services with land, cattle and gold, and held a very high position in the chief's court among his advisors. The poet could exercise considerable control over the chief by choosing to eulogise or satirise him. If the chief ruled well, the society would be at peace and would prosper. If he held his position unfairly, or ruled unwisely, disorder would break out and the tribe would suffer. Therefore, it was in the interests of all – chief, poet and people – that each understood their mutual obligations to one another.

In composing their works, poets sought not to portray the chief realistically, but to present him as the ideal ruler. Thus, a panegyric code was developed and to a large extent, was the one employed by all professional poets. In these works, poets would recount the lineage which made the chief the rightful ruler and list the alliances which resulted from his lineage. The chief had to be shown as the pre-eminent defender of his clan on the battlefield and as the provider for his clan on the hunting-ground. These sections would praise the chief's pride, ferocity and fine physique, as well as his marksmanship and the excellent quality of his weapons. The social role of the chief also had to be praised, for it was in his drinking-hall that new alliances were forged and old ones consolidated, so qualities of conviviality and generosity were of prime importance. Similarly, spiritual qualities such as gentleness, piety and the ability to give good counsel were also stressed. The chief is pictured surrounded by beautiful, jewel-adorned women, drinking and gambling warriors, and poet bands drawn from afar who were attracted to the hall by the chief's generosity and who will spread news of his reputation abroad.

Because this work was formulaic, originality of thought and innovation had no place in its estimation. The appreciation of the cognoscenti was reserved for the elegant conveying of detail within the confines of strict metrical forms. By the thirteenth century, the professional poets had evolved and standardised a literary form of Irish which was used as a lingua franca in both Ireland and Scotland, a form which was to remain unchanged for the next four hundred and fifty years. Poets undertook a seven-year training in the use of this Classical Gaelic, a period deemed necessary for them to master the poetic codes and complicated metres of the form. Gaelic is a stressed language, but the metres used by the professional poets were based on the number of syllables in each line. Ornate rhyme schemes were codified too, and both internal and end rhymes were used. Professional poets continued to compose in these syllabic metres (*dán díreach*) until about 1650 when the mediaeval order of Gaelic society collapsed and with it the stability required for training bards.

As far as is known, no women poets were trained in the bardic schools, but a small number of aristocratic women did master classical forms (presumably through emulation of the court poets) and composed their own works in *dán díreach*. For example, Aithbreac Inghean Corcadail (who was the wife of the MacNeill chief and constable of Castle Sween on Gigha) in her eulogy for her husband draws heavily on the panegyric code in praising his influence and generosity, but departs from conventional expressions of grief in the opening stanza where one of her husband's personal possessions – his rosary – evokes the memory of him and the sadness she feels at his death.

Similarly, 'Lament for MacGregor of Glenstrae' was composed by a Campbell woman whose husband was betrayed and beheaded by her own people. The poem is remarkable for the way in which the poet keeps artistic control over the widely-ranging emotions of grief, despair and desire for revenge through the use of images.

A somewhat different example of the use of classical metres is that of Isabel, Countess of Argyll. Her poems are in the continental tradition of courtly love songs, which had been spread to Ireland and Scotland by travelling clerics. These works are short and understated, and her themes are those of clandestine or unspoken love. These may well have been composed as *jeux d'esprit*, rather than from personal experience, just as in a third poem (not printed in this collection) she obviously relishes telling the household (in graphic terms) of her priest's prodigious sexual endowments.

However, such poems as the above do not form the main corpus of women's work in the Gaelic tradition. This distinction belongs to the folksong tradition which flourished from the fifteenth to the eighteenth century. Although the poets who composed this work were ignorant of the language and metre of the professional poets, they shared the heroic values of the classical poets. These songmakers are often described as non-literate or unlearned, terms which are accurate only when they do not carry the pejorative associations they have accrued in modern society. Such poets were non-literate in the sense that they did not depend upon writing for either the composition or the transmission of their songs. While they did not study the poetic forms of the chief's court, they were certainly familiar with the conventions of their own folksong, for these works seem to have been composed using certain sets of formulae and conventions.

The songs owe their survival to the fact that they were work songs; they were sung to accompany communally performed tasks such as milking, spinning, weaving and, in particular, waulking cloth. The symbiotic relationship between song and task ensured both the frequent repetition of the works and their transmission to the next generation. When cloth was woven, the web was taken off the loom and washed and shrunk to an appropriate length to increase its warmth and water-tightness. The job of shrinking the cloth was performed exclusively by women and it was during these sessions (which lasted about three hours) that many of the songs were first composed or were adapted from older songs. As the cloth was pounded, the song provided a rhythmical accompaniment. Sometimes established tunes were used and these were identified by means of the chorus, which usually consisted of meaningless vocables. The chorus was sung by all, while individuals would sing the verses, sometimes well-known, sometimes newly-invented. As would be expected, by far the majority of the songs are about women's experiences. In matchmaking songs, young women are teased about prospective marriage partners, and they respond by rejecting or accepting the suitor with humorous or bawdy replies. In some of the songs, an unmarried woman will tell of her rape or seduction, or of her pregnancy and subsequent abandonment by her lover. The songs give expression to feelings of jealousy, or desire, or grief over the death of a lover. Songs which praise the lover often use the same formulas as the professional poets, but such works may also be accompanied by an erotic note which is quite foreign to the work of the professional poets. The subjects of the six waulking songs presented in this anthology are all concerned with human relationships, but the tradition is very wide-ranging and includes songs on religious, satirical, convivial and political themes, as well as songs describing hunting, home, faeries and the supernatural.

The great attraction of these songs is their directness, sensuousness and frankness. There is nothing that is affected or self-conscious, perhaps because the works were often composed extempore and yet they succeed in conveying depths of emotion. A modern reader, coming to these folksongs with notions of the necessity of originality, may well be surprised by the powerful and disturbing tensions these poems convey.

One unexplained characteristic of these folksongs is the sudden change of theme within the one song. It has been suggested that these sudden changes represent different singers, yet the sections are not arbitrarily strung together, for when the same song is collected from oral sources in widely different areas, the same type of changes in theme and diction occur.

The metre of the folksong is a stressed metre. In early examples of the form, lines would be grouped into stanzas of irregular length, linked by the assonance of the final stressed syllable. The refrain would follow every line, or even half-line, often breaking into the sense and syntax of the line. Many songs were sung in couplets which were followed by rephrasing, so that the second line of each couplet became the first line of the next. Such repetition does not come across in printed versions where, after the first few couplets, the lines are printed in stanzas. Of course, it must be borne in mind that up until this century poetry and song were not separate in the Gaelic tradition.

The third group of work represented in this selection is that of the vernacular poets. This group used the vernacular language and stressed metres of the unlearned poets, but took on much of the business of the professional poets, to the degree that they did have some social influence. In fact, they rose to fill the vacuum left by the professional poets after the dissolution of the bardic schools. This is shown in both 'Cumha do Sheumas MacGillean' ('Lament for James MacLean') and 'Alasdair a Gleanna Garadh' ('Alasdair of Glengarry'), two poems which have nothing in their content that could not have been composed in a syllabic metre four hundred years earlier. Of course the difference is that the later poems were composed by women who were seen as holding at least the unofficial role of court poet, a situation which would not have been countenanced in the earlier period.

Sileas Nighean Mhic Raghnaill (Sheila MacDonald) and Catriona Nic Gilleain (Catherine MacLean) both enjoyed considerable influence and seem to have lived secure and peaceful lives. However, Mairi Nighean Alasdair Ruaidh (Mary MacLeod) was at one point banished from Skye to Mull by the chief of her clan and was only allowed to return on the understanding that she would compose no more. The reasons for her banishment are disputed, but obviously her role as poet was an uneasy one. It may have been that her songs were bawdy or that she trespassed on areas of poetry felt to be suitable only for men. Both she and Mairearad Nighean Lachainn (whose work does not appear in this collection) remained unmarried and kept company mainly with other women who recited their works. They were buried face down under a heap of stones, a custom introduced by the Norse for the burial of witches.

The fourth group included in this selection (the work of poets of the nineteenth and twentieth centuries) is the one in which the effects of the modern world on Gaelic culture are most in evidence. By the nineteenth century, the order of Gaelic society had been disrupted by forced clearances and emigration, thus breaking irretrievably the link between clan and chief. Many works of this period lament the passing of the old ways. A few poets were able to use their skill in adjusting to the change. 'Brosnachadh nan Gaidheal' ('Incitement of the Gaels') composed by Mairi Nic a'Phearsain (Mary MacPherson, 'Big Mary of the Songs') is a poem of praise to the political leaders chosen to champion the cause of the crofters.

As a result of the strong evangelical movement in the Protestant islands, much religious poetry was, and still is, produced, which shows the influence of earlier Gaelic song.

I am alone among the four contemporary poets represented in this selection in not being a native speaker of Gaelic. As a girl, I was fascinated by the thought of other cultures existing in this country alongside my own, and I went on to study Gaelic at university. I became knowledgeable about Gaelic poetry in a way I am still not about English-language poetry, and so when I started to write poetry myself I wrote it in Gaelic. I expect I am a product of a deep change in attitude in Scotland. Ten years ago all the signs indicated that Gaelic was dying. Now no such certainty is possible. More official support in broadcasting, education and publishing is available than ever before. Throughout Scotland people express the idea that Gaelic should be cherished as a unique window on the world, our inheritance from many generations. I suggest that 'green' attitudes, rather than nationalist ones (though indeed they may be part and parcel), form the basis of this kind of thinking. It seems inevitable now that we will see very much more creativity in Gaelic singing and writing as more people make those deeply resonant characteristics of the tradition their own.

In translating the poetry, my aim has been to preserve the rhythm of the Gaelic and, in most cases, I have tried to preserve the rhymes at the end of couplets. Gaelic rhyme is based on assonance and this is the sort of rhyme I have used in the English. By and large I have avoided 'poetic language', for the keynote of Gaelic poetry is the simplicity and directness of its statement. The effect of the poems as song cannot really be reproduced on the printed page even with musical notation, because the rhythm of the melody is constantly varied according to the speech rhythms of the words. It is my hope that readers will have the opportunity to hear a good traditional singer pass on some of these songs.

Meg Bateman

TEXTUAL NOTE

The orthography of the Gaelic texts displays considerable variation because spelling conventions have not yet been standardised. The forms used in this anthology are those established by the poets' various editors.

SOURCES

J. L. Campbell and Francis Collinson, *Hebridean Folksongs* (3 vols., 1969, 1977, 1981).

A. and A. MacDonald, *The MacDonald collection of Gaelic Poetry* (1911).

D. C. MacPherson, *An Duanaire* (1868).

Archibald Sinclair, *An t-Oranaiche* (1876-79).

Frances Tolmie, a collection in *The Journal of the Folk Song Society* (1911).

THE GAELIC TRADITION – FOLKSONG
Anonymous
c. 1650

TALADH DHOMHNAILL GHUIRM

LE A MHUIME

Nàile bho hì nàile bho h-àrd
Nàile bho hì nàile bho h-àrd
Ar leam gur h-ì   a' ghrian 's i ag éirigh
Nàile bho h-àrd   's i a' cur smàl
Nàile bho h-ì air na reultaibh.

Nàile nàile nàile ri triall *hò*
Gu cùirt Dhòmhnaill   nan sgiath ballbhreac
Nan lann ceanngheal   nan saighead siùbhlach
Nan long seòlach   nam fear meanmnach.

Nàile nàile hò nàile gu triall
Moch a màireach.   Gun d' fhaighnich a' bhean
De' n mhnaoi eile: Na, có i an long ud,
Siar an eirthir   'sa' chuan Chanach?
Don-bìdh ort!   C' uim' an ceilinn?
Có ach long Dhòmhnaill   long mo leinibh
Long mo rìgh-sa   long nan Eilean.
Is mór leam an trom   atà 'san eathar.
Tha stiùir òir oirr'   trì chroinn sheilich.
Gu bheil tobar fìona   shìos 'na deireadh
Is tobar fìoruisg   'sa' cheann eile.

Hó nàile nàile nàile ri triall
Moch a màireach.   Nàil chuirinn geall
Is mo shean-gheall: Am faod sibh àicheadh?
An uair théid mac mo   rìgh-sa dh' Alba
Ge bè caladh   tàimh no àite
Gum bi mire   cluiche is gàire
Bualadh bhròg   is leòis air deàrnaibh
Bidh sud is iomairt *hò*   air an tàileasg
Air na cairtean   breaca bàna
Is air na dìsnean   geala chnàmha.

THE GAELIC TRADITION – FOLKSONG
Anonymous
c. 1650

DONALD GORM'S LULLABY

BY HIS NURSE

Nàile from Iona, Nàile from above,
Nàile from Iona, Nàile from above,
I think that it is   the sun as it rises
Nàile from above   that is casting a haze
Nàile from Iona   over the stars.

Nàile Nàile Nàile travelling *hó*
to the court of Donald   of the studded targes,
of the swords bright-pointed,   of the flying arrows,
of the many-sailed birlins,   of the spirited clansmen.

Nàile Nàile *hó* Nàile travelling
early tomorrow.   The woman questioned
the other woman,   'Well, what is that vessel
west of the coastline   in the Sea of Canna?'
Starvation take you!   why should I hide it?
Whose ship but Donald's,   the ship of my baby,
ship of my own King,   ship of the Islands?
Heavy the cargo   she carries within her.
She has a golden rudder,   three masts of willow,
there's a well of wine   down at her sternage,
and a well of spring-water   up at the bowsprit.

Hó Nàile Nàile Nàile travelling
early tomorrow.   Nàile I'd wager
with my old bet,   can you refuse it?
When my King's son   reaches Scotland
whatever the port of   call or lodging,
there will be merriment,   sport and laughter,
beatings with slippers   and palms with blisters,
that, and playing   *hó* at back-gammon,
gambling at cards   patterned and gleaming,
and throwing of dice of   white ivory.

19

Hó nàile nàile nàile le chéile
Ge bè àite   an tàmh thu an Alba
Bidh sud mar ghnàths ann   ceòl is seanchas
Pìob is clàrsach   àbhachd 's dannsa
Bidh cairt uisge   suas air phlanga,
Ol fiona is   beòir ad champa
Is gur lìonmhor triubhas   saoithreach seang ann.

Nàile nàile   nàile hó nàile
An uair théid mac *hó*   mor rìgh-sa deiseil
Chan ann air chóignear   chan ann air sheisear
Chann ann air naoinear   chan ann air dheichnear:
Ceud 'nan suidhe leat   ceud 'nan seasamh leat.

Ceud eile, *hó*, bhith cur   a' chupa deiseal dhut
Dà cheud deug bhith   dèanamh chleasa leat
Dà cheud deug bhith   cur a' bhuill-choise leat
Da cheud deug bhith   'n òrdugh gleaca leat.

Nàile nàile hó nàile so hugaibh i
An uair théid mac mo   rìgh fo uigheam
Chan i a' Mhórthir   a cheann-uidhe
Ile is Cinn-tìre   an Ròimh 's a' Mhumhan
Dùthaich MhicShuibhne   is dùthaich MhicAoidh
  cuide riutha.

Cha liutha dris   air an droigheann
No sguab choirce air   achadh foghair
No sop seann-todhair   air taobh taighe
Na an cùirt Dhòmhnaill   sgiath is claidheamh
Clogaide gormdheas   is balg-shaighead
Bogha iubhrach   is tuagh chatha.
Gur lìonmhor bonaid   ghorm air staing ann
Is coinnle chéire   laiste an lanndair.

Nàile nàile hó nàile le chéile
An uair théid mac mo   righ-s' na éideadh
Gu robh gach dùil mar   tha mi fhéin da.
Ciod e ma bhios? Cha   tachair beud da.
Gu bheil mi dhut mar   tha do phiuthar:
Mur 'eil mi bàrr   tha mi uibhir.

Hó Nàile Nàile Nàile together,
whatever the place you   stay in Scotland
this will be usual: music and talking,
piping and harping,   mirth and dancing,
quarts of whisky   up on the table,
drinking of wine and   beer in encampment,
and many pairs of breeches   tight and well-fashioned.

Nàile Nàile   Nàile *hó* Nàile
when the son of   my King travels southwards
it isn't with five men,   it isn't with six men,
it isn't with nine men,   it isn't with ten men,
but one hundred with you sitting,   one hundred standing.

A hundred sending   sunwise the cup to you,
twelve hundred others   to frisk and sport with you,
twelve hundred driving   the football across to you,
twelve hundred standing   in battle array with you.

Nàile Nàile *hó* Nàile to you with this,
when the son of   my King goes on board ship
not the mainland   his destination,
but Kintyre and Islay,   Rome and Munster,
the land of MacSween   and MacKay as well.

Not more the prickles   on the blackthorn
or stooks of corn sheaves   on a field in autumn,
or wisps of old straw   at the side of a bothy,
than the swords and targes   in the court of Donald,
the bows of yew-wood   and battle-axes;
many the blue-bonnet   hanging on the stand there
and waxen candles   blazing in lanterns.

Nàile Nàile *hó* Nàile together
when the son of   my King is in armour
may every being   be as I am to him.
What if it is? No   harm will befall him.
I am to you   like your sister,
if not as much   then I am more so.

Neart na gile   neart na gréine
Bhith eadar Dòmhnall   Gorm 's a léine.
Neart an fhochainn   anns a' Chéitean
Bhith eadar Dòmhnall   Gorm 's a léine.
Neart nan tonna   troma treubhach
Bhith eadar Dòmhnall   Gorm 's a léine.
Neart a' bhradain as   braise leumas
Bhith eadar Dòmhnall   Gorm 's a léine.
Neart Chon Chùlainn   fa làn éideadh
Bhith eadar Dòmhnall   Gorm 's a léine.
Neart sheachd cathan   feachd na Féine
Bhith eadar Dòmhnall   Gorm 's a léine.
Neart Oisein bhinn neart   Osgair euchdaich
Bhith eadar Dòmhnall   Gorm 's a léine.
Neart na stoirm' 's na   toirmghaoith reubaich
Bhith eadar Dòmhnall   Gorm 's a léine.
Neart an torrainn is na   beithreach éitigh
Bhith eadar Dòmhnall   Gorm 's a léine.
Neart na miala   móire a' séideadh
Bhith eadar Dòmhnall   Gorm 's a léine.
Neart nan dùl is   chlanna-speura
Bhith eadar Dòmhnall   Gorm 's a léine.
Gach aon diubh sud   is neart Mhic Dhé
Bhith eadar Dòmhnall   Gorm 's a léine.
Ciod e ma bhios? Cha   tachair beud dut.

Ar leam gur h-ì   a' ghrian 's i ag éirigh
Nàile bho hì nàile bho hò h-àrd.

Might of the brightness,   might of the sun's rays
be between Donald   Gorm and his shirting,
might of the green corn   in May time
be between Donald   Gorm and his shirting,
might of the breakers,   heavy and hurtling,
be between Donald   Gorm and his shirting,
might of the salmon,   boldly leaping,
be between Donald   Gorm and his shirting,
might of Cu Chulainn,   dressed for battle,
be between Donald   Gorm and his shirting,
might of the seven   bands of the Fenians
be between Donald   Gorm and his shirting,
might of sweet Ossian   and valorous Oscar
be between Donald   Gorm and his shirting,
might of the storm and   ripping tempest
be between Donald   Gorm and his shirting,
might of the thunder   and lurid lightning
be between Donald   Gorm and his shirting,
might of the monstrous   whale blowing
be between Donald   Gorm and his shirting,
might of the elements   and hosts of Heaven
be between Donald   Gorm and his shirting,
every one of those and   the might of God's Son
be between Donald   Gorm and his shirting,
What if it is? No   harm can befall you.

I think that it is   the sun as it rises
Nàile from Iona, Nàile from above.

Anonymous
c. 1700

BOTHAN AIRIGH AM BRAIGH RAITHNEACH

ORAN LE NIGHINN OIG D'A LEANNAN

Gur e m'anam is m'eudail
Chaidh an dé do Ghleann Garadh:

Fear na gruaige mar an t-òr
Is na pòig air bhlas meala.

Is tu as feàrr do'n tig deise
De na sheasadh air thalamh;

Is tu as feàrr do'n tig culaidh
De na chunna mi dh' fhearaibh.

Is tu as feàrr do'n tig osan
Is bròg shocrach nam barriall:

Còtan Lunnainneach dùbhghorm,
Is bidh na crùintean 'ga cheannach.

An uair a ruigeadh tu an fhéill
Is e mo *ghear*-sa a thig dhachaigh.

Mo chriosan is mo chìre
Is mo stiomag chaol cheangail,

Mo làmhainne bòidheach
Is déis òir air am barraibh,

Mo sporan donn iallach
Mar ri sgian nan cas ainneamh.

Thig mo chrios a Dùn Eideann
Is mo bhréid a Dùn Chailleann.

Cuime am bìomaid gun eudail
Agus spréidh aig na Gallaibh?

Gheibh sinn crodh as a' Mhaorainn
Agus caoirich a Gallaibh.

Is ann a bhios sinn 'gan àrach
Air àirigh am Bràigh Raithneach,

Anonymous
c. 1700

THE SHEILING IN BRAE RANNOCH

A SONG BY A YOUNG GIRL TO HER SWEETHEART

My darling and my treasure
went yesterday to Glengarry,

The man with the hair like gold
and the kiss like honey.

You look best in suiting
of all who walked the wide earth.

You look the best in armour
of all men I've ever looked on.

You look the best in hose
and soft shoes with laces,

In a navy London coat
bought with heaps of sovereigns.

When you go to the fair
it's my gear that comes homewards:

My girdle and my comb,
my finely-knotted hair fillet,

My beautiful gloves
with gold tips to the fingers,

My brown thonged purse
and knife with wrought handle.

My kertch comes from Dunkeld,
my belt from Edinburgh.

Why should we want for riches
when the Lowlanders have cattle?

We'll get beasts from the Mearns
and sheep from Caithness.

We'll raise them and fatten them
on a shieling in Brae Rannoch.

Ann am bothan an t-sùgraidh,
Is gur e bu dùnadh dha barrach.

Bhiodh a' chuthag 's an smùdan
A' gabhail ciùil duinn air chrannaibh;

Bhiodh an damh donn 'sa' bhùireadh
'Gar dùsgadh 'sa' mhadainn.

26

In the bothy of courtship,
closed over with brushwood,

With the cuckoo and ringdove
singing in the branches,

And the brown rutting stag
arousing us at morning.

Anonymous
17th century
CRAOBH AN IUBHAIR

'S e Mac Aoidh an duine treubhach,
O, chraobh an iubhair, *o ho,*

Nì e sìoda dha'n chloimh cheutaich,
O, chraobh an iubhair, *o ho,*

Nì e sìoda dha'n chloimh cheutaich,
O, chraobh an iubhair, *o ho.*

Nì e fion a dh'uisg' an t-sléibhe,
O, chraobh, *etc.*

Copanan dearg air a' chréadhaich,
Lìon air bhàrr an fhraoich nam b'fheudar,
Muileann air gach sruthan sléibhe,
Tobar fion' air bhruaich gach féithe,
Caisteal air gach cnoc 's leis fhéin 'ad.

'S e Mac Aoidh a' chòtain eangaich
Nach iarradh an t-earradh trom,
Chuireadh coisiche 'na dheannaibh,
Mharcraicheadh an t-each 'na dheann.

Nam biodh Mac Aoidh 'san àite,
No Niall anabharrach a bhràthair,
Cha bhiodh mo thochradh gun phàigheadh;
Bhiodh crodh-laoigh ann 's aighean dàra,
'S na seasgaich air chùl a' ghàrraidh.

Mo ghaol fhìn an cùirteir feucannt,
'S tric a thog 'ad oirnn na breugan
Far nach biomaid fhìn 'gan éisdeachd.

Mo ghaol 's mo ghràdh an t-òg beadarrach,
Dhannsadh gu grinn lùthmhor aigeanntach;
Air ùrlar gum biomaid suigeanta,
Air chnoc àrd gum biomaid beadarrach.

Anonymous
17th century

THE YEW TREE

MacKay it is who's the man of valour,
    o tree of yew, o ho,

He makes silk of wool most handsome,
    o tree of yew, o ho,

He makes silk of wool most handsome,
    o tree of yew, o ho.

He makes wine of moorland water,
    o tree of yew, etc.

Out of the clay he makes brass cups,
lint to grow on heath if he had to,
a mill on every mountain rapid,
a well of wine by every marshland,
on every hill one of his castles.

MacKay it is of the skirted frock-coat,
he would not want heavy armour,
he could outstrip any walker,
he would ride a horse at the gallop.

If MacKay were in his country
or young Niall, his excelling brother,
not unpaid would be my dowry,
there'd be cows with calf and heifers bulling
and young stock beyond the townland.

My own dear's a charming lover,
often they spread tales about us,
but we'd be gone and wouldn't bother.

My young love's a wanton darling,
he danced nimbly and with spirit,
we'd be gambolling over the dance-floor,
on the hillock we'd be kissing.

29

'S math thig dhut an deise chothlamaidh,
'S léine chaol dha'n anart Ghailmhinn,
Clogad cruadhach 's suaicheantas dearg ort
'S paidhir mhath phiostal air chrios nam ball airgid.

Chraobh nan ubhal, gheug nan abhal,
Chraobh nan ubhal, gu robh Dia leat,
Gu robh Moire 's gu robh Crìosda,
Gu robh ghealach, gu robh ghrian leat,
Gu robh gaoth an ear 's an iar leat,
Gu robh m'athair fhìn 's a thriall leat.

Ach ma théid thu dha'n choill' iùbhraich
Aithnich fhéin a' chraobh as liùmsa.
Chraobh as mìlse 's as buig' ùbhlan,
Chraobh mheanganach pheurach ùbhlach,
Bun a' fàs 's a bàrr a' lùbadh
'S a meangannan air gach tùbh dhi,
Ùbhlan troma, donna, dlùthmhor.

Ach ma théid thu 'na choill' fhiosraich
Foighnich a' chraobh am bi mise,
Chraobh a thilg a bàrr 's a miosan,
Chraobh a thilg a peighinn phisich.

Well you suit clothes of colourful tweed,
a fine-spun shirt of Galway linen,
a steel helmet with a bright red crest
and a good pair of pistols on a belt studded silver.

O tree of fruit, O branch of apples,
O tree of fruit, may God be with you,
may Christ and Mary both be with you,
may the moon and the sun be with you,
may the wind of the East and the West,
and my own father and his herds be with you.

If you go to the wood of yews
recognise yourself which tree is mine,
the tree of the sweetest softest fruit,
branching tree of apples and pears,
its trunk thickening, its crest bowing,
branches spreading all around it,
its apples heavy, thick-set, russet.

But if you go to the wood of knowledge,
ask for the tree where I am watching,
tree that dropped its leaves and produce,
tree that dropped its penny of fortune.

31

Anonymous
c. 1600

'S FLIUCH AN OIDHCHE 'N NOCHD 'S GUR FUAR I

Éileadh na ùrabh o ho,
'S fliuch an oidhche, *o hù o ho,*
Éileadh na ùrabh o ho,
'A nochd 's gur fuar i, *o hù o ho,*
Éileadh na ùrabh o ho,

Thug am bàta, *o hù etc.*   bàn an cuan oirr', *o hù etc.*
'S beag mo chùram   as a fuadach,
'S mo leannan air   bhòrd a fuaraidh,
Òganach deas   do dhuin' uasal,
Làmh air an stiùir   nuair bu chruaidhe,
Cha b'fhear cearraig   bheireadh uat i,
No fear làimhe deis'   is fuachd air.
Guma slàn do'n   làimh a dh'fhuaigh i,
Dh'fhàg e luchdmhor   làidir luath i,
Fulangach gu   siubhal chuantan,
'N saoil sibh péin na   nach mór an truaighe,
Do m' leithid fhìn   do gheala-ghruagaich
Bhith 'm bothaig bhig   an iomall tuatha,
Fo dhiolanas   mhic duin' uasail,
Gun òl cupa, o hù o ho,

Éileadh na ùrabh o ho,
Gun òl cuaiche, *o hù o ho.*

32

Anonymous
c. 1600

WET THE NIGHT IS, FULL OF COLDNESS

Eileadh na ùrabh o ho,
Wet the night is, *o hù o ho,*
Eileadh na ùrabh o ho,
Tonight it is cold, *o hù o ho,*
Eileadh na ùrabh o ho.

The white boat set off, *o hù o ho,*   over the ocean *o hù o ho,*
little my fear   she'll not make where she's bound for,
with my sweetheart on board,   by the windward gunnel,
a handsome youth   of noble mother,
hand on the tiller   when it blows strongest,
no left-handed man   could take her from you,
nor right-handed man   when the numbing cold comes,
health to the hand   who saw her seams bonded,
he made her strong,   fast and roomy,
worthy to   sail the oceans.
Do you not think it   a matter for sorrow
that the likes of me,   a fair young woman,
sits in a hut   at the edge of the country,
heavy with child   to the son of a noble,
with no drinking from goblet, *o hù o ho,*

Eileadh na ùrabh o ho,
with no drinking from saucer *o hù o ho.*

Anonymous
c. 1600

DH'EIRICH MISE MOCH DI-DOMHNAICH

Ì hoireann ò hi ri o ho,
Ù hoireann ò hi ri ri u,
Ì hoireann ò hi ri o ho.

Dh'éirich mise moch Di-Dòmhnaich,
Chaidh mi sgiobalta 'nam chòmhdach.
Ì hoireann ò etc.

Chaidh mi sgiobalta 'nam chòmhdach,
Ann am stocainnean 's am' bhrògan,
Ì hoireann ò etc.

Ann am stocainnean 's am' bhrògan,
Cha robh uisge mór no ceò ann,
Ì hoireann ò etc.

Grian gheal air aghaidh nam mòrbheann;
Thug mi gu siubhal na mòintich,
Thànaig mo leannan am chòmhdhail,
'S shuidh sinn air taobh cnocain còmhla,
'S theann sinn ri mire 's ri gòraich'
Mar as minic a rinn ar seòrsa;
'S e thànaig as a sin dòibheirt,
Bhagair e mo léine shròiceadh,
Rinn e liadan beag' am chòta,
Chuir e stìom mo chinn 'na h-òrdan -
Chunnaic thu, Rìgh! nach b'i chòir i!

Fhir ud a shiùbhlas a' mhòinteach,
Fois orr 'o cheum, biomaid còmhla -
Thoir mo shoiridh-sa gu m'eòlas,
Bhuam do Sgorabreac an eòrna,
'S thoir fios gu m' phiuthair a Chnòideart,
'S innis dhi mar dh'éirich dhòmhsa,
Rinn mi 'n dìolanas ro'n phòsadh,
Laigh mi le glas-ghiollan gòrach,
Nach dug cìr no stìom no bròg dhomh,
Nach dug fàinne far a mheòir dhomh,
Cha dug, no 'm bréid, 's e bu chòir dha.

34

Anonymous
c. 1600

I ROSE EARLY ON SUNDAY MORNING

I hoireann ò hi ri o ho,
U hoireann ò hi ri rì u,
I hoireann ò hi ri o ho.

I rose early on Sunday morning,
and quickly put on my clothing.
  I hoireann ò etc.

and quickly put on my clothing,
and my shoes and my stockings,
  I hoireann ò etc.

and my shoes and my stockings,
it was neither raining nor foggy,
  I hoireann ò etc.

the sun bright on the mountains;
I set off for the moorland,
then my sweetheart came across me,
we sat together on a hummock,
and started romping and sporting
as our likes are often wont to;
thus arose the misfortune,
he made to rip down my bodice,
and left rents in my clothing,
and my fillet disordered –
you saw, oh King, how he scorned it!

Oh man who roams the moorland,
stop a a while and I'll join you,
take my greetings to my homestead,
to Sgorabreac of barley-growing,
tell my sister in Knoydart
how these things have befallen,
I've got a baby without a promise,
I lay with a foolish green youngster,
he gave me no ribbon, comb or footwear,
nor a ring to show his honour,
nor yet the kertch that he owed me.

Ach nam bithinn-sa 's taigh-òsda
Dh'aithnghinn fear mhealladh na h-òinsich,
Làmh air a cìochan 's 'ga pògadh,
Paidirean is preasain bhòidheach,
'S muladach caileag 'na h-ònar
Am bothan beag an iomall mòintich,
Chleachd bhith 'n cuideachd nam fear òga.

Iain Mhic Chaluim 'ic Dhòmhnaill,
Cha digeadh tu nuair bu chòir dhut,
Tacan beag mun rinn mi 'n còrdadh,
Gun laighinn leat an déidh còrdaidh,
Dhianainn bainis is mór-phòsadh
An taigh mór an ùrlair chòmhnard,
Far am bi daoin' uaisle mu bhòrdaibh.

If I'd ever been in the hostel
I'd have known the false lover,
kissing with his hand on a girl's bosom,
deceiving with trinkets and baubles;
sad is a woman all lonesome,
in a bothy by the moorland
who young men used to throng round.

John, son of Malcolm, son of Donald,
you came when you ought not to,
before I ever made the contract,
with you I'd lie if we'd done so,
I'd make a wedding with great rejoicing,
in the big house with smooth flooring,
and round the tables there'd sit nobles.

Anonymous
c. 1690

CLANN GHRIOGAIR AIR FOGRADH

Is mi suidhe an so am ònar
    Air còmhnard an rathaid,

Dh'fheuch am faic mi fear-fuadain,
    Tighinn o Chruachan a' cheathaich,

Bheir dhomh sgeul ar Clann Ghriogair
    No fios cia an do ghabh iad.

Cha d'fhuair mi d'an sgeulaibh
    Ach iad bhith 'n dé air na Sraithibh.

Thall 's a bhos mu Loch Fìne,
    Masa fìor mo luchd bratha;

Ann an Clachan an Dìseirt
    Ag òl fìon air na maithibh.

Bha Griogair mór ruadh ann,
    Làmh chruaidh air chùl claidhimh;

Agus Griogair mór meadhrach,
    Ceann-feadhna ar luchd-taighe.

Mhic an Fhir a Srath h-Ardail,
    Bhiodh na bàird ort a' tathaich;

Is a bheireadh greis air a' chlàrsaich
    Is air an tàileasg gu h-aighear;

Is a sheinneadh an fhidheall,
    Chuireadh fioghair fo mhnathaibh.

Is ann a rinn sibh an t-sidheann anmoch
    Anns a' ghleann am bi an ceathach.

Dh'fhàg sibh an t-Eòin bòidheach
    Air a' mhòintich 'na laighe,

'Na starsnaich air féithe
    An déidh a reubadh le claidheamh.

Anonymous
c. 1690

CLAN GREGOR IN EXILE

I am sitting by myself
by the level of the road,

looking out for a fugitive,
coming from Cruachan of the fog,

who has word of Clan Gregor
or can tell me where they've gone.

That they were yesterday in the Straths
is all their news I know.

Here and there about Loch Fyne,
if my spies are any good;

in the Clachan of Dysart
drinking wine with the nobles.

Big red Gregor was there,
a hand, deadly with sword;

and big merry Gregor,
the head of our house.

Son of the Laird of Strathardle,
where the bards used to flock;

you'd spend a while at the harp
and gladly gamble at the boards;

and you'd play the fiddle,
filling the women with hope.

It was late you made venison
in the glen where there's fog.

You left Handsome John slumped
face down on the moor,

a great lump on the marsh
hacked by a sword.

Is ann thog sibh ghreigh dhùbhghorm
O Lùban na h-abhann.

Ann am Bothan na Dìge
Ghabh sibh dìon air an rathad;

Far an d'fhàg sibh mo bhiodag
Agus crios mo bhuilg-shaighead.

Gur i saighead na h-àraich
So thàrmaich am leathar.

Chaidh saighead am shliasaid,
Crann fiar air dhroch shnaidheadh.

Gun seachnadh Righ nan Dùl sibh
O fhùdar caol neimhe,

O shradagan teine,
O pheileir 's o shaighid,

O sgian na rinn caoile,
Is o fhaobhar geur claidhimh.

Is ann bha bhuidheann gun chòmhradh
Di-dòmhnaich am bràighe bhaile.

Is cha dèan mi gàir éibhinn
An am éirigh no laighe.

Is beag an t-iongnadh dhomh féin sud,
Is mi bhith 'n déidh mo luchd-taighe.

You lifted the blue-black stud
from the Loops of the Lyon.

In the bothy of the Ditch
you hid from the road;

there you left my dirk
with my quiver of bolts.

In my side, the arrow
from the battle is lodged.

My thigh is pierced,
by a squint-shafted bolt.

May the King of All protect you
from fine venomous powder,

from bullet and dart,
from sparks red-hot,

from sword's keen blade,
and sharp knife's point.

The company was silent
above the village on Sunday.

On going to bed or rising
I desire no sport.

For me that's no wonder,
since my household is lost.

Anonymous
c. 1500

NACH FHREAGAIR THU, CHAIRISTIANA?

É hó hì ura bhì
Ho ro ho ì, ó ho ro ho,
É hó hì ura bhì

Nach fhreagair thu, Chairistiana?
É hó, etc.

Nam freagradh, gun cluinninn fhin thu,
É hó, etc.

Bha mi bliadhna 'n cùirt an rìgh leat,
'S ged chanainn e, bha mi a trì ann -
Fuaigheal anairt 'g gearradh shìoda,
'S a' cur gràinne air léintean rìomhach.

Thug mi turus do Ghleann Comhann,
'S bha 'm muir àrd 's an caolas domhain
Gheàrr mi leum 's cha d'rinn mi thomhas,
Gun leum na h-uiseagan romham,
'S thuirt iad rium nach dianainn gnothach,
Nach fhaighinn mo mhuime romham,
Ceann na céille, beul na comhairl',
Sgrìobhadh 's a leughadh an leobhar;
Bhiodh na h-uaislean ort a' tadhal
Cha b'ann gu mealladh an gnothaich.

'S iomadh long is bàrc is biaoirlinn
Is luingeas a tha 'm bial Chaol Ìle
Tighinn a dh'iarraidh Cairistiana;
Cha n-ann gu pùsadh mhic rìgh leat,
Gus do chur 'san talamh ìseal,
Fo leaca troma na dìleann.

Fhleasgaich òig na gruaige duibhe,
'S ann an nochd as mór do mhulad;
Do leannan a staigh fo dhubhar
An ciste nam bòrd air a cumadh,
An déidh na saoir a bhith 'ga dubhadh.

Anonymous
c. 1500

WON'T YOU ANSWER, CAIRISTÌONA?

E hó hì ura bhì
Ho ro ho ì, ó ho ro ho,
E hó hì ura bhì.

Won't you answer, Cairistìona?
    E hó etc.

If you would, I myself would hear you,
    E hó etc.

I spent a year with you in the King's court,
as it was, I spent full three there,
trimming silk, sewing linen,
embroidering the shirts of my kinsmen.

To Glencoe I made a journey,
the Kyle was deep and the sea was stormy,
I took a leap but didn't judge it,
the larks rose up, startled before me,
they told me I wouldn't be lucky,
that I wouldn't find my foster-mother,
head of wisdom, mouth of counsel,
you could write and read the good Book,
you often had visits from the nobles,
they were never disappointed.

There's many a ship and boat and galley,
and fleet at the mouth of the Kyle of Islay,
coming to fetch Cairistìona,
not in order to wed you to a king's son,
but to lay you to rest in the deep ground,
under flagstones, heavy, dripping.

Young man whose hair is blackest,
it is tonight your mood is saddest,
your sweetheart hidden away in darkness,
locked in the coffin of deal planking,
coated by the joiners with black lacquer.

Anonymous
c. 1700

AN T-EUDACH

Gur a mise tha iar mo chlisgeadh,
Tha loch uisge fo m' chluasaig.

Ged a théid mi do m' leabaidh
Chan e an cadal as dual domh,

Is a' bhean tha an Ile
Sìor mhiadachadh m'euda;

Bhean thug uamsa mo roghainn,
Is gun taghainn thar cheud e.

Ach nam bithinn 'na fianuis,
Gum biodh spìonadh air bhréidean.

Chì mi an Fhionnairigh thall ud
Is ì gun earras fo 'n ghréin oirr'.

Gum faca mise uair a
Bha daoine-uaisle mu d'réidhlean.

Rachadh cuid do'n bheinn-sheilg dhiubh,
Cuid a mharbhadh an éisg dhiubh,

Air Linne na Ciste
Am bi na bric anns an leumraich.

Tha mo chean air an lasgair,
Saighdear sgairteil fo sgéith thu.

An uair a thig thu do'n chaisteal
Bheir thu dhachaidh do cheud ghràdh.

Ged a tha mi air m'aineol
O 'n bhaile fo éislean,

Chan ion do 'n bhan-Ilich
Bhith strìth rium mu d'dhéidhinn.

Anonymous
c. 1700

THE JEALOUS ONE

It is I who am shaken,
there's a loch of tears beneath my pillow.

Though I lie down on my mattress,
sleep is not likely,

While the woman in Islay
forever makes me jealous;

The woman who robbed me of my darling
whom I'd choose before a hundred.

If I were ever to meet her
there'd be the tearing of kertches.

I see Fiunary yonder
without any provision,

Though once I saw it
with nobles on your greensward.

Some would go hunting,
some to kill fishes,

At the Pool of the Coffin
where trout are leaping.

My desire is for the soldier,
you nimble youth with buckler.

When you come to the castle
you will take home your first love.

Though I'm in a strange country,
far from home, dejected,

It isn't fitting that that woman
contends with me about you.

Anna Campbell of Scalpay, Harris
fl. 1773

AILEIN DUINN, O HO HI, SHIUBHLAINN LEAT

Ailein Duinn, *o hó hì*, shiùbhlainn leat
Hi ri ri, ri u ó, hi o hùg hòireann ó,
Ailein Duinn, *o hó hì*, shiùbhlainn leat.

'S bochd an nochd na bheil air m'aire,
Miad na sìne, fuachd na gaillinn
Ailein Duinn, *etc.*

Miad na sìne, fuachd na gaillinn
Dh'fhuadaicheadh na fir o 'n charraig,
Ailein Duinn, *etc.*

Dh'fhuadaicheadh na fir o 'n charraig,
Chuireadh iad a' bhòid dha'n aindeoin
Ailein Duinn, *etc.*

Far an trom an laigh a' ghailleann,
Cha b'e siod leam ar dìol caladh,
Ach Caolas Diadhair anns na Hearadh,
Far am bi na féidh air bhearradh,
Dóbhran donn is laogh breac ballach.

Gura mise th'air mo léireadh
Cha n-e bàs a' chruidh 'sa Chéitein,
No tainead mo bhuaile spréidhe,
Ach a fhlichead 's tha do léine,
'S tu bhith 'm bàrr nan tonn ag éirigh
Mucan mara bhith 'gad reubadh,
Bhith 'gad ghearradh as a chéile;
Ailein Duinn, a laoigh mo chéilleadh,
Gura h-òg a thug mi spéis dhut,
Nuair a bha thu 'n sgoil na Beurla
Nuair a bha sinn ann le chéile;

Gum pàigheadh Dia siod ri t'anam
Mhiad 's a fhuair mi d' chuid gun cheannach,
Pìosan caola geal' an anart,
Nèapagain do 'n t-síoda bhallach,
Thug thu fhéin, a ghaoil, a Manainn.

Anna Campbell of Scalpay, Harris
fl. 1773

BROWN-HAIRED ALLAN, I'D GO WITH YOU

Brown-haired Allan, *o hó hì*, I'd go with you,
Hi ri ri, ri u ó, hi o hùg hòireann ó,
Brown-haired Allan, *o hó hì*, I'd go with you.

Sad tonight what lies on my spirit,
the strength of the storm, the cold of the tempest,
Brown-haired Allan, *o hó hì*, I'd go with you.

The strength of the storm, the cold of the tempest,
that could drive the men from the headland,
Brown-haired Allan, *o hó hì*, I'd go with you.

That could drive the men from the headland,
they would take the pledge regardless,
Brown-haired Allan, *o hó hì*, I'd go with you.

Where the storm fiercely rages,
I doubt that as our choice harbour,
but the Sound of Diadhair in Harris
where the deer are on the hilltops,
the dappled fawn and dark-brown otter.

Alas, it is me who is sorely wounded
not by the deaths of stock in the springtime,
nor by the leanness of my herd of cattle,
but by the wetness of your clothing,
with you on the crests of waves rising,
with sea-monsters rending your body,
ripping and tearing your limbs asunder;
brown-haired Allan, calf of my senses,
young I was when first I loved you,
when you were getting English schooling,
when we were going to school together.

May God reward your soul its kindness,
for what I got of your store without paying,
for fine silver cups wrapped in linen,
handkerchiefs of spotted satin,
brought by you, love, from the Isle of Manann.

Ailein Duinn, a mhiann nan leannan,
Chuala mi gun deach thu fairis
Air a' bhàta làidir dharaich;
Ma 's fhìor siod, cha bhi mi fallain,
Gu là bràch cha dian mi bainis.
M'iarrtas air Rìgh na Cathrach
Gun mo chur an ùir no 'n gaineamh,
An talamh toll no 'n àite falaich,
'N seòmbar cùil no 'n àite daingeann,
Ach 's bhall am bheil thu, Ailein!

'S truagh, a Rìgh! nach mi bha 'n làimh riut,
Ge bè bàgh no sgeir an tràigh thu,
Ge bè tiùrr am fàg an làn thu,
'S cùl do chinn air bhac mo làimhe,
Do chùl dualach, cuachach, fàinneach.
Dh'òlainn deoch, ge b'oil le càch e,
Cha b'ann do bhùrn no do shàile,
No do dh'fhìon dearg na Spàinte,
Ach fuil do chuim 's tu 'n déidh do bhàthadh;
Gura buidhe nochd dha d' mhàthair,
Bho nach 'eil thu beò 's tu bàite.

Ailein Duinn, *o hó hì*, shiùbhlainn leat,
Hi ri ri, ri u ó, hi o hùg hoireann ó,
Ailein Duinn, *o hó hì*, shiùbhlainn leat.

Brown-haired Allan, choice of sweethearts,
I have heard that you crossed over
in the strong oaken vessel;
if that is true, I'll not recover,
till Doomsday I'll make no wedding.
This is my plea to the King of Heaven:
not in soil or sand my burial,
nor in earthen hole or place of hiding,
nor in back-room, nor in fortress,
but in the place where you are, Allan!

Alas, Oh King, I was not beside you,
whatever bay or rock you'll land on,
whatever beach the tide will cast you,
your head lying in the crook of my elbow,
your head of thick curling ringlets;
I'd take a drink, though others would hate it,
not of the sea, nor of fresh water,
nor of red Spanish claret,
but of your breast's blood after your drowning;
lucky tonight for your mother's passing
since you are drowned and live no longer.

Brown-haired Allan, *o hó hì*, I'd go with you,
Hi ri ri, ri u ó, hi o hùg hòireann ó,
Brown-haired Allan, *o hó hì*, I'd go with you.

49

Anna Nic Ealair
c. 1800

LUINNEAG ANNA NIC EALAIR

Is ann am bothan bochd a' bhròin
   A chuir mi eòlas ort an toiseach;
A's thug mi thu gu tigh mo mhàth'r
   'S an d' rinn mi d' àrach car tamuill.

> *'S e do ghaol-sa, a ghaoil, -*
>   *'S e do ghaol-sa rinn mo tharruing;*
> *'S e do ghràdh-sa, a rùin,*
>   *Rinn mo dhùsgadh 's a' mhadainn.*

Tha thu mar dhubhar carraig mhòir
   Am fearann sgìth is mi làn airsneil;
'N uair a thionndaidh riut mo shùil
   'S ann bha thu an rùn mo ghlacadh.

'S ann a thug thu dhomh do ghaol
   Fo dhubhar craobh an aiteil;
A's comh-chomunn do rùin
   Ann an gàradh nan ubhall.

Is millse leam do ghaol na'm fìon, -
   Seadh am fìon, 'nuair is treis' e,
'S 'n uair a thug thu dhomh do ghràdh
   'S ann a dh' fhàilnich mo phearsa.

'S ann a thug thu dhomh do d' ghràdh
   Gus an d'fhàilnich mo phearsa;
'S gus am b' éigin domh a ràdh
   'Cum air do làimh a charaid.'

'S ann a dh' éirich thu le buaidh
   As an uaigh suas le cabhaig,
Amhluidh dhùisgeas do shluagh
   Suas le buaidh anns a' mhadainn.

'S chaidh thu suas air ionad àrd
   Dh' ullach' àite do m' anam;
'S tha thu 'g ràdh gu 'n tig thu rìs
   A choimh-lìonadh do gheallaidh.

Anna Nic Ealair
c. 1800

ANNA NIC EALAIR'S SONG

It was in the wretched poor stall
that I first came to know you;
and I took you to my mother's house
where for a while I nursed you.

> *It was your love, my love,*
> *it was your love that drew me,*
> *it was your love, my dear,*
> *that awoke me in the morning.*

You're like the shade of a great rock
in a troubled land where I walk in sadness;
when I looked to you for help
you desired my encapture.

You gave me your love
in the juniper's shadow,
and the company of your regard
in the garden of apples.

Sweeter to me your love than wine,
even wine at its strongest;
when you showed me your esteem
it made my body falter.

You gave me of your love
until it overwhelmed me
and I had to call out
'Friend, stop your caresses.'

You have risen up with haste
from the grave, victorious;
likewise will your host awake,
triumphant in the morning.

And you went up to a place on high
to prepare my soul a lodging,
and you say you'll come back again
to bring about your promise.

LEARNED ARISTOCRATIC VERSE
Aithbhreac Inghean Corcadail
fl. 1460

A PHAIDRIN DO DHUISG MO DHEAR

A Phaidrín do dhúisg mo dhéar,
 ionmhain méar do bhitheadh ort;
ionmhain cridhe fáilteach fial
 'gá raibhe riamh gus a nocht.

Dá éag is tuirseach atáim,
 an lámh má mbítheá gach n-uair,
nach cluinim a beith i gclí
 agus nach bhfaicim í uaim.

Mo chridhe-se is tinn atá
 ó theacht go crích an lá dhúinn;
ba ghoirid do éist ré ghlóir,
 ré h-agallaimh an óig úir.

Béal asa ndob aobhdha glór,
 dhéantaidhe a ghó is gach tír:
leómhan Muile na múr ngeal,
 seabhag Íle na magh mín.

Fear ba ghéar meabhair ar dhán,
 ó nach deachaidh dámh gan díol;
taoiseach deigh-einigh suairc séimh,
 agá bhfaightí méin mheic ríogh.

Dámh ag teacht ó Dhún an Óir
 is dámh ón Bhóinn go a fholt fiar:
minic thánaig iad fá theist,
 ná mionca ná leis a riar.

Seabhag seangglan Sléibhe Gaoil,
 fear do chuir a chaoin ré cléir;
dreagan Leódhuis na learg ngeal,
 éigne Sanais na sreabh séimh.

A h-éagmhais aon duine a mháin
 im aonar atáim dá éis,
gan chluiche, gan chomhrádh caoin,
 gan ábhacht, gan aoibh i gcéill.

LEARNED ARISTOCRATIC VERSE
Aithbhreac Inghean Corcadail
fl. 1460

OH ROSARY THAT WOKE MY TEARS

Oh rosary that woke my tears,
beloved the finger that on you did lie,
beloved the kindly generous heart
that you belonged to till tonight.

For the death of him I am sad,
whose hand you encircled every hour,
alas I do not hear it move
or see it lying before me now.

My heart has been smarting and sore
since this day came to a close;
short was the time I listened to his voice,
to the conversation of the lovely youth.

Mouth of the most delightful voice,
whose whims were conceded in every land,
Lion of Mull of the white walls,
Hawk of Islay of the smooth plains.

No poet-band left without reward
the man whose memory for song was keen,
he had the bearing of a prince,
hospitable, courteous, gentle chief.

Poet-bands coming from Dùn an Oir,
poets from the Boyne to the man of curling hair,
often did they come drawn by his fame,
not less often they got their desire.

Bright slender hawk of Sliabh Gaoil,
man who showed his kindness to the Church,
Dragon of Lewis of the sunny slopes,
Salmon of Sanas of the peaceful burns.

For want of only this one man
I am alone, longing for him,
without diversion or kindly talk,
without gladness or sign of mirth.

Gan duine ris dtig mo mhiann
  as sliocht na Niall ó Niall óg;
gan mhuirn gan mheadhair ag mnáibh,
  gan aoibhneas an dáin im dhóigh.

Mar thá Giodha an fhuinn mhín,
  Dún Suibhne do-chím gan cheól,
faithche longphuirt na bhfear bhfial:
  aithmhéala na Niall a n-eól.

Cúis a lúthgháire má seach,
  gusa mbímis ag teacht mall:
's nach fuilngim a nois, mo nuar,
  a fhaicinn uam ar gach ard.

Má bhrisis, a Mheic Dhé bhí,
  ar bagaide na dtrí gcnó,
fa fíor do ghabhais ar ngiall:
  do bhainis an trian ba mhó.

Cnú mhullaigh a mogaill féin
  bhaineadh do Chloinn Néill go nua:
is tric roighne na bhfear bhfial
  go leabaidh na Niall a nuas.

An rogha fá deireadh díbh
  's é thug gan mo bhrígh an sgéal:
do sgar riom mo leathchuing rúin,
  a phaidrín do dhúisg mo dhéar.

Is briste mo chridhe im chlí,
  agus bídh nó go dtí m'éag,
ar éis an abhradh dhuibh úir,
  a phaidrín do dhúisg mo dhéar.

Muire mháthair, muime an Ríogh,
  go robh 'gam dhíon ar gach séad,
's a Mac do chruthuigh gach dúil,
  a phaidrín do dhúisg mo dhéar.

Not one man of Clan MacNeill
takes my fancy with young Neil gone;
women lack all happiness and joy,
I cannot hope for cheer in song.

Sad is Gigha of the smooth soils,
I see Dùn Suibhne standing on its green,
fort of the fine men now without a tune,
they know the sorrow of Clan MacNeill.

Place we used to approach in state,
which brought us merriment every time,
now alas I cannot bear
to see it rise up from every height.

If Thou, Oh Son of the living God,
hast breached the cluster of nuts on the trees,
Thou hast taken hostage our choicest man,
Thou hast taken the greatest of the three.

The topmost nut of Clan MacNeill
has been stripped away from the generous men;
often does the choicest of their bunch
fall down to the MacNeill's last bed.

The most recent, finest of them all,
the tale of him has cost me dear,
my beloved yokefellow has parted from me,
Oh rosary that woke my tears.

Broken is my heart within my breast,
and will remain so until my death,
longing for the fresh dark-lashed man,
Oh rosary that woke my tears.

Mary, Mother, nurse of the King,
may she protect me far and near,
and also her Son who created every beast,
Oh rosary that woke my tears.

Anonymous
c. 1570

CUMHA GHRIOGAIR MHICGHRIOGAIR GHLINN SREITH

A DHÌTHCHEANNADH 'SA' BHLIADHNA 1570

Moch madainn air latha Lùnasd'
Bha mi sùgradh mar ri m'ghràdh,
Ach mun tàinig meadhon latha
Bha mo chridhe air a 'chràdh.

Ochain, ochain, ochain uiridh
Is goirt mo chridhe, a laoigh,
Ochain, ochain, ochain uiridh
Cha chluinn t' athair ar caoidh.

Mallachd aig maithibh is aig càirdean
Rinn mo chràdh air an-dòigh,
Thàinig gun fhios air mo ghràdh-sa
Is a thug fo smachd e le foill.

Nam biodh dà fhear dheug d'a chinneadh
Is mo Ghriogair air an ceann,
Cha bhiodh mo shùil a' sileadh dheur,
No mo leanabh féin gun dàimh.

Chuir iad a cheann air ploc daraich,
Is dhòirt iad fhuil mu làr:
Nam biodh agam-sa an sin cupan
Dh'òlainn dith mo shàth.

Is truagh nach robh m'athair an galar,
Agus Cailean Liath am plàigh,
Ged bhiodh nighean an Ruadhanaich
Suathadh bas is làmh.

Chuirinn Cailean Liath fo ghlasaibh,
Is Donnchadh Dubh an làimh;
'S gach Caimbeulach th' ann am Bealach
Gu giùlan nan glas-làmh.

Ràinig mise réidhlean Bhealaich,
Is cha d'fhuair mi ann tàmh:
Cha d'fhàg mi ròin de m'fhalt gun tarraing
No craiceann air mo làimh.

Anonymous
c. 1570

LAMENT FOR MACGREGOR OF GLENSTRAE

WHO WAS BEHEADED IN 1570

Early on Lammas morning
I was sporting with my love,
but before noon came upon us
my heart had been crushed.

Alas, alas, alas and alack,
sore is my heart, my child,
alas, alas, alas and alack,
your father won't hear our cries.

A curse on nobles and relations
who brought me to this grief,
who came on my love unawares
and took him by deceit.

Had there been twelve of his kindred
and my Gregor at their head,
my eye would not be weeping
nor my child without a friend.

They put his head on an oaken block
and spilled his blood on the ground,
if I had had a cup there
I'd have drunk my fill down.

A pity my father was not diseased
and Grey Colin stricken with plague,
even though Ruthven's daughter
would wring her hands dismayed.

I'd put Grey Colin under lock and key
and Black Duncan in heavy irons,
and every Campbell in Taymouth
I'd set to wearing chains.

I reached the lawn of Taymouth
but for me that was no balm,
I left no hair of my head unpulled
nor skin upon my palms.

Is truagh nach robh mi an riochd na h-uiseig,
Spionnadh Ghriogair ann mo làimh:
Is i a' chlach a b'àirde anns a' chaisteal
A' chlach a b'fhaisge do'n bhlàr.

Is ged tha mi gun ùbhlan agam
Is ùbhlan uile aig càch,
Is ann tha m' ubhal cùbhraidh grinn
Is cùl a chinn ri làr.

Ged tha mnathan chàich aig baile
'Nan laighe is 'nan cadal sàmh,
Is ann bhios mise aig bruaich do lice
A' bualadh mo dhà làimh.

Is mór a b'annsa bhith aig Griogair
Air feadh coille is fraoich,
Na bhith aig Baran crìon na Dalach
An taigh cloiche is aoil.

Is mòr a b'annsa bhith aig Griogair
Cur a' chruidh do'n ghleann,
Na bhith aig Baran crìon na Dalach
Ag òl air fìon is air leann.

Is mòr a b'annsa bhith aig Griogair
Fo bhrata ruibeach ròin,
Na bhith aig Baran crìon na Dalach
A' giùlan sìoda is sròil.

Ged a bhiodh ann cur is cathadh
Is latha nan seachd sìon,
Gheibheadh Griogair dhòmh-sa cragan
'S an caidlimid fo dhìon.

Ba hu, ba hu, àsrain bhig,
Chan 'eil thu fhathast ach tlàth:
Is eagal leam nach tig an latha
Gun dìol thu t'athair gu bràth.

If only I had the flight of the lark
with Gregor's strength in my arm,
the highest stone in the castle
would be the closest to the ground.

Though now I'm left without apples
and the others have them all,
my apple is fair and fragrant
with the back of his head on the mould.

Though others' wives are safe at home
lying sound asleep,
I am at the edge of your grave
beating my hands in grief.

I'd far rather be with Gregor
roaming moor and copse
than be with the niggardly Baron of Dull
in a house of lime and stone.

I'd far rather be with Gregor
driving the cattle to the glen
than be with the niggardly Baron of Dull
drinking beer and wine.

I'd far rather be with Gregor
under a rough hairy skin
than be with the niggardly Baron of Dull
dressed in satin and silk.

Even on a day of driving snow
when the seven elements reel
Gregor would find me a little hollow
where we would snugly sleep.

Ba hu, ba hu, little waif,
you are still only young,
but the day when you revenge your father
I fear will never come.

Iseabail Ní Mheic Cailéin
fl. 1500

ATA FLEASGACH AR MO THI

Atá fleasgach ar mo thí,
  a Rí na ríogh go rí leis!
a bheith sínte ré mo bhroinn
  agus a choim ré mo chneis:

Dá mbeith gach ní mar mo mhian,
  ní bhiadh cian eadrainn go bráth,
gé beag sin dá chur i gcéill,
  's nach tuigeann sé féin, mar tá.

Acht ní éadtrom gan a luing,
  sgéal as truaighe linn 'nar ndís:
esan soir is mise siar,
  mar nach dtig ar riar a rís.

IS MAIRG DÁ NGALAR AN GRÁDH

Is mairg dá ngalar an grádh,
  gé bé fáth fá n-abrainn é;
deacair sgarachtainn ré pháirt;
  truagh an cás i bhfeilim féin.

An grádh-soin tugas gan fhios,
  ó's é mo leas gan a luadh,
mara bhfaigh mé furtacht tráth,
  biaidh mo bhláth go tana truagh.

An fear-soin dá dtugas grádh,
  's nach féadtar a rádh ós n-aird,
dá gcuireadh sé mise i bpéin,
  gomadh dó féin bhus céad mairg.

60

Isabel, Countess of Argyll
fl. 1500

THERE'S A YOUNG MAN IN PURSUIT OF ME

There's a young man in pursuit of me,
Oh King of Kings, may he have success!
Would he were stretched out by my side
with his body pressing against my breast!

If everything were as I would wish,
no distance would ever cause us separation,
though that is all too little to say
with him not yet knowing the situation.

But it isn't easy if his ship doesn't come,
for the two of us it's a wretched matter:
he is East and I am West,
so what we desire can never again happen.

WOE TO THE ONE WHOSE SICKNESS IS LOVE

Woe to the one whose sickness is love,
no matter the grounds I might present,
hard it is to get free of its hold,
sorry the lot I have myself.

That love I have given in secret,
it being better not to declare it,
unless I find relief before long,
my flowering will grow wan, withered and wretched.

That man to whom I have given love,
(this should not be said out loud)
if he should ever cause me hurt,
may he suffer a hundred times the woe.

VERNACULAR POETS
Màiri Nighean Alasdair Ruaidh
c. 1615-1706

AN TALLA AM BU GHNATH LE MAC LEOID

Gur muladach thà mi,
Is mi gun mhire gun mhànran
Anns an talla am bu ghnàth le Mac Leòid.

Tigh mór macnasach meadhrach
Nam macaomh 's nam maighdean,
Far am bu tartarach gleadhraich nan còrn.

Tha do thalla mór prìseil
Gun fhasgadh gun dìon ann,
Far am faca mi am fìon bhith 'ga òl.

Och mo dhìobhail mar thachair,
Thàinig dìle air an aitribh:
Is ann is cianail leam tachairt 'na còir.

Shir Tormoid nam bratach,
Fear do dhealbh-sa bu tearc e,
Gun sgeilm a chur asad no bòsd.

Fhuair thu teist is deagh urram
Ann am freasdal gach duine,
Air dheiseachd 's air uirghioll beòil.

Leat bu mhiannach coin lùthmhor
Dhol a shiubhal nan stùcbheann,
Is an gunna nach diùltadh ri h-òrd.

Is i do làmh nach robh tuisleach
Dhol a chaitheamh a' chuspair
Le do bhogha cruaidh ruiteach deagh-neòil.

Glac throm air do shliasaid
An déidh a snaidheadh gun fhiaradh,
Is bàrr dosrach de sgiathaibh an eòin.

Bhiodh céir ris na crannaibh
Bu neo-éisleanach tarruing,
An uair a leumadh an taifeid o d' mheòir.

VERNACULAR POETS
Mary MacLeod
c. 1615-1706

THE HALL OF MACLEOD

I am filled with sorrow,
with no merriment or sporting,
in the hall that belonged to MacLeod.

Great joyful blithe mansion,
of youths and of maidens,
where drinking horns' clanking was heard.

Your brilliant building
without roof or timbers
where I used to see wine being drunk.

My ruination, what happened,
a disaster came on the mansion,
and it makes me so sad on approach.

Sir Norman of the banners,
rare a man of your appearance,
with never a word of arrogance nor boast.

You won honour and fine record
in everyone's service,
for your elegance and eloquence of mouth.

You delighted in deerhounds,
with you roaming the peaked hills,
with the gun that quickly yielded to the lock.

Your hand didn't falter,
taking aim at the target
with your bow, red and hard of good hue.

On your thigh, a heavy quiver,
arrows without blemish whittled,
with plumed tips from the wings of the fowl.

Their shafts, sealed with beeswax,
were not sluggish in leaping
when the bowstring was released from your hold.

63

An uair a leigte o d' làimh i
Cha bhiodh òirleach gun bhàdhadh
Eadar corran a gàinne is an smeòirn.

Ceud soraidh le dùrachd
Uam gu leannan an t-sùgraidh:
Gum b'e m'aighear 's mo rùn bhith 'nad chòir.

An ám dhuit tighinn gu d' bhaile
Is tu bu tighearnail gabhail
An uair a shuidheadh gach caraid mu d' bhòrd.

Bha thu measail aig uaislean,
Is cha robh beagan mar chruas ort:
Sud an cleachdamh a fhuair thu ad aois òig.

Gum biodh farum air thàilisg
Agus fuaim air a' chlàrsaich,
Mar a bhuineadh do shàr mhac Mhic Leòid.

Gur h-e bu eachdraidh 'na dhéidh sin
Greis air ursgeil na Féinne,
Is air chuideachda chéirghil nan cròc.

When the dart flew from your fingers,
every inch would get hidden
from the pointed tip to the notch.

A hundred farewells and blessings
to the lover of revelling
whose company was my pleasure and joy.

At the time of your home-coming,
your demeanour would be lordly
with all your friends ensconsed around your board.

Nobles esteemed you,
you knew nothing of meanness,
that's the custom you learnt when young.

There'd be the clatter of draughtsmen,
and the clarsach resounding
as was fitting for MacLeod's fine son.

Then there'd be the telling of stories,
about the Fenian warriors,
and the antlered white-bottomed throng.

Catrìona Nic Gilleain
fl. 1680

CUMHA DO SHEUMAS MAC-GILLEAIN, A FEAR

Gur h-e mise 'tha pràmhail
'S fhuair mi fàth air 'bhi dubhach.
Tha mi 'feitheamh an àite
Far 'm bu ghnàs dhuit 'bhith 'd shuidhe,
'S gun do ghunn' ann air ealachainn,
'Chuireadh earba bho shiubhal. –
Mo chreach dhuilich gun d'eug thu,
Nàmhaid féidh anns a' bhruthach.

Nuair a bha mi gad chàradh,
Ged bu shàr-mhath mo mhisneach,
Gun robh saighead am àirnean,
'S i gam shàthadh gu 'h-itich,
Mu 'n fhear churanta, làidir,
Nach robh fàilinn 'na ghliocas.
Cha robh 'n saoghal mar chàs ort
Nam biodh t' àilleas fo t' iochd dheth.

Cha do rinn mi riut fàilte
Ged a thàinig thu, Sheumais.
Gur h-e mise 'tha cràiteach,
Is cha slànaich an léigh mi.
Bho nach bheil thusa maireann,
'Fhir 'bu cheanalt' 's bu bheusaich';
Gur h-e mise nach sòradh
Ni bu deònach le d' bheul-sa.

Ormsa thàinig am fuathas
O 'n Di-luain so 'chaidh tharam;
Bhon a chunnaic mo shùilean
Thu gad ghiùlan aig fearaibh,
Gun robh mnai air bheag céille,
'S fir gu deurach gad ghearan.
Bhon a dh' fhag iad 'sa chìll thu,
Och, mo dhìobhail, 's trom m' eallach.

Nuair a thug iad gu tilleadh
Gun robh 'n iomairt ud cruaidh leam,
'S tus', a rùin, air do chàradh
Ann an càrnaich na fuarachd.

66

Catherine MacLean
fl. 1680

LAMENT FOR HER HUSBAND, JAMES MACLEAN

It is I who am dejected
and have reason to be dismal,
as I look up expectant
at the place you used to sit at,
at the rack with your gun missing
which checked the flight of the roe-deer,
my harsh ruin that you have perished,
enemy of the stag on the hill-side.

When I was laying you out,
though I showed great courage,
there was an arrow in my liver
embedded to its feather,
for the fate of the hero
whose wisdom had no failing,
the world could never have harmed you
had you less pride than forbearance.

I composed you no welcome
though you came here, Seumas,
it is I who am wounded
and the leech cannot cure me,
for you are living no longer
Oh man most kind and gentle,
I begrudged you nothing
your mouth ever wanted.

Dread has overcome me
since this last Monday,
when my eyes beheld you
being borne by others,
with women grown distracted
and tearful men lamenting.
Since they left you in the graveyard,
alas my burden has grown heavy.

When they made to go homewards,
for me that was not easy,
with you, my love, buried
in the ground, damp and stony.

Com cho geal ris a' chanach
Fo chúl clannach, cas, dualach;
'S truagh nach robh mise mar-riut,
'S mi gun anam, 's an fhuar leab'!

Nuair a ràinig mi 'n clachan
Chaidh am braisid mo dheuraibh;
Bho nach d' leigeadh a steach mi
'Dh-ionns' na leap' a robh m'eudail.
Ach nam bitheadh tu maireann,
Chaoidh cha dhealaicheadh tu-fhéin sinn.
Ochain, ochain, mo sgaradh!
'S i mo bharail a thréig mi.

Air Di-dòmhnaich 'sa chlachan,
Och! cha 'n fhaic mi mo ghràdh ann.
Bidh gach aon té gu h-éibhinn
Is a céile fhéin làmh-rith';
Ach bidh mise gad ghearan-s',
'Fhir 'bu cheanalta nàdar.
Mo theinn thruagh 'bhith gad chumhadh,
'S tu 'n leab' chumhainn nan clàran.

Tha mi 'm ònrachd 's an fheasgar,
'Ghaoil, cha deasaich mi t' àite.
'S gun mo dhùil ri thu 'thighinn;
'S e, 'fhir cridhe, so 'chràidh mi.
Do chorp glé gheal th' air dubhadh,
'S do chul buidh' th' air dhroch chàradh.
Ged a dh' fhàg mi thu 'm dheoghainn,
B' e mo roghainn bhith làmh-riut.

Nam biodh fios air mo smaointinn
Aig gach aon dha bheil céile,
'S fad mun dèanadh iad gearan,
Fhad 's a dh' fhanadh iad-fhéin daibh.
Ged a gheibhinn de dh-òig'
Air achd 's gum pòsadh dhà-dheug mi,
'S dearbh nach faicinn bho thoiseach
Aon bu docha na 'n ceud fhear.

Body white as bog cotton
below thick curling ringlets,
a pity I was not beside you
in the cold bed, lifeless.

When I reached the kirkyard
my tears came more quickly,
for they didn't let me down to
the bed of my treasure,
but if you had been living
you would never have had us parted.
Alas, alas, my separation!
My senses have left me.

On Sunday in the kirktown
I won't see my darling,
every woman will be cheerful
with her husband beside her,
but I will be mourning
for the man of kindest nature.
What misery to keen you
in the narrow bed of deal-boards.

I am alone in the evening,
I'll set no place for you, dear one,
being without hope of your coming
has been my sore undoing.
Your bright white body has darkened,
your yellow hair's dishevelled.
Though I left you behind me,
I'd sooner be lying with you.

If everyone who is married
knew how I'm feeling,
they'd think long before complaining
while their spouses were living.
Even had I youth unstinted,
so twelve men could wed me,
it's certain I would not see any
dearer than the first one.

Nan do ghabhadh leat fògar,
'S barail bheò bhith aig càch ort,
'S grad a rachainn an tòir ort;
B' e sin sòlas mo shlàinte,
'N dùil gun deanadh tu tilleadh
'Dh-ionns' an iònaid a dh ' fhàg thu –
'S fheudar fhulang mar thachair;
'S ann a ghlais iad fo 'n chlàr thu.

Och a Righ, ghleidh mo chiall dhomh,
'S mi ga t' iargainn-s', a ghràidhein.
'Fhir 'bu tuigsich' 's bu chiallaich',
'S mór 'bha 'chiatabh 'co-fhàs riut. –
Tha mi 'nis mar Mhaol Ciarain,
Gad ghnàth-iarraidh 's mi cràiteach.
Math mo laigsinn, a Dhia, dhomh;
Gur h-e t' iasad a chràidh mi.

If you had been banished
and the others believed you living,
I'd set off at once to find you
– that'd restore my well-being –
in the hope you would return to
the place you have forsaken.
What has happened must be accepted:
they've locked you beneath the deal-board.

Oh King, preserve my senses,
as I long for you, beloved,
Oh man most sound in understanding,
His satisfaction in you was growing,
I am now like Maol Ciarain,
pining constantly, tormented,
Oh God, forgive my weakness,
it is the loan of you that broke me.

Sileas Nighean Mhic Raghnaill
c. 1660-1729

ALASDAIR A GLEANNA GARADH

Alasdair a Gleanna Garadh,
Thug thu 'n diugh gal air mo shùilibh;
'S beag ionghnadh mi bhith fo chreuchdaibh
'S gur tric 'gan reubadh as ùr iad;
'S beag ionghnadh mi bhith trom-osnach,
'S meud an dosgaidh th' air mo chàirdibh;
Gur tric an t-eug uainn a' gearradh
Rogha nan darag as àirde.

Chaill sinn ionann agus còmhla
Sir Dòmhnall 's a mhac 's a bhràthair;
Ciod e 'n stà dhuinn bhith 'gan gearan?
Thuit Mac Mhic Ailein 's a' bhlàr uainn;
Chaill sinn darag làidir liath-ghlas
A chumadh dìon air ar càirdean,
Capull-coille bhàrr na giùthsaich,
Seobhag sùil-ghorm lùthmhor làidir.

Bu tu ceann air céill 's air comhairl'
Anns gach gnothach am biodh cùram,
Aghaidh shoilleir sholta thlachdmhor,
Cridhe fial farsaing mu 'n chùinneadh;
Bu tu roghainn nan sàr-ghaisgeach,
Ar guala thaice 's tu b' fhiùghail;
Leómhann smiorail fearail feumail,
Ceann feachda chaill Seumas Stiùbhart.

Nam b' ionann duit-se 's do Dhòmhnall,
An uair a chuir e 'n long air muir,
Cha tigeadh tu dhachaidh gu bràth
Gun fhios dé 'm fàth as 'n do chuir:
Nuair a chunncas air an tràigh sibh
A bhith 'gur fàgail air faondradh,
Thuit ar cridheachan fo mhulad:
'S léir a bhuil – cha robh sibh saogh'lach.

Bu tu 'n lasair dhearg 'gan losgadh,
Bu tu sgoltadh iad gu 'n sàiltibh,
Bu tu curaidh cur a' chatha,
Bu tu 'n laoch gun athadh làimhe;

72

Sheila MacDonald
c. 1660-1729

ALASDAIR OF GLENGARRY

Alasdair of Glengarry
today you've set my tears dropping;
small wonder that I'm wounded,
with the wounds again torn open;
small wonder that I'm sighing
with my people in such misfortune;
often is Death found felling
the pick of our tallest oak-trees.

We lost, almost together,
Sir Donald, his son and brother;
what good is it to mourn them?
Clan Ranald fell in the slaughter,
our kin have lost their protector,
a strong grey-green oak-tree,
the capercailzie from the pine-wood,
a blue-eyed hawk, strong and powerful.

You were the wisest in giving counsel
in every matter that was troubling,
a bright face, mild and pleasant,
a generous heart, kind with money;
you were the choice of fine fighters,
a shoulder worthy to support us,
a courageous lion, capable and manly,
a leader lost for James Stuart.

If it had been the same for you as Donald
when he launched the galley,
you would never have come homewards
without finishing the matter;
when you were seen on the foreshore,
left there abandoned,
our hearts fell into sorrow,
clearly your life wasn't lasting.

You were the red torch to scorch them,
you'd cleave them to the ankles,
you were the battle-waging warrior,
the hero whose hand wouldn't falter;

73

Bu tu 'm bradan anns an fhìor-uisg,
Fireun air an eunlaith 's àirde,
Bu tu 'n leómhann thar gach beathach,
Bu tu damh leathan na cràice.

Bu tu 'n loch nach fhaoidte thaomadh,
Bu tu tobar faoilidh na slàinte,
Bu tu Beinn Nibheis thar gach aonach,
Bu tu chreag nach fhaoidte theàrnadh;
Bu tu clach uachdair a' chaisteil,
Bu tu leac leathan na sràide,
Bu tu leug lòghmhor nam buadhan,
Bu tu clach uasal an fhàinne.

Bu tu 'n t-iubhar thar gach coillidh,
Bu tu 'n darach daingean làidir,
Bu tu 'n cuileann 's bu tu 'n draigheann,
Bu tu 'n t-abhall molach blàthmhor;
Cha robh do dhàimh ris a' chritheann
Na do dhligheadh ris an fheàrna;
Cha robh bheag ionnad de 'n leamhan;
Bu tu leannan nam ban àlainn.

Bu tu céile na mnà prìseil,
'S oil leam fhéin d' a dìth an dràsd thu;
Ged nach ionann domh-sa 's dhi-se,
'S goirt a fhuair mise mo chàradh;
H-uile bean a bhios gun chéile,
Guidheadh i Mac Dé 'n a àite,
O 's E 's urra bhith 'ga còmhnadh
Anns gach bròn a chuireas càs oirr'.

Guidheam t' anam a bhith sàbhailt
Ona chàradh anns an ùir thu;
Guidheam sonas air na dh'fhàg thu
Ann ad àros 's ann ad dhùthaich:
Gum faic mi do mhac ad àite
Ann an sàibhreas 's ann an cùram:
Alasdair a Gleanna Garadh,
Thug thu 'n diugh gal air mo shùilibh.

the eagle in the flock that flies highest,
you were the salmon in fresh water,
the lion over all creatures,
the sturdy stag with great antlers.

You were the bountiful well of healing,
you were the loch that can't be emptied,
you were Ben Nevis over every summit,
the crag that can't be descended;
you were the topmost stone of the castle,
you were the broad flagstone of the cellar,
you were the priceless magic jewel,
in the ring you were the gem-stone.

You were the oak, strong and steadfast,
you were the yew over every forest,
you were the holly and the blackthorn,
the gnarled apple-tree in blossom;
you had no kinship with the aspen,
you owed nothing to the alder,
you had no connection with the lime tree;
you were the darling of lovely women.

You were the spouse of a precious lady
whose loss of you harms me,
though she and I are different
my lot has brought me anguish;
let every woman who has no husband,
pray to the Son of the Father,
since it is He who can help her
in every sorrow and hardship.

I pray your soul may find salvation
now that you lie buried;
I pray for happiness for your people
in your house and your country;
may I see your son in your position,
in wealth and importance;
Alasdair of Glengarry,
today you've set my tears dropping.

COMHAIRLE AIR NA NIGHEANAN OGA

An toiseach m' aimsir is mo dhòigh ri bargan
Gun robh mi 'g earbsa nach cealgte orm;
Cha chòmhradh cearbach air ro-bheag leanmhuinn
Bho aois mo leanbaidh chaidh fheuchainn dhòmhs';
Ach nis bho chì mi cor nan daoine,
An comunn gaolach gur faoin a ghlòr,
Cha dèan mi m' aontadh ri neach fo 'n t-saoghal;
Chan eil gach aon diùbh air aon chainnt beòil.

Nach fhaic sibh òig-fhear nam meall-shùil bòidheach,
Le theangaidh leòmaich 's e labhairt rium,
Le spuir 's le bhòtan, le ad 's le chleòca,
Le chora-cheann spòrsail an òr-fhuilt duinn;
Saoilidh gòrag le bhriathraibh mòrach
'Ga cur an dòchas le glòr a chinn:
"A ghaoil, gabh truas rium 's na leig gu h-uaigh mi:
Do ghaol a bhuair mi bho ghluais mi fhìn.

"Le d' theangaidh leacaich nam briathran tearca,
'S e saobhadh t' fhacail dh'fhàg sac 'gam leòn;
Gu bheil mi 'g altrum am thaobh an tacaid
A rinn mo ghlacadh 's mo ghreas' fo 'n fhòid."
Mar shamhladh dhà sud gaoth a' Mhàirt ud,
Thig bho na h-àirdibh 's nach taobh i seòl:
'Nuair gheobh e mhiann di gun toir e bhriathra
Nach fhac e riamh i, 's car fiar 'n a shròin.

Na geallan breugach air bheag reusan,
Fallsail, eucorach, neo-ghlan rùn,
Air eagal bhreugan no masladh fhaotainn
'S ann leam nach b' éibhinn taobhsann riù;
A chlann, na éisdibh ri 'n glòr gun éifeachd,
'S na toiribh spéis do fhear caogaidh shùil;
Gur h-aobhar reusain dhuibhs' an tréigeadh –
'S ann annta fhéin a bhios gné nan lùb.

Bha mi uair 'nuair a bha mi 'm ghruagaich
Gum fuighinn uaigneas gun fhios do chàch;
Mar shamhladh bruadair an diugh 'ga luaidh rium,
Gun dad de bhuanachd ach buaidh mar ghnàth,
Na geallan glé-mhór a gheobhainn fhéin bhuap'
Air chor 's nach tréigeadh iad mi gu bràth;
A nis is léir dhomh na rinn mi dh' eucoir
'S a' mheud 's a dh'éisd mi d' am breugan bàth.

76

ADVICE TO YOUNG GIRLS

When I was a young girl, and hoping for a bargain,
I had confidence that I wouldn't be deceived;
improper overtures, lacking in candour,
never in my childhood were tried on me;
but now I'm acquainted with men's behaviour,
and know that the voice of love is weak,
I won't unite myself with anyone in the wide world,
they are not all sincere in what they speak.

Don't you see that young man, with his winning glances,
and persuasive tongue when he's conversing with me,
with his spurs and his boots, his hat and his mantle,
his swaggering head and golden-brown locks;
a silly young maiden will think from his fawning
that she has reason to place hope in his talk,
'Oh love, have pity, don't send me to my Maker,
I've been ill with love for you since first I walked.

'With your mild speech and shy prattling,
your misleading words have put me in pain;
at the side of my breast I'm nursing an arrow
that pierced me and hurries me into the grave.'
Just like that fellow is the squalling March-wind,
dropping from the heights and helping no sail,
he'll get his way with her, and then he'll clear off,
swearing he never saw her, with his nose in the air.

For fear of disgrace or causing gossip,
I think it no joke when a girl attends
to their false promises, without any grounding,
of lying, wrong and impure intent.
Girls, don't heed their empty vaunting,
don't fall for the man who winks at you;
you have good reason to forsake them –
they are all rotten, right to the core.

There was a time when I was a young girl
when I'd need to get peace away from the rest;
today it's like a dream for me to say so
when nothing remains but the abiding effect
of the great big promises they used to give me,
that they would never leave me forlorn,
now it is clear to me I was mistaken,
in listening so much to their foolish fraud.

Ach a fhearaibh òga, ge mór nur bòlaich,
'S math 's aithne dhòmh-sa cuid mhór d' ur gnàths:
Gu barrail, bòidheach sibh tighinn am chòmh-dhail,
Le 'r teangaidh leòmaich 's le 'r còmhradh tlàth;
Ghabhte ceòl leibh an aodann gòraig,
'S mur bidh i eòlach gun gabh i à:
'Nuair bhios e stòlda 's 'nuair gheobh e leòr dhi,
Gum bidh Ochòin aic' an lorg bhith bàth.

A ghruagach chéillidh na creid fhéin iad,
An car-fo'n-sgéith sin bhios ann an gràdh;
Chan eil 's an t-saoghal nach creid an saoradh,
Ach 's mise dh'fhaodadh a chaochladh ràdh;
Taobh an inntinn mar as cinnteach,
Is theirig aotrom air ghaol thoirt dàibh:
Dh' aindheoin fhocail 's a bhriathra brosguil,
Na dèan do lochd leis an t-sochar-dhàil.

A ghruagach dheud-gheal an fhuilt theud-bhuidhe,
Cum do cheutaidh fo d' cheud-bharr ùr;
Na creid am breugan 's na tog droch-sgeula,
Ged robh fear leumnach 'n an déidh mar chùl;
Dh' aindheoin uaigneis is raspars uasal,
Na leig e 'n uachdar air chruas a ghlùin,
Ach cum e 'n ìochdar ge b' oil le fhiacaill,
Mur toir e bhriathar gur fhiach leis thu.

Am fear a thriallas a dhol a dh'iarraidh
Na mnà as miannaiche bhios d' a réir,
Gur cailinn shuairc i nach fhuilig mì-stuamachd,
Na dhol an uaigneas le neach fo 'n ghréin;
Mar shamhladh bhà sud, a bhrìgh a nàire,
Dhol nas dàine na mànran béil;
Bheir fear gun riaghailt an sin a bhriathar
Gu bheil i fiadhta 's nach fhiach a gné.

Ma bhios i gléidhteach air nì 's air feudail,
Their fear gun reusan gum bidh i crìon,
'S ma bhios i pàirteach air nithe àraidh,
Gun abair càch rith' gum b' fheàrrd' i ciall;
An té tha stròdhail, cha bhuin i dhòmh-sa
Mar chéile pòsta bhon tha i fial;
Gur cailinn shàmhach nach fhuilig tàmailt,
A mòid no mànran an àirde miann.

But young men, though great your bombast,
well I'm acquainted with much of your style,
handsome and cocky, coming to see me,
with your affected speech and honeyed lies;
you'd address songs to a foolish girl's beauty,
which, if she's naïve, she will not decline,
and when he's calmed and has had enough of her,
she will cry 'Alas' for being unwise.

Oh prudent maiden, do not trust them,
or that dissemblance in their wiles;
everyone on earth believes their protest,
but I am able to say otherwise.
Trust the intellect as it is certain,
and go careful in giving your plight,
despite his words and encouraging prattle,
don't harm yourself with some silly intrigue.

White-toothed maiden with hair yellow like harp-strings,
keep your affections fresh in your heart,
don't believe their lies or raise scandal,
even if a plausible man can make them match;
despite his loneliness and vain swanking
don't let him get on top however hard his knee,
but keep him under in spite of his gnashing,
unless he swears that you're good enough to keep.

The man who sets out to find and bring back
the perfect woman he most desires
will choose a meek girl, who can't stand lewdness
or going apart with a man to flirt;
who accordingly, because of her virtue,
will allow nothing bolder than a murmured word;
but an unbridled man will make the assertion
that she is surly and of a worthless kind.

If she's thrifty with her belongings and cattle
a stupid man will say she's tight;
and if she's generous with her assets,
everyone will tell her she should have more sense;
the one who's lavish does not attract me
as a marriage partner just because she's kind;
but the quiet girl who will cause no scandal,
her vows and honour of the highest intent.

DO RIGH SEUMAS

'S binn an sgeul so tha 'd ag ràdhainn,
  Mo Mhaili bheag Ò,
Ma sheasas e gun fhàillinn,
  Mo nighean rùin Ò;
Rìgh Seumas a bhith air sàile
'S a' tighinn a steach gun dàil oirnn
Chur misneach ann a chàirdibh,
  Mo Mhaili bheag Ò.

Nan tigeadh oirnne Seumas,
  Mo Mhaili bheag Ò,
Le chabhlach làidir ghleusta,
  Mo nighean rùin Ò,
Ge fada sinn 'n ar n-éiginn
Fo ainneart Cuigse 's cléire,
'S e sud a dhèanadh feum dhuinn,
  Mo Mhaili bheag Ò.

'S e sud a thogadh sunnd oirnn,
  Mo Mhaili bheag Ò,
Nam b' fhìor na bheil mi cluinntinn,
  Mo nighean rùin Ò;
Do loingeasan 'gam bréideadh
'S an cuan a bhith 'ga reubadh,
'S do nàimhdean duit a' géilleadh,
  Mo Mhaili bheag Ò.

Tha do chathair aig *Hanòver,*
  Mo Mhaili bheag Ò,
Do chrùn 's do chlaidheamh còrach,
  Mo nighean rùin Ò;
Tha 'n sean-fhacal cho cinnteach
'S gur barail leam gur fìor e,
Nach marcach muc an dìollaid,
  Mo Mhaili bheag Ò.

Ach Alba éiribh còmhla,
  Mo Mhaili bheag Ò,
Mun geàrr Sasunnaich ur sgòrnan,
  Mo nighean rùin Ò;
'Nuair thug iad air son òir uaibh
Ur creideas is ur stòras,
'S nach eil e 'n diugh 'n ur pòca,
  Mo Mhaili bheag Ò.

TO KING JAMES

Sweet this news they are telling,
My little Mollie O,
if it proves true without defect,
My darling girl O,
that King James is on the ocean,
even now approaching,
bringing hope to his supporters,
My little Mollie O.

If King James would come and help us,
My little Mollie O,
with his powerful fleet of vessels,
My darling girl O,
though we've suffered long oppression
under tyrant Whigs and clergy
it would truly be a blessing,
My little Mollie O.

That's what would raise our spirits,
My little Mollie O,
if it's true what I am hearing,
My darling girl O,
that your ships with their rigging,
the oceans are cleaving,
and your enemies are yielding,
My little Mollie O.

Hanover had taken your throne too,
My little Mollie O,
your crown and sword of justice,
My darling girl O,
the proverb's so appropriate
I think it now stands proven –
a pig in a saddle's no horseman,
My little Mollie O.

Scotland, rise as one body,
My little Mollie O,
before the English cut your throttles,
My darling girl O,
since your credit and resources
they bought off you with a coinage
that's no longer in your pockets
My little Mollie O.

Gur goirt leam thug iad sgrìob oirbh,
  Mo Mhaili bheag Ò,
'Nuair a dheasaich iad ur dìnneir,
  Mo nighean rùin Ò;
'Nuair chuir iad uinnean puinnsein
'Ga gheàrradh air gach truinnsear:
Ma 's fiach sibh bidh se cuimhnichte,
  Mo Mhaili bheag Ò.

Chaill Sasunnaich an nàire,
  Mo Mhaili bheag Ò,
A' ruith air beart mi-ghnàthaichte,
  Mo nighean rùin Ò:
Tha mo dhòchas anns an Àrd-rìgh,
An rìgh tha tighinn air sàil' oirnn,
Gun réitich sibh *Whitehall* dhà,
  Mo Mhaili bheag Ò.

I regret they brought disaster,
   My little Mollie O,
when they prepared you your banquet
   My darling girl O,
when they put a poisoned onion
sliced up in every portion,
you won't forget it if you've honour
   My little Mollie O.

The English behave most crassly
   My little Mollie O,
in pursuing this wrong action,
   My darling girl O,
I trust the King of Heaven
you'll soon have Whitehall ready
for the king who's on the water,
   My little Mollie O.

NINETEENTH- AND TWENTIETH-CENTURY VERSE
Mary MacKellar of Lochaber
1836-90

AN IARRAIDH DIOMHAIN

C' àit am bheil fois, agus c' àit am bheil tàmh,
C' àit am bheil fois, agus c' àit am bheil tàmh,
C' àit am bheil ìoc-shlaint do chridhe fo phràmh
No c' àit am bheil suaimhneas o uamhann 's o chràdh?

Mar thonnan na fairge a' bualadh gu dlùth,
'S e nuallan, is monmhur, mu oirean nan stùc,
Tha luasgan is gluasad 's an t-saoghal mu 'n cuairt,
'S gach ni cho beag socair ri broilleach nan stuagh.

Chuir mi flùr, 's rinn e fàs ann an gàradh ri deas,
'S nuair shaoil mi e cùmhraidh le driùchd agus teas,
'S ann thàinig gaoth reòt' 's air mo ròs thàinig bàs,
'S bha dhuilleagan caoin a' dol aog air a bhàrr.

Thug mi eun as a' choill dhèanamh seinn dhomh gu binn,
'S nuair shaoil mi bhi 'g éisdeachd a cheileiridh ghrinn,
'S ann shuidh e air géig, 's e gu h-éisleanach trom,
Gu marbh-shuileach tùrsach, 's e tùchte gun phong.

Sheall mi 's a' ghleann air son fois agus tàimh
Ri latha geal samhraidh 's a' ghrian anns an àird;
'S mu 'n deach i 's an iar, gu'n robh 'n iarmailt fo ghruaim,
Is beithir, 's beum-sléibhe, a' reubadh nam bruach.

Dh' iarr mi gu fois agus dh' iarr mi gu sìth,
Dh' iarr mi gu teicheadh o chogadh 's o strìth;
'S nuair shaoil mi gu 'n d' fhuair mi gu cala nam buadh,
'S ann bha mi gu h-anrach air taisdeal nan stuagh.

Dh' iarr mi gu fois, is gun fhois air an t-saogh'l,
Is leag mi mo cheann air geal-bhroilleach mo ghaoil,
'S bha chluasag ud làn de chaoin-dhuilleach nan ròs
Ach, ochan, 'nam measg gu 'n robh 'n dris mar bu nòs.

O ciamar bhiodh fois ann an àrfhaich nan tuagh,
'S gur cruaidh bhios an cogadh, mu 'n coisinn sinn buaidh,
Bidh leagadh, is leònadh, is dò-bheairt, 's an strìth
'S ged 's truagh e, gur dìomhain bhi 'g iarraidh na sìth.

NINETEENTH- AND TWENTIETH-CENTURY VERSE
Mary MacKellar of Lochaber
1836-1890

THE VAIN SEARCH

Where is there peace and where is there quiet,
where is there peace and where is there quiet,
where is a cure for the heart that's oppressed,
and where is there ease from horror and dread?

Like the waves of the ocean that break on the shore,
and murmur and moan at the foot of the rocks,
is the tossing and turning all over the world,
with everything as restless as the breast of the surge.

I planted a flower in a bower where it grew,
and when it smelled sweet with the sun and the dew
death came and destroyed it with a frost-laden wind,
and its tender young leaves turned yellow to the tips.

I brought a bird from the wood to sing sweetly to me,
and when I would listen to the small bird's glee
it was dull and dejected, sitting on the mould,
its eyes without lustre, its reed without note.

I searched the glen for peace and for quiet
one bright summer's day with the sun in the sky,
and before it moved west, the heavens turned black,
and lightning and thunder shattered the crags.

I wanted to find rest and I wanted to find quiet,
I wanted to flee from war and from strife,
and when I thought I'd reached the port of the brave,
I found I'd gone wrong travelling the waves.

I wanted rest though none exists on this earth,
and I lay my head down on my love's white breast,
and that pillow was full of the petals of the rose,
but, alas, in their midst there was also the thorn.

Oh, how could there be peace on the battle-field,
when the clashes must be hard before we're set free,
there'll be felling and wounding, iniquity and feuds,
and though sad, it's vain to be looking for a truce.

85

Ach nuair choisneas sinn buaidh mar is dual do gach sonn,
Air a' gheal-ghaineamh airgid tha thall thar nan tonn,
Gheibh sinn suaimhneas bhios buan thar gach uamhunn is strìth,
'S bidh sinn crùinte le gaol an tigh aobhach na sìth.

But when we win victory as everyone should
on the silvery sand that lies over the flood,
we'll find a tranquillity that cures every breach,
and be crowned with love in the joyous hall of peace.

Màiri Nic A' Phearsain
1821-98

NUAIR BHA MI OG

Moch 's mi 'g éirigh air bheagan éislein,
  Air madainn Chéitein 's mi ann an Os,
Bha spréidh a' geumnaich an ceann a chéile,
  'S a' ghrian ag éirigh air Leac-an-Stòrr;
Bha gath a' boillsgeadh air slios nam beanntan,
  Cur tuar na h-oidhche 'na dheann fo sgòd,
Is os mo chionn sheinn an uiseag ghreannmhor,
  Toirt 'na mo chuimhne nuair bha mi òg.

Toirt 'na mo chuimhne le bròn is aoibhneas,
  Nach fhaigh mi cainnt gus a chur air dòigh,
Gach car is tionndadh an corp 's an inntinn,
  Bho'n dh'fhàg mi 'n gleann 'n robh sinn gun ghò;
Bha sruth na h-aibhne dol sìos cho tàimhidh,
  Is toirm nan allt freagairt cainnt mo bheòil,
'S an smeòrach bhinn suidhe seinn air meanglan,
  Toirt 'na mo chuimhne nuair bha mi òg.

Nuair bha mi gòrach a' siubhal mòintich,
  'S am fraoch a' sròiceadh mo chòta bàn,
Feadh thoman còinnich gun snàthainn a bhrògan,
  'S an eigh 'na còsan air lochan tàimh;
A' falbh an aonaich ag iarraidh chaorach,
  'S mi cheart cho aotrom ri naosg air lòn,
Gach bot is poll agus talamh toll,
  Toirt 'na mo chuimhne nuair bha mi òg.

Toirt 'na mo chuimhn' iomadh nì a rinn mi,
  Nach faigh mi 'm bann gu ceann thall mo sgeòil,
A' falbh 'sa gheamhradh gu luaidh is bainnsean
  Gun solus lainnteir ach ceann an fhòid;
Bhiodh òigridh ghreannmhor ri ceòl is dannsa,
  Ach dh'fhalbh an t-ám sin 's tha 'n gleann fo bhròn;
Bha 'n tobht aig Anndra 's e làn de fheanntaig,
  Toirt 'na mo chuimhne nuair bha mi òg.

Mary MacPherson, 'Big Mary of the Songs'
1821-98

WHEN I WAS YOUNG

I rose up early, with little worry,
  one May morning in Os,
the cattle lowing to one another,
  the sun rising on Leac-an-Stòrr;
its rays engulfing the hillsides,
  hurrying away night's dark clouds,
and above me sang the skylark,
  reminding me of when I was young.

Bringing to mind with a joy and sorrow
  that I cannot quite put into words,
every change to mind and body
  since I left the glen without fraud;
with the river flowing by gently
  and the burns babbling to my talk,
and the thrush singing sweetly,
  reminding me of when I was young.

When I heedlessly roamed the moorland,
  the heather tugging my petticoat,
over mossy mounds without footwear,
  ice in crannies on stagnant pools;
fetching sheep from the hilltops,
  light as the snipe in the marsh,
every bog and hummock and hollow
  reminding me of when I was young.

Bringing to mind the things I did then,
  I won't unravel till my days have run,
going in winter to waulkings, weddings,
  with no lantern but a glowing turf;
there'd be young folk singing and dancing,
  but that time's past and the glen's in gloom;
Andrew's croft, overgrown with nettles,
  reminding me of when I was young.

Nuair chuir mi cuairt air gach gleann is cruachan,
    Far 'n robh mi suaimhneach a' cuallach bhó,
Le òigridh ghuanach tha nis air fuadach,
    De shliochd na tuath bha gun uaill gun ghò,
Na raoin 's na cluaintean fo fhraoch is luachair,
    Far 'n tric na bhuaineadh leam sguab is dlò,
'S nam faicinn sluagh agus tighean suas annt',
    Gum fàsainn suaimhneach mar bha mi òg.

An uair a dhìrich mi gual an t-Sìthein,
    Gun leig mi sgìos dhiom air bruaich an lòin;
Bha buadhan m'inntinn a' triall le sìnteig,
    Is sùil mo chinn faicinn loinn gach pòir;
Bha 'n t-sóbhrach mhìn-bhuidh' 's am beàrnan-brìghde,
    An cluaran rìoghail, is lus an òir,
'S gach bileag aoibhneach fo bhraon na h-oidhche,
    Toirt 'na mo chuimhne nuair bha mi òg.

Nuair chuir mi cùl ris an eilean chùbhraidh,
    'S a ghabh mi iùbhrach na smùid gun seòl,
Nuair shéid i 'n dùdach 's a shìn an ùspairt,
    'S a thog i cùrsa o Thìr a' Cheò;
Mo chridhe brùite 's na deòir le m' shùilean,
    A' falbh gu dùthaich gun sùrd, gun cheòl,
Far nach faic mi cluaran no neòinean guanach,
    No fraoch no luachair air bruaich no lòn.

BROSNACHADH NAN GAIDHEAL

Cuiribh Teàrlach suas le aighear,
    'S deagh MhacPhàrlain suas le caithreim,
Cuiribh Aonghas suas le buaidh,
    Air ceann an t-sluaigh far 'n d'fhuair e aran.

Chuidich sud le neart nan Gàidheal,
    Air taobh Theàrlaich Bhàin gun mhearachd,
Na sgeith an *Courier* de chlàbar,
    'S ann am fàbhor ri Sir Coinneach.

Cuiribh Teàrlach suas le cliù,
    Oir dhearbh e dhuibh a dhùrachd cheana,
Is gheibh sibh cead air féidh nan stùc,
    Is còir ás ùr air bhur cuid fearainn.

I travelled each glen and headland
   where once carefree I tended cows,
with playful children now in exile,
   stock of the people without pride or grudge;
the fields and plains under rush and heather
   where I've reaped swathes and sheaves of corn,
had I seen houses and people there still
   I'd be happy as I was when young.

When I'd climbed the Sìthean's shoulder
   I rested a while beside the burn,
my thoughts were skipping and jumping,
   my eyes on the beauty of every flower,
the dandelion and pale-yellow primrose,
   the thistle royal and marigold,
dew sparkling on every grass blade,
   reminding me of when I was young.

When I turned my back on the fragrant island,
   and boarded the steam-ship which has no jib,
when she blew her horn and began her churning
   and made her way from the Isle of Mist,
my heart was broken, my eyes tear-filled,
   leaving for a land without cheer or song,
where I see no thistle nor joyful daisy,
   no heather nor rushes on brae or lawn.

INCITEMENT OF THE GAELS

Put up Charles with glad exulting
   and good MacFarlane with joyful cheer,
put up Angus with hope and courage
   to stand for the people where he was reared.

That will help the strength of the Gaels
   ranked behind Charles who has no blemish;
the filth and claptrap the *Courier* spewed out
   is only to the advantage of Sir Kenneth.

Put up Charles and sing his praise,
   his sincerity he's proved to you before,
he'll win you the right to the deer on the braes
   and a new title to your plot of the land.

'Sa cheàrn 's na dh'àithneadh dhuinn de Dia,
  Chan fhaod sinn triall air sliabh no gaineimh,
A h-ùile nì robh smear no luach,
  Gun spùinn iad uainn le lagh an fhearainn.

Chan eil bileag ghorm no uaine,
  Far 'n robh dualachas mo sheanar,
Leis na bric tha snàmh fo'n chuan,
  Nach tug iad uainn, a dheòin no dh'aindeoin.

Ma thog neach eisir ann an cliabh,
  No maorach ann am meadhon mara,
Théid an cur fo ghlais 's fo dhìon,
  Le laghan diongmhalt' dìon an fhearainn.

Faodaidh gu bheil a' chainnt so garbh,
  Ach 's tric tha 'n fhìrinn searbh ri labhairt,
Chaidh luingeas-chogaidh 's sluagh fo airm,
  A dhìon 's a theàrmunn lagh an fhearainn.

Nuair a bha na h-uachdarain cruinn,
  Ann am baile-cinn na siorrachd,
Cuimhnichear ri iomadh linn,
  An guim a rinn iad gus ar mealladh.

Sgrìobh iad àithne dhaingeann dhian,
  Do'n ionad air nach dèan sinn labhairt,
Na h-aingle is am fear nach b'fhiach
  A thighinn a riaghladh lagh an fhearainn.

Nuair leugh Ivory an àithne,
  Chùnnt e chuid a b'fheàrr d'a aingil,
Ach dh'fhàg e chuid thàinig an Bhràighe,
  Oir bha'n cnàmhan air am prannadh.

"Togaidh sinn òirnn do na glinn,
  Leis na tha de Ghoill fainear dhuinn,
'S ma bhios sibhse fo m'chomannd,
  Théid an ceannsachadh dha'n aindeoin."

Nuair a ràinig iad na glinn,
  'S ann bha na suinn nach dèanadh mearachd
Air an crioslachadh le fìrinn,
  'S cha robh innleachd air am prannadh.

In the country granted us by the Father
we may not wander the moor or strand,
everything of any worth or value
they deprived us of by the law of the land.

No blade of grass, new sprung or older,
growing on my grandfather's hereditary patch,
nor spotted trout swimming in the ocean
have they not stolen despite our stand.

If someone lifts a creel with an oyster,
or in the open sea they find a clam,
they'll be apprehended and locked away
under the law protecting the land.

This talk may seem a little harsh,
but often the truth is bitter to say,
a fleet of battle-ships and troops with arms
set off to safeguard the law of the land.

Many a generation will now remember
how in the main town of the parish
a plan was hatched in order to deceive us
by the landowners there gathered.

They wrote an urgent pressing letter
to the accursed angels and that scurrilous man
stationed at the place we will not mention
to come and enforce the law of the land.

Ivory counted out the best of his angels
having read all that was in the demand,
but the lot that came, he left in the Braes here
for that's where their bones were hammered.

'With all the Lowlanders we can muster
and all of you under my command,
we'll make for the glens just as I order,
and sort them out or I'll be damned.'

When Ivory and his army reached the glens
before them stood the men that wouldn't falter,
girded about with righteousness,
evil had not made *them* slacken.

Ghlaoidh Ivory an sin le gruaim,
  Ris na truaghain, a chuid aingeal –
"Chan fhaigh sinn am feasd a' bhuaidh,
  'S e seo an sluagh a fhuair a' bheannachd.

"Cha till mise gun mo dhiùmbadh,
  Nì mi cùirt am measg nan aingeal,
Bheir mi bheathachadh bho Dhùghall,
  'S cuiridh mi an crùn air Calum."

Dh'ainmichinn iad air an cinn,
  Bha seinn air ainneart luchd an fhearainn,
A thionndaidh 'n còta air an druim,
  'S a dh'ith na rainn dhe'n d'rinn iad ealain.

Falbh le leabhraichean 's 'gan seinn
  Dha na suinn a bh'aig a' bhaile –
"Gheibh sibh mil air bhàrr an fheòir
  Am Manitòba, is na fanaibh."

Phàidh na h-uachdarain dhaibh duais
  Mas do ghluais iad o'n a' bhaile,
Ach 's e 'n gad air an robh 'n t-iasg
  A fhuair na sìochairean, 's iad falamh.

Then Ivory shouted in a rage
  to the poor wretches, his troop of angels,
'Over this lot we'll never win the day,
  they are the ones who have the advantage.

'Turning back would cause me sorrow,
  I'll hold a court among my angels,
I'll take his livelihood away from Donald
  and I'll set the crown myself on Calum.'

I could name them one by one,
  who sang against the owners of the land
and turned their coats upon their backs
  and ate the words which had been their art.

Who went with books, declaiming loudly
  to the young men working the homelands,
'Why stay here when you can reap honey
  from the top of the grass in Manitoba?'

The landowners offered to pay a reward
  to the young men if they'd leave the township,
but it was only the withe where the fish had hung
  the wretches got when they were starving.

Màiri NicDhòmhnaill

MO LORGAN FHIN

Dé chòrdadh ruibh a Mhàthair?
'Riumsa? O chreutair!
Iarrtas mo chridhe an diugh –
Seasamh air mo dhà chois
Cead mo chas a shìneadh
Agus mo lorgan fhìn
Fhaicinn
San tràigh ghil ud.
Nam chadal 's nam dhùsgadh
Tha mo rathad fom chomhair
S mi feitheamh sa feitheamh.
Aitean m'òige
Na lorgan gan cuartachadh...'

A cridhe glaiste 's e caoidh

Théid sinn ann gheall mo chridhe-sa
Théid sinn ann san t-Samhradh
Gun dochan sam bith dha na cnàmhan ciùrramach
Cuiridh sinn sibh nur suidhe
Far an gluais am muran
Agus chì sibh na lorgan.

'An siaban blàth fo mo làmhan
Gach gràinean mar mhìle bliadhna
Am muran a' gluasad
Agus chluinninn iad
Na guthan a dh'fhalbh.
Chraithinn a' ghainmheach far m'aodaich
Agus choisichinn
Mo cheumanan dìreach
Oir bha fios agam
Gun robh mi dol dhachaidh.'

Thuit i na cadal a raoir
An sneachda fhathast air an làr
Cha tig Samhradh dhuinn tuilleadh
S tha mo chridhe-sa caoidh.

Mary MacDonald

MY OWN FOOTPRINTS

What is your wish, Mother?
'My wish? O child!
The desire of my heart today
To stand on my own two feet
Strength to step out
And see my own footprints
In that white sand.
Waking and sleeping
My road is before me,
Waiting, waiting.
The places of my youth
Foot prints encircling.'

Her heart locked and sorrowing

We will go there
Promised my heart
We will go when the Summer comes
Without injury to fragile bones
We will place you gently
Where the bent grass moves.
You shall see your foot prints.

'The drift sand warm under my hands
Each grain like a thousand years
The bent grass moving
And I would hear them
The voices of the departed.
I would shake the sand from my clothing
And walk
My footprints straight
For I knew that I was going home.'

She fell asleep last night
The snow still on the ground
Our Summer will not come
And my heart is sorrowing.

CRAOBHAN

Nach eil e iongantach
Gur anns na craobhan
A nis tha bheatha
Craobhan
Air an dluth-chur
S air fàs suas
Am muchadh a' ghlinne
'S a' dubhadh na gréine.

Chuir iad as
Dha na caoraich
S tha an cìobair
Air fhògradh
Tobhta a shinnsrean
Fuar falamh
S an gleann fo na
Craobhan.

AM BOLA BEAG

S ann leatsa
Bha am bola beag air an sgeilp
Oir ghabh thu còir air
Cheud là shìn thu mach do làmh:
'Faigh mi bola eile dheth?'
Ceannruisgt' agus casruisgt'
Shuidh tu
Aig a' ghriosaich.

Dh'fhalbh thu uainn
Mar a dh'fhalbh do cho-aoisean eile
Nuair a chuireadh fios ort.
Cha b'ann ceannruisgt' neo casruisgt'
Agus
Cha b'e bola beag
A bha nad làimh
Ach Bìobull ùr
Agus sgrìobhte air an duilleig
An làimh sgrìobhaidh m'athar:
Gu'm beannaicheadh Dia thu agus
Gu'n gleidheadh E thu.'

Gun gleidheadh E thu...

98

TREES

Is it not strange
That it is in the trees
There now is life
Trees
Planted close
Now grown high
Choking the glen
Darkening the sun.

The sheep
Are gone
The shepherd
In exile
The house of his forebears
Cold-empty
The glen under
Trees.

THE LITTLE BOWL

Yours
The little bowl on the shelf
You made it yours
The first day you reached out your hand:
'Another bowl of it?'
Barehead and barefoot
You sat
By the fire's heart.

You went from us
With your generation
When you were called
Not bareheaded nor barefoot.
And
In your hand
Not the little bowl –
A new Bible.
Written on the white page
In my father's hand:
'Gum beannaicheadh Dia thu agus
Gu'n gleidheadh E thu.'

'May He protect you...'

Thill do Bhìobull dhachaidh
An sgrìobhadh fhathast air an duilleig
Agus thill do ghuth:
'Faigh mi bola eile dheth?'

Your Bible came back to us
The words still on the page
And your voice:
'Another bowl of it?'

Catriona NicGumaraid

GUN STIUIR

Uair, 's am bruaillean na bu theotha
chaidh mi iomrall anns a' cheòthach,
m'uilebheistean ag èirigh na mo choinneamh,
a' dannsa mun cuairt an dannsa cathaich.
Ged a dh'fhiach mi sabaid riutha
cha d'rinn mi'n gnothach am mùchadh buileach.
Dhùisg mi às a' mheara- chadal
's mi air mo chlaoidh, 's mi grìseach prapach,
gun chreud gun bhàt' a stiùirinn romham,
gun bhrèid ri crathadh air a' mhunadh.
Thionndaidh mi a-bhos is tharam
cha d' fhuair mi Dia no fiù's dia coimheach.

Ochoin, a Rìgh, an e sabaid fhalamh
a bhith sgrìobadh an fhìrinn às an talamh?

EILIDH

Bha dùil agam gum biodh tu agam
measg chreag is tiùrr is glinn,
's gun ionnsaicheadh tu cainnt Dhiarmaid
gu siùbhlach bhuamsa fhèin;
chan ann an seo san Ear-Bhaile
far nach tuig mi cleas na cloinn'
ach a-nochd gur dlùth an dàimh, a chagair
's tu torghan air a' chìch.

HOWFF

Nan cròileagan aig ceann a' bhàr,
làmh thar làimh a' togail pinnt,
an godail air tighinn gu drabasdachd.
'O, dùin do bheul, Iain Mhòir –
cuimhnich, tha boireannach sa chuideachd sa.'
Balgam cabhagach de lionn
's thionndaidh an còmhradh gu iasgach chudaigean.

Nan cròileagan an Dùn Dèagh,
tom taobh tuim sa chladh cruinn,
tha na mairbh fo ghiuthaisean ribeagach,
ach fad air falbh air an taobh a-muigh
tha saighdear bochd air adhlacadh
far nach dèan e air a' chuideachd cron,
oir bhàsaich e le cholera!

Catriona Montgomery

RUDDERLESS

Once when the sultry heat was more oppressive
I went astray in the mist,
my demons rising up to meet me,
writhing in mad, savage dance.
Although I tried to struggle with them
I did not manage to subdue them completely.
I woke from the delirium,
exhausted, shivering and bleary-eyed,
without creed, without a boat that I could steer before me;
without as much as a sail flapping on the horizon.
I turned this way and that and did not find God or even a false god.

My God, is it an empty fight
to be eternally scratching truth from the earth?

EILIDH

I thought that I would have you
midst rock, sea-wrack and glen,
and that you would learn Diarmaid's language
fluently from myself.
Not here, in this east-coast city,
where I don't understand the children's play.
But tonight the kinship is close
as you gurgle at the breast.

HOWFF

Huddling at the bar
a fankle of hands lifting pints,
the chatter soon becoming bawdy.
'Oh shut your mouth, Big Jock,
remember there's a woman in the company.'
A quick slug of beer
and the topic turns to cuddy-fishing.

Huddling in Dundee,
mound beside mound in the graveyard,
the dead sleep underneath ragged yew-trees,
but on the outside, far apart from the others,
a poor soldier is buried
where he will not harm the company
because he died of cholera.

103

Meg Bateman
b. 1959

A CHIONN 'S GUN ROBH MI MEASAIL AIR

Thigeadh e thugam
nuair a bha e air mhisg
a chionn's gun robh mi measail air.

Dhèanainn tì dha
is dh'èisdinn ris
a chionn's gun robh mi measail air.

Sguir e a dh'òl
is rinn mi gàirdeachas leis
a chionn's gun robh mi measail air.

Nist cha tig e tuilleadh
is nì e tàir orm
a chionn's gun robh mi measail air.

A'CAOINEADH BRIDE

Nighean an sìoda,
air dath nan speuran,
nighean chuimir òg uallach,
ciall an luchd-èisdeachd,
òran Mhahler ga fhuasgladh leat,
a chràdh 's iargain,
do ghuth domhainn dòrainneach,
t'ùidh dian.

Leug theàrainte,
dara bean ghràdhaichte,
a-nochd bithidh làmhan
mu do chom bog àlainn.

Cràdh na ciad mhnà
a-rithist ag èirigh annam –
cràdh a pòsaidh ghaisich
's nam bliadhnachan falamh,
cràdh a sàrachaidh
am bailtean glasa Shasainn,
cràdh a chràidh fhalaicht'
's a bàis gun stàth,

Meg Bateman
b. 1959

BECAUSE I WAS SO FOND OF HIM

He used to visit me
when he was drunk
   because I was so fond of him.

I'd make him tea
and listen to him
   because I was so fond of him.

He stopped drinking
and I was happy for him
   because I was so fond of him.

Now he visits me no more,
indeed he despises me
   because I was so fond of him.

KEENING BIDDY

Girl in silk
the colour of the skies,
shapely, young, lightsome girl,
darling of the audience,
you singing Mahler,
his pain and his turbulence,
your voice low and anguished,
your concentration intense.

Treasured jewel,
beloved second wife,
tonight arms will encircle
your soft white waist.

The pain of the first wife
again welling up in me,
the pain of her blighted marriage
and the years of emptiness,
the pain of her grinding work
in the grey towns of England,
the pain of her hidden pain
and her needless death,

cràdh san òran
na luasganaich,
cràdh air seachran
ga shireadh,
cràdh ga ruagadh,
ga lèireadh,
's ga iomairt an dèinnead –

cràdh
glaicte
ann am pong fada cagarach

is sìth.

Is chaidil nam chridhe
mo chràdh claoidhte,
an call do-innse agamsa
air a làn chaoineadh
agadsa.

Flùraichean
dhan nighinn loinneil fheartaich,
bas-bhualadh is
pògan.

DEALBH MO MHATHAR

Bha mo mhàthair ag innse dhomh
gun tig eilid gach feasgar
a-mach às a' choille dhan achadh fheòir,
an aon tè, 's dòcha,
a dh'àraich iad an-uiridh,
is i a'tilleadh a-nist le a h-àl.

Chan e gràs an fhèidh fhìnealta
a'gluasad thar na leargainn
a leanas ri m'inntinn, na fòs
a dà mheann, crùibte còmhla,
ach aodann mo mhàthar 's i a' bruidhinn,
is a guth, cho toilicht' cho blàth.

FHIR LURAICH, IS FHIR ALAINN

Fhir luraich, is fhir àlainn
's tu thug dàn dha mo bhilean

pain tossing
in the song,
pain straying
sought out,
pain pursued,
pain bullied,
pain driven to the edge –

pain
caught
in a long, whispering note

then peace.

And in my heart
my spent pain slept;
the loss
I could not say
fully keened
by you.

Flowers
for the lovely, talented girl,
applause and
kisses.

PICTURE OF MY MOTHER

My mother was telling me
that a hind comes every evening
out of the wood into the hay-field,
the same one probably
they fed last year,
returning now with her young.

It isn't the grace of the doe
moving across the slope
that lingers in my mind, nor yet
the two fawns huddled together,
but my mother's face as she spoke,
and her voice, so excited, so warm.

O BONNIE MAN, LOVELY MAN

O bonnie man, lovely man,
you've brought a song to my lips

tobar uisge ghil chraobhaich
a'taomadh thar nan creagan

feur caoin agus raithneach
a'glasadh mo shliosan

do leabaidh, canach m'uchd-sa
is gairm ghuilbneach air iteig

ceòban meala do bhàidhe
a'teàrnadh mu mo thimcheall

's i a'toirt suilt agus gutha
dha m'fhuinn fada dìomhain.

Fhir luraich, 's fhir àlainn,
's tu thug dàn dha mo bhilean.

o hì o ho hù o
o hì o ho hù o
hi ri ri o ho èile
o hì ri ri rio iall bho.

a spring of bright spreading water
spilling over the rocks

soft grasses and bracken
covering my slopes with green

your bed, my breast of bog-cotton
with the call of curlews in flight

the honey drizzle of your affection
settles around me

giving mirth and voice
to my uplands long barren.

O bonnie man, lovely man,
you've brought a song to my lips.

o *hì o ho hù o*
o hì o ho hù o
hi ri ri o ho èile
o hì ri ri rio iall bho

109

Anne Frater

SNATHAD NA DOILLE

'Am faic thu', chanadh iad
'San uairsin tosd –
Mì–chomhfhurtail
A' cuimhneachadh
Gun robh thu dall...
Is bhruidhneadh iad a rithist
Ach an dràsd
A'dol a-mach air rudan beag
Rudan air nach robh an aire
Gus nach biodh tu faireachdain
Na bha thu 'call.

Ach sheall thusa dhaibh
Na do bheachd fhéin
Is dh'fhuaigheil thu am beòil
Agus, ged 'bha thusa dall
Bha iadsan balbh.
Is dh'fhairich thu
Gun robh thusa nis nas fheàrr
Gun robh rud a nise agad-sa
Nach robh aca-san
Is bhruidhinn thu riutha on h-àrd.
Ach, chan fhaic thu am bilean
Gus am freagairt a leughadh
No gus na snàithlein a ghearradh
A tha ga'n cumail nan tosd.

SMUAIN

'Alba saor no na fàsach.'
Saorsa no gainmheach
canaidh iad ruinn an aon rud:
'Gheibh sibh sin ...
ach cumaidh sinne an ola.'

9MH DEN T-SAMHAINN 1989

Danns' air a' bhalla ...
Casan saor a' cluich puirt
air clachan cruaidh,
's a' uèir-ghathach air a lomadh

110

Anne Frater

THE NEEDLE OF BLINDNESS

'Can you see', they would say
And then silence –
Uncomfortable,
Remembering
That you were blind...
And they would speak again
But now
Going on about trivial things
Things that did not interest them
So that you would not feel
How much you were missing.

But you showed them
Or so you thought
And you sewed up their mouths
And though you were blind
They were mute
And you felt
That you were superior
That you had something
Which they lacked
And you talked loudly to them.
But you cannot see their lips
To read their reply
Or to cut the threads
That keep them silent.

A THOUGHT

'Scotland free or a desert.'
Freedom or sand
they'll say the same thing to us:
'You can have that ...
but we'll keep the oil.'

9TH NOVEMBER 1989

Dancing on the wall ...
Feet freely playing tunes
on hard stones,
the barbed wire made smooth

111

le bualadh nam bas ...
No man's land
loma-làn le daoine
's iad a' dol seachad air Teàrlach –
chan ann gun fhiost
ach gun sgrùdadh –
agus na càirdean a' feitheamh
le gàire nan gàirdean ...
agus gàir' aig na gàrdan
's gun fleum ac' air gunna
airson bacadh a thogail
agus blocan a leagail ...
Cailleach a' tighinn
gu geata Brandenburg,
nach eil fhathast air fhosgladh
cho farsaing ri càch,
saighdear òg a' dol thuice
's i a' seasamh, gu daingeann
's a' coimhead a slighe
mar cheumannan ceadachaidh
na chlàr fo a casan,
ga slaodadh,
ga tarraing,
's i gluasad a-rithist,
's a' coimhead an òigeir,
s' a' toirt dùbhlan dha
a tilleadh air ais.
Làmh air a gualainn,
greim air a h-uilinn,
's i gun chothrom
a dhol an aghaidh a' churaidh
bha ga stiùireadh dìreach
gu Brandenburg,
gu teampall a saorsa ...

A-raoir
gun imcheist
bhiodh e air peilear a chur innt'.

by the beating of hands ...
No man's land
brimming over with people
as they pass Charlie –
not furtively
but without scrutiny –
and their friends wait
with a smile in their arms ...
and the guards laugh,
as they need no guns
to lift barriers
and knock down bricks ...
An old woman comes
to the Brandenburg Gate,
which is not yet open
as wide as the rest,
a young solider goes to her
and she stands firm
looking at her path
laid out at her feet
like steps of permission,
pulling her,
drawing her,
and she moves again,
and she watches the youth
daring him
to turn her back.
A hand on her shoulder,
a grip on her elbow,
and she is powerless
to resist the brave
who leads her straight
to Brandenburg,
to her temple of freedom ...

Last night
without hesitation
he would have shot her.

THE BALLAD TRADITION
Anonymous

THE BONNY HYN

O may she comes, and may she goes,
  Down by yon gardens green,
And there she spied a gallant squire
  As squire had ever been.

And may she comes, and may she goes,
  Down by yon hollin tree,
And there she spied a brisk young squire,
  And a brisk young squire was he.

'Give me your green manteel, fair maid,
  Give me your maidenhead;
Gif ye winna gie me your green manteel,
  Gi me your maidenhead.'

He has taen her by the milk-white hand,
  And softly laid her down,
And when he's lifted her up again
  Given her a silver kaim.

'Perhaps there may be bairns, kind sir,
  Perhaps there may be nane;
But if you be a courtier,
  You'll tell to me your name.'

'I am nae courtier, fair maid,
  But new come frae the sea;
I am nae courtier, fair maid.
  But when I court 'ith thee.

'They call me Jack when I'm abroad,
  Sometimes they call me John;
But when I'm in my father's bower
  Jock Randal is my name.'

'Ye lee, ye lee, ye bonny lad,
  Sae loud's I hear ye lee!
For I'm Lord Randal's yae daughter,
  He has nae mair nor me.'

'Ye lee, ye lee, ye bonny may,
  Sae loud's I hear ye lee!
For I'm Lord Randal's yae yae son,
  Just now come oer the sea.'

She's putten her hand down by her spare,
　　And out she's taen a knife,
And she has putn't in her heart's bluid,
　　And taen away her life.

And he's taen up his bonny sister,
　　With the big tear in his een,
And he has buried his bonny sister
　　Amang the hollins green.

And syne he's hyed him oer the dale,
　　His father dear to see:
'Sing O and O for my bonny hind,
　　Beneath yon hollin tree!'

'What needs you care for your bonny hyn?
　　For it you needna care;
There's aught score hyns in yonder park,
　　And five score hyns to spare.

'Four score of them are siller-shod,
　　Of thae ye may get three;'
'But O and O for my bonny hyn,
　　Beneath yon hollin tree!'

'What needs you care for your bonny hyn?
　　For it you need na care;
Take you the best, gi me the warst,
　　Since plenty is to spare.'

'I care na for your hyns, my lord,
　　I care na for your fee;
But O and O for my bonny hyn,
　　Beneath the hollin tree!'

'O were ye at your sister's bower,
　　Your sister fair to see,
Ye'll think na mair o your bonny hyn
　　Beneath the hollin tree.'

THE GYPSY LADDIE

The gypsies came to our good lord's gate,
　　And wow but they sang sweetly!
They sang sae sweet and sae very compleat
　　That down came the fair lady.

And she came tripping down the stair,
   And a' her maids before her;
As soon as they saw her well-far'd face,
   They coost the glamer oer her.

'Gae tak frae me this gay mantile,
   And bring to me a plaidie;
For if kith and kin and a' had sworn,
   I'll follow the gypsie laddie.

'Yestreen I lay in a well-made bed,
   And my good lord beside me;
This night I'll ly in a tenant's barn,
   Whatever shall betide me.'

'Come to your bed,' says Johny Faa,
   'Oh come to your bed, my deary;
For I vow and I swear, by the hilt of my sword,
   That your lord shall nae mair come near ye.'

'I'll go to bed to my Johny Faa,
   I'll go to bed to my deary;
For I vow and I swear, by what past yestreen,
   That my lord shall nae mair come near me.

'I'll mak a hap to my Johnny Faa,
   And I'll mak a hap to my deary;
And he's get a' the coat gaes round,
   'And my lord shall nae mair come near me.'

And when our lord came hame at een,
   And speir'd for his fair lady,
The tane she cry'd, and the other reply'd,
   'She's away with the gypsie laddie.'

'Gae saddle to me the black, black steed,
   Gae saddle and make him ready;
Before that I either eat or sleep,
   I'll gae seek my fair lady.'

And we wer fifteen well-made men,
   Altho we were nae bonny;
And we were a' put down for ane,
   A fair young wanton lady.

LADY DAISY

There was a king, and a very great king,
   And a king of meikle fame;
He had not a child in the world but ane,
   Lady Daisy was her name.

He had a very bonnie kitchen-boy,
   And William was his name;
He never lay out o Lady Daisy's bower,
   Till he brought her body to shame.

When een-birds sung, and een-bells rung,
   And a' men were boune to rest,
The king went on to Lady Daisy's bower,
   Just like a wandering ghaist.

He has drawn the curtains round and round,
   And there he has sat him down;
'To whom is this, Lady Daisy,' he says,
   'That now you gae so round?

'Is it to a laird? or is it to a lord?
   Or a baron of high degree?
Or is it William, my bonnie kitchen-boy?
   Tell now the truth to me.'

'It's no to a laird, and it's no to a lord,
   Nor a baron of high degree;
But it's to William, your bonnie kitchen-boy:
   What cause hae I to lee?'

'O where is all my merry, merry men,
   That I pay meat and fee,
That they will not take out this kitchen-boy,
   And kill him presentlie?'

They hae taen out this bonnie kitchen-boy,
   And killd him on the plain;
His hair was like the threads o gold,
   His een like crystal stane;
His hair was like the threads o gold,
   His teeth like ivory bane.

They hae taen out this bonnie boy's heart,
   Put it in a cup o gold;
'Take that to Lady Daisy,' he said,
   'For she's impudent and bold; '
And she washd it with the tears that ran from her eye
   Into the cup of gold.

'Now fare ye weel, my father the king!
   You hae taen my earthly joy;
Since he's died for me, I'll die for him,
   My bonnie kitchen-boy.'

'O where is all my merry, merry men,
    That I pay meat and wage,
That they could not withold my cruel hand,
    When I was mad with rage?

'I think nae wonder, Lady Daisy,' he said,
    'That he brought your body to shame;
For there never was man of woman born
    Sae fair as him that is slain.'

THE WYLIE WIFE OF THE HIE TOUN HIE

It fell about the Martinmas,
    When the gentlemen were drinking there wine,
And a' the discourse that they had
    Was about the ladies they gude fine.

It's up and spake a tall young man,
    The tallest o the companie;
'The bonniest lass that I ken off
    She lives into the hee toun hee.

'O I would give a guinea of gold,
    A guinea and a pint of wine,
I would give it to the hostler's wife,
    For to wile that bonny lassie in.'

The hostler's wife gaed down the stair,
    And she's looked hersell round near by,
And there she spied the bonny handsom girl,
    Coming walking down the hee town high.

'Come in, come in, my bonny handsom girl,
    Come speak one word with me;
Come taste a little of our wine,
    For it's new come out of Italie.'

So willillie she wil'd her up,
    And so willillie she wil'd her in,
And so cunningly she's locked the door,
    And she's comd down the stair again.

One of them took her by the milk-white hand,
    And he's laid her body on the ground,
And aye she sighed, and said, Alass,
    T is a sin to do me wrong!

'But since ye hae done sae muckle to me,
    And brought me to so muckle shame,
O wad ye be so kind to me
    As to tell to me your name.'

118

'O if I tell to you my name,
  It's a thing I never did to none;
But I will tell to the, my dear;
  I am the Earl of Beaton's son.'

When two years were past and gone,
  This gentleman came walking by,
And there he spied the bonny handsome girl,
  Coming walking down the hie town high.

'To whom belongs that pretty child,
  That blinks with its pretty eye?'
'His father's from home and has left me alone,
  And I have been at the fold milking my ky.'

'You lie, you lie, my bonny handsome girl,
  So loudlie I hear you lie;
O do not you mind that happie day
  When ye was drinking the wine wi me?'

He's lighted off his milk-white steed,
  He's kissd her both cheeck and chin;
He's made a' the servants in Beaton castle
  To welcome this fair lady in.

GET UP AND BAR THE DOOR

It fell about the Martinmas time,
  And a gay time it was then,
When our goodwife got puddings to make,
  And she's boild them in the pan.

The wind sae cauld blew south and north,
  And blew into the floor;
Quoth our goodman to our goodwife,
  'Gae out and bar the door.'

'My hand is in my hussyfskap,
  Goodman, as ye may see;
An it shoud nae be barrd this hundred year,
  It's no be barrd for me.'

They made a paction tween them twa,
  They made it firm and sure,
That the first word whaeer shoud speak,
  Shoud rise and bar the door.

Then by there came two gentlemen,
  At twelve o clock at night,
And they could neither see house nor hall,
  Nor coal nor candle-light.

'Now whether is this a rich man's house,
    Or whether is it a poor?'
But neer a word wad ane o them speak,
    For barring of the door.

And first they ate the white puddings,
    And then they ate the black;
Tho muckle thought the goodwife to hersel,
    Yet neer a word she spake.

Then said the one unto the other,
    Here, man, tak ye my knife;
Do ye tak aff the auld man's beard,
    And I'll kiss the goodwife.'

'But there's nae water in the house,
    And what shall we do than?'
'What ails yue at the pudding-broo,
    That boils into the pan?'

O up then started our goodman,
    An angry man was he:
'Will ye kiss my wife before my een,
    And scad me wi pudding-bree?'

Then up and started our goodwife,
    Gied three skips on the floor:
'Goodman, you've spoken the foremost word,
    Get up and bar the door.'

Mrs Walker

THE FOUR MARYS

Last nicth there were four Marys
This night the'll be but three
There was Mary Sitten and Mary Beten
And Mary Kermyckle and me.

Oh little did my mither think
When first she cradeld me
That I wide be sae fare frae
And hang on a gallows tree.

Theey tied a napin roon my een
To nae lat me see to dee
They niether tellt my father and mither
That I wis awa owr the see.

But I my sell are Mary Mill
The flower oh a the three
But I hae killed my boney wee son
And well deserved to dee.

But ye'll bury me in the auld kirkyard
Beaneath the auld uew tree
Where wee pulled the gowens and ringed the strones   *daisies*
My sisters and brother and me.

Oh what care I for a nameless grave
If I've hope for etrinity
For it was for the blood of the dying lamb
That's granted through grace unto me.

121

Meg Walker
(Mrs Margaret Caldwell of Lochwinnoch)

JAMIE DOUGLAS

O I am sike and very sike
A Frind of mind came to visit me
The Blackemore whisperd in my Lords ears
That he was too lang in my Companey

In the morning when he arase
As well a pleas'd Lord as ear could be
But when that he came back again
Never a word he woud speak to me

In the morning when I arase
A my pretty palace's for to vew
I whisper'd in at my Lord window
But the never a word he wou'd ansure me

When my father heard of the dispute
That was between my good Lord and me
He sent five score of his soilders brave
To conduct me hame to my own Country

Come doun the stairs my Jimie Duglas
Come doun the stairs and drink tea with me
Ill set thee in a chair of gold
And not one farthing it will cost thee

When cockel shells grows siller bells
And mussals grows on every tree
When frost and snow turns red bolts of Iron
Then will I come doun and drink tea we thee

When I sat in my coach and six
Its no delight that ilded me
. . . .
I wish I was in my own countrey

Of a the Birds flee's in the air
The Hawk flee's farest frea its nest
And a the world may plainly see
Its Jimie Duglas I like best

Fare you well my Jeamie Duglas
And fare ye well my childreen three
May a that's new still attend you
Till I see you a safe in my ain cuntrey

She looked out at her father window
To take a view of the countrey
Wha did she see but Jemie Duglas
And alang with him her childreen three

There cam a soilder to the gate
And he did knock right hasteley
If Lady Duglas be within
Bid her come and speak to me

Come away my Lady fair
Come away now alang with me
For I have hanged the Blackemoor
The verey place where he tald the lie

JOCK T' LEG AND THE MERRY MERCHANT

Jock the Leg and the merry merchant
Are up to England gane
He had a Pack upon his back
And it was well buckled on, on, on,
And it was well bucklit on

As they came in by yon tavern house
Where quarterers were wont to dine
Make readie a supper said Jock t' Leg
Gae ready it gude ane fine, fine, fine,
Gae readie it gude ane fine,

For the merrie merchant will pay for it
Altho it were crowns three
Never a bit quoth the merry merchant
For hauffers thou sal be, be, be,
For hauffers thou sal be.

At night when they went to their bed
Thinking upon a sleep
Up and starts muckle lang Jock to Leg
At the merry merchant's bed feet, feet, feet,
At the merrie merchant's bed feet.

123

Rise up rise up thou merrie merchant
Thou might a been miles three
Ne'er a bit quoth the merrie merchant
Till day light come that I see, see, see,
Till day light come that I see

Never a bit quo the merrie merchant
Till day light come that I see
For Jockteleg is a rank robber
He'll take my pack frae me, me, me,
He'll take my pack frae me

As they came in by Nottingham
And down by yon green bay tree
Repent repent thou merrie merchant
For what thou said of me, me, me,
For what thou said of me

Never a bit quo the merrie merchant
For a rank robber thou be
Jockteleg set a whistle to his mouth
And he gave whistles three, three, three
And he gave whistles three,

Till four and twenty well armed men
Came linking owr the lee
O what is yon quo the merry merchant
O what is yon that I see, see, see,
O what is yon that I see

It's four and twentie well armed men
That'll tak thy pack frae thee
Tak eleven o thy well armed men
Thy sell the twelfth to be, be, be,
Thysell the twelfth to be

. . . .
. . . .
And put me but one inch from my pack
And all sall go wi thee, thee, thee,
And all shall go with thee

He took eleven o his well armed men
Himsell the twelfth to be
And to put him but one inch frae his Pack
Was a thing they coudna do, do, do,
Was a thing they coudna do

Will thou gie me as muckle of thy light links
As clead my men and me
And when we come to Nottingham
Gude billy bairns we sall be, be, be,
Gude billy bairns we sall be

I'll no gie thee as muckle of my light links
As clead thy men and thee
And when we come to Nottingham
Neir a farthing care I thee, thee, thee,
Neir a farthing care I thee

BONNIE BELLEEN

O did ye e'er hear of Bonnie Belleen
The flower o' Avonwood lee
And did ye e'er hear o' her brothers brave
Wha fought by the Warlock tree
And did ye e'er hear o Todecliff Tower
That frowns o'er the dashing tide
Or of gallant Ross, its statly Lord
The Lothian's boast and pride

The bonnie Bellien sat in her bower
And O she was fair to see
For her skin was white and her een was bright
As the stars in the lift sae hie
The gallant Ross was a hunting then
And he stepp'd her bower within
And he daff'd his cap and he bent his knee
Her heart's trew love to win

And they ha'e met by the moon yellow light
And he's kiss'd below the tree
O come wi me my bonnie Belleen
And Lady Ross thou shalt be
He blew a blast, till glen and shaw
Powr'd out his merry men bold
And they plac'd her on a milk white steed
And borr her to Todecliff hold

125

O she has sat in Todecliff Tower
And a weary wife was she
For the Ross was proud and her friends were gane
And there faces she dar'd na see
And the seamaw skriegh'd o'er the Castel wa
And the waves dash'd wearilee
And she thought o her hame and her brothers brave
And the bonnie braes o Avonwood lee

A Lady gay came doun frae the south
Wi riches and jewels most precious to see
O leeze me she said on the gallant Ross
For I love the glance o his bright black ee
And he's te'an her east and he's tean her west
And he's seated her in ha and bower
But little he thought on his bonnie dame
That mournd in gloomy Todecliff Tower

The merry bells did ring and the tapers did blaze
When he wedded the Southern Lady gay
But a weird voice was heard boon the revelrie
Saying wo to the Ross for the deid done this day

O mirk was the night and fearfu the storm
When the pud Belleen frae her lanley bed
And percingly she shriek'd and the watter spirit laugh'd
As the green sie swirled o'er her bonnie head
For they ha'e dround the bonnie Belleen
And nae mair she'll chant by Avonwood lee
And her brother's hae slain they cruel Ross
Where his ghost still howls by the Warlock Tree

126

Anna Gordon (Mrs Brown of Falkland)
1747-1810

THE TWA SISTERS

There was twa sisters in a bowr,
  Edinburgh, Edinburgh
There was twa sisters in a bowr,
  Stirling for ay
There was twa sisters in a bowr,
There came a knight to be their wooer.
  Bonny Saint Johnston stands upon Tay.

He courted the eldest wi glove an ring,
But he lovd the youngest above a' thing.

He courted the eldest wi brotch an knife,
But lovd the youngest as his life.

The eldest she was vexed sair,
An much envi'd her sister fair.

Into her bowr she could not rest,
Wi grief an spite she almos brast.

Upon a morning fair an clear,
She cried upon her sister dear:

'O sister, come to yon sea stran,
An see our father's ships come to lan.'

She's taen her by the milk-white han,
An led her down to yon sea stran.

The younges[t] stood upon a stane,
The eldest came an threw her in.

She tooke her by the middle sma,
An dashd her bonny back to the jaw.

'O sister, sister, tak my han,
An Ise mack you heir to a' my lan.

'O sister, sister, tak my middle,
An yes get my goud and my gouden girdle.

'O sister, sister, save my life,
An I swear Ise never be nae man's wife.'

'Foul fa the han that I should tacke,
It twin'd me an my wardles make.

'Your cherry cheeks an yallow hair
Gars me gae maiden for evermair.'

Sometimes she sank, an sometimes she swam,
Till she came down yon bonny mill-dam.

O out it came the miller's son,
An saw the fair maid swimmin in.

'O father, father, draw your dam,
Here's either a mermaid or a swan.'

The miller quickly drew the dam,
An there he found a drownd woman.

You couldna see her yellow hair
For gold and pearle that were so rare.

You couldna see her middle sma
For gouden girdle that was sae braw.

You couldna see her fingers white
For gouden rings that was saw gryte.

An by there came a harper fine,
That harped to the king at dine.

When he did look that lady upon,
He sighed and made a heavy moan.

He's taen three locks o her yallow hair,
An wi them strung his harp sae fair.

Tne first tune he did play and sing,
Was, 'Farewell to my father the king.'

The nextin tune that he playd syne,
Was, 'Farewell to my mother the queen.'

The lasten tune that he played then,
Was, 'Wae to my sister, fair Ellen.'

ALLISON GROSS

O Allison Gross, that lives in yon towr,
  The ugliest witch i the north country,
Has trysted me ae day up till her bowr,
  An monny fair speech she made to me.

She stroaked my head, an she kembed my hair,
  An she set me down saftly on her knee;
Says, Gin ye will be my lemman so true,   *lover*
  Sae monny braw things as I woud you gi.

She showd me a mantle o red scarlet,
  Wi gouden flowrs an fringes fine;
Says, Gin ye will be my lemman so true,
  This goodly gift it sal be thine.

'Awa, awa, ye ugly witch,
  Haud far awa, an lat me be;
I never will be your lemman sae true,
  An I wish I were out o your company.'

She neist brought a sark o the saftest silk,
  Well wrought wi pearles about the ban;
Says, Gin you will be my ain true love,
  This goodly gift you sal comman.

She showd me a cup of the good red gold,
  Well set wi jewls sae fair to see;
Says, Gin you will be my lemman sae true,
  This goodly gift I will you gi.

'Awa, awa, ye ugly witch,
  Had far awa, and lat me be;
For I woudna ance kiss your ugly mouth
  For a' the gifts that ye coud gi.'

She's turnd her right and roun about,
  An thrice she blaw on a grass-green horn,
An she sware by the meen and the stars abeen,
  That she'd gar me rue the day I was born.

Then out has she taen a silver wand,
  An she's turnd her three times roun and roun;
She's muttered sich words till my strength it faild,
  An I fell down senceless upon the groun.

She's turnd me into an ugly worm,
  An gard me toddle about the tree;
An ay, on ilka Saturdays night,
  My sister Maisry came to me,

Wi silver bason an silver kemb,
  To kemb my heady upon her knee;
But or I had kissd her ugly mouth,
  I'd rather a toddled about the tree.

But as it fell out on last Hallow-even,
  When the seely court was ridin by,
The queen lighted down on a gowany bank,
  Nae far frae the tree where I wont to lye.

She took me up in her milk-white han,
  An she's stroakd me three times oer her knee;
She chang'd me again to my ain proper shape,
  An I nae mair maun toddle about the tree.

FAIR ANNIE

'O wha will bake my bridal bread,
  And brew my bridal ale?
Wha will welcome my bright bride,
  That I bring oer the dale?'

'O I will bake your bridal bread,
  An brew your bridal ale;
An I will welcome your bright bride,
  That you bring oer the dale.'

'O she that welcomes my bright bride
  Maun gang like maiden fair;
She maun lace her in her green cloathin,
  An braid her yallow hair.'

'O how can I gang maiden like,
  Whan maiden I am nane?
Whan I ha born you seven sons,
  An am wi bairn again?'

The lady stood in her bowr door
  An lookit oer the lan,
An there she saw her ain good lord,
  Leadin his bride by the han.

She's dressd her sons i the scarlet red,
   Hersel i the dainty green,
An tho her cheek lookd pale and wan,
   She well might ha been a queen.

She calld upon her eldest son:
   'Look yonder what you see;
For yonder comes your father dear,
   Your step-mother him wi.

'O you'r welcome hame, my ain good lord,
   To your ha's but an your bowrs;
You'r welcome hame, my ain good lord,
   To your castles an your towrs:
Sae is your bright bride you beside,
   She's fairer nor the flowers.'

'O whatn a lady's that?' she says,
   'That welcoms you an me?
If I'm lang lady about this place,
   Some good I will her dee.
She looks sae like my sister Jane,
   Was stoln i the bowr frae me.'

O she has servd the lang tables,
   Wi the white bread an the wine;
But ay she drank the wan water,
   Tb keep her colour fine.

An she gid by the first table,
   An leugh amo them a';
But ere she reachd the second table,
   She let the tears down fa.

She's taen a napkin lang an white,
   An hung't upon a pin;
It was to dry her watry eyes,
   As she went out and in.

Whan bells were rung, an mass was sung,
   An a' man boun to bed,
The bride but an the bonny bridegroom
   In ae chamber was laid.

She's taen her harp intill her han,
  To harp this twa asleep;
An ay as she harped an she sang,
  Full sorely did she weep.

'O seven fu fair sons I have born
  To the good lord o this place,
An I wish that they were seven hares,
  Tb run the castle race,
An I mysel a good gray houn,
  An I woud gi them chase.

'O seven fu fair sons I have born
  To the good lord o this ha;
I wish that they were seven rottons,
  To rin the castle wa,
An I mysell a good gray cat,
  I wot I woud worry them a'.

'The earle o Richmond was my father,
  An the lady was my mother,
An a' the bairns bisides mysel
  Was a sister an a brother.'

'Sing on, sing on, ye gay lady,
  I wot ye hae sung in time;
Gin the earle o Richmond was your father,
  I wot sae was he mine.'

'Rise up, rise up, my bierly bride;
  I think my bed's but caul'
I woudna hear my lady lament
  For your tocher ten times taul.   *dowry*

'O seven ships did bring you here,
  An an sal tak you hame;
The leve I'll keep to your sister Jane,
  For tocher she gat nane.'

FAIR MARY OF WALLINGTON

'O we were sisters seven, Maisry,
  And five are dead wi child;
There is nane but you and I, Maisry,
  And we'll go maidens mild.'

She hardly had the word spoken,
   And turned her round about,
When the bonny Earl of Livingston
   Was calling Maisry out.

Upon a bonny milk-white steed,
   That drank out of the Tay,
And a' was for her Ladie Maisry,
   To take her hyne and hyne.   *far away*

Upon a bonny milk-white steed,
   That drank out of the Tay,
And a' was for her Lady Maisry,
   To carry her away.

She had not been at Livingston
   A twelve month and a day,
Until she was as big wi bairn
   As any ladie coud gae.

She calld upon her little foot-page,
   Says, Ye maun run wi speed,
And bid my mother come to me,
   For of her I'll soon have need.

'See, there is the brootch frae my hause-bane,   *collarbone*
   It is of gowd sae ried;
Gin she winna come when I'm alive,
   Bid her come when I am dead.'

But ere she wan to Livingston,
   As fast as she coud ride,
The gaggs they were in Maisry's mouth,
   And the sharp sheers in her side.

Her good lord wrang his milk-white hands,
   Till the gowd rings flaw in three:
'Let ha's and bowers and a' gae waste,
   My bonny love's taen frae me!'

'O hold your tongue, Lord Livingston,
   Let a' your mourning be;
For I bare the bird between my sides,
   Yet I maun thole her to die.'   *suffer*

Then out it spake her sister dear,
    As she sat at her head:
'That man is not in Christendoom
    Shall gar me die sicken dead.'

'O hold your tongue, my ae daughter,
    Let a' your folly be,
For ye shall be married ere this day week
    Tho the same death you should die.'

LAMKIN

It's Lamkin was a mason good
    as ever built wi stane;
He built Lord Wearie's castle,
    but payment got he nane.

'O pay me, Lord Wearie,
    come, pay me my fee:'
'I canna pay you, Lamkin,
    for I maun gang oer the sea.'

'O pay me now, Lord Wearie,
    come, pay me out o hand:'
'I canna pay you, Lamkin,
    unless I sell my land.'

'O gin ye winna pay me,
    I here sall mak a vow,
Before that ye come hame again,
    ye sall hae cause to rue.'

Lord Wearie got a bonny ship,
    to sail the saut sea faem;
Bade his lady weel the castle keep,
    ay till he should come hame.

But the nourice was a fause limmer
    as eer hung on a tree;
She laid a plot wi Lamkin,
    whan her lord was oer the sea.

She laid a plot wi Lamkin,
    when the servants were awa,
Loot him in at a little shot-window,
    and brought him to the ha.

'O whare's a' the men o this house,
   that ca me Lamkin?'
'They're at the barn-well thrashing;
   't will be lang ere they come in.'

'And whare's the women o this house,
   that ca me Lamkin?'
'They're at the far well washing;
   ''t will be lang ere they come in.'

'And whare's the bairns o this house,
   that ca me Lamkin?'
'They're at the school reading;
   't will be night or they come hame.'

'O whare's the lady o this house,
   that ca's me Lamkin?'
'She's up in her bower sewing,
   but we soon can bring her down.'

Then Lamkin's tane a sharp knife,
   that hang down by his gaire,
And he has gien the bonny babe
   a deep wound and a sair.

Then Lamkin he rocked
   and the fause nourice sang,
Till frae ilkae bore o the cradle
   the red blood out sprang.

Mary MacQueen (Mrs Storie)
1786-1854

THE HAWTHORN GREEN

A lady as fair as fair could be
Sat marvelling under yon hawthorn tree
She marvelled much how things could be
To see the grein leaves on yon hawthorn tree

Then out bespak the hawthorn tree
What makes you marvel sae much at me
The finest dew that ever was seen
Does faw on me and keep me green

What if I wud cut you doun
And carry you hence to yonder town
The next year after ye woudna be seen
To spread forth your leaves baith fresh and green

To cut me down I put nae doubt
But ye dinna cut me by the root
The neist year after I will be seen
To spread my leaves baith fresh and green

But you fair maids you ar not so
When ance that your virginity go
The next year after you may be seen
But never to flourish sae fresh again

This fair maid she hearing this
She turned her back to the hawthorn buss
The neist year after she was near seen
To talk onie mair to the hawthorn grein

THE CRUEL STEPMOTHER

A noble lord of Exeter
A hunting did ride
An he took wi him aw his train
O gentry by his side

He had ane only daughter fair
A beauty bricht was she
She was her father's delight an joy
As ye may after see

But woe be to her stepmother
Wha envied her sae much
That day by day she sought her life
Her malice it was such

She bargain'd wi the master cook
To tack her life away
An cuming to her daughter deir
This to her did say

O daughter ye maun gang hame
The cook for to tell
That he maun dress the dove
The dove he knows full well

This lady deir fearand nae harm
Obayed her mother's will
An presently she hastened hame
Her mind for to fulfil

She says ye maun dress
This pure and milk white dove
That in the park does shine sae bricht
There's nane so fair doth prove

O' ye'r the dove that I maun dress
Behold here is my knife
Baith sharp and keep an ready too
To end you o your life

Then out bespak the scullion boy
An this began to cry
O maister maister save her life
An mak o me your pye

O now I winna save her life
Nor make my pye of thee
But if these words you do declare
Your butcher to I'll be

When the good lord cam hame at noon
An at his dinner sat
He called for his daughter deir
That she might carve the meet

Than out bespak her stepmother
As by his side she sat
Yer daughter's to some nunnery gane
Your daughter I pray forget

The lord he made a solemn vow
Before the company
That he would neither eat nor drink
Till his daughter he would see

Then out bespak the scullion boy
And this began to cry
If that your daughter ye maun see
My lord break up the pye

Ye'r daughter she is minched sma
An peirsand by the fire
Aw caused by her stepmother
Wha did her life desire

The lord he went in mourning then
Aw for his daughter's sake
An caused her cursed stepmother
To be burned at a stake

An next he caused the master cook
In boing lead to stand
An made the little scullion boy
The heir o aw his land

THE BUSH OF BROOM

As I went out on a May morning
A May morning it happened to be
O there I spied a very bonny lass
She was asking the road to her ain country

O where is your country my bonny lass
Or whatna town do ye come frae
Frae London I came kind Sir she says
And for Newcastle I do stray

If from London you came my very bonny lass
Wat and weary might you be
I wad hae you sit down by yon bonny buss o Broom
And bear a young man company

138

O faun wad I sit down by yon bony buss o broom
But I'm afraid you wad injure me
The night is dark I am afraid it will be wet
And it's O but I am far frae my ain countrie

He's tane her by the green gown sleeve
And by the lily white hand
And he's tane her down to yon bony buss o Broom
To a silent shade whaur no one seen

He put his hand into his purse
And then he gied her guineas three
Saying take ye that my very bony lass
It will help ye ham to your ain country

He put his hand into his purse
And there he gied her guineas ten
Saying Take ye that my very bony lass
It will fee a nurse aw for your bairn

But what will ye say my very bonny lass
When ye gae hame to your ain country
O I'll take a cup and I'll fill it to the top
And I'll drink to the bony buss o broom and thee

But nine lang months had scarce been gone
Nine lang months and scarcely three
Till she sent him a bottle of the wine sae red
And a braw lad bairn to divert him wi

He took the young thing in his arms
And there he gied it kisses three
Saying weel do I mind o the bonny buss of broom
And the braw faced lass that I sportit wi

If I had her here as I had her there
Richt happy happy would I be
I'd make her heir of my houses and lands
And a braw lad bairn to devert her wi

THE MASON'S DOCHTER

Doun in Oxford city lived a mason to trade
An he had a dochter a beautiful maid
The fairest o faces but the fausest o hearts
That ever was known in our neighbouring parts

She feed wi a lady upon her to wait
She was her companion baith early and late
She had the good will o her mistress therefore
An the finest o garments she commonly wore

She had na been there a month or above
Until their young Steward being Isabel's love
He said now come wad I'll mak you my wife
For I vow that I luve you as deir as my life

O as for my part I'll no marry yet
I hae nae muckle money and far less wit
An ye hae as little as me for my life
An I laugh when I hear a cloun caw for a wife

But this being nane o his cunning design
He was pleased to treat her wi plenty of wine
As muckle as laid her secure fast asleep
That into her arms he might cosily creep

Some part of the night in his arms she has lain
Until her senses returned again
Awa frae his arms in a passion she flew
Sayand was I ordained to be ruined by you

Ae day he said to her he said to her then
My dearest come wad I'll mak ye my ain
My dearest come was I'll mak ye my wife
For I vow that I love you as dear as my life
I am no wi bairn I'll no be your wife
I avow I'll never wad you a' the days of my life

But nevertheless he kent it was so
And he did watch her wherear she did go
He fixed a net and he fixed it weel
An he fixed a net out owr the draw well

Supposing she woud murder or smother there
And he did watch her with abundance of care
When her appointed time began to draw nigh
Ae night at her window a light he did spy

Which made him come speedily doun frae the shore
An he saw his true love coming out at the door
Wi something in her hand in the draw well she threw
An when she retired frae it her true lover drew

He drew up the nett fand the infant alive
This was an invention that he did contrive
He tuke the babe and he kept it likewyse
Till by good fortune he fand out a nurse
Till by good fortune he fand out a nurse
Till whom he paid money out of his purse

He beg'd o the nurse to be tender and free
And for his babie muckle siller he'd gie
And for this babie much siller in store
The like was never paid before

In twa years after he said to her then
My dear I am gaun for a visit a friend
Though she wad na wed yet her favour to shaw
A walking wi him did she offer to go

An this bonnie babe stood tender and free
As it stands prattling by his mother's knie
She uttered her words an she said wi amaze
I'm sure I near saw as braw a bairn in aw my days

He said if it were na for lying your lane
Ye might hae had as braw a bairn o your ain
O that's what I do and I will do that still
An lead my life single let you say what you will

But as thay were walking dune by yonder field
He said my dear jewel lang hae I concealed
Your intended murder shall never be known
Rejoice and be thankfu yon babie is your ain

O little she said or naething at all
She raise in the next morning wi a heart ful of gaw
She gade to the house cryde the nurse to the door
And she murdered the babie left it lying on the floor

O grippit she was and suffered lykewyse
Which made the salt tears to run frae his eyes
For he lued the bairn weel and the mamma for its sake
And just for them baith his heart was readie to break

Come all you true lovers o beautiful charms
If ever your true love does fa in your arms
Dinna slight there kind offer or if you do
Perhaps it'll prove a sad ruin unto you

Bell Robertson

THE FRASERBURGH MEAL RIOT

Charlie, Charlie, rise and rin,
The fisher wives is makin' din,
It's best to sleep in a hale skin,
It'll be a bluidy mornin'.

Charlie Wemyss wi' his lang mou
He lap the dyke like ony coo,
And to Newmill he did pursue
For shippin' the meal in the mornin'.

THE BEAUTY OF BUCHAN

Come all my relations with deep lamentations,
Ye shepherds o' Buchan come listen I pray,
Let my song be respected since sheep is rejected
And they from their pastures are banished away.

I hae seen our green fountains on wild heathy mountains,
Wi' flocks all clad over how pleasant were they;
But now they are lonely for want o' flocks only
Since the beauty from Buchan is banished away.

I hae heard lasses liltin' when met at ewe milkin'
Each one with her sweetheart in innocent play,
But now they want leisure to crack wi' their treasure
Since the beauty frae Buchan is banished away.

I hae seen the rams sporting and corams resorting   *groups*
And nothing disturbing their innocent play,
But now they go mourning both evening and morning
Since the beauty frae Buchan is banished away.

I hae seen the lambs bleating their careful dams weeping,
To guard them frae Lowrie that made them his prey,
Now Lowrie is starvin', it's what he's deservin'
Since the beauty frae Buchan is banished away.

I hae seen at sheep shearin' sportin' and jeerin'
Their sunny white fleeces how pleasant were they,
But now we maun buy them frae merchants that cry them,
Since the beauty frae Buchan is banished away.

Woe to our gentry, they're ruined a' our country,
And brought our fine pasture so deep in decay
Mong hedges and ditches they've spent a' our riches,
And banished our beauty entirely away.

Lament all ye shepherds for want o' your clipherds,
Wi' sighing and sobbing and sorrow for aye;
Let my song be respected since sheep is rejected,
And they from their pastures are banished away.

Mrs Margaret Gillespie

HOOLY AND FAIRLY

Oh, neighbours! what had I ado for to marry?
My wife she drinks possets and wine o' Canary,   *milk curdled with wine*
And ca's me a niggardly, thrawn-gabbit cairly,   *sour-faced old man*
O gin my wife wad drink hooly and fairly!   *moderately, simply*
Hooly and fairly, hooly and fairly;
O gin my wife wad drink hooly and fairly!

She feasts wi' her kimmers on dainties enew,   *friends*
Aye bowsing and smirking and wiping her mou',
While I sit aside and am helpit but sparely.
O gin my wife wad feast hooly and fairly!
Hooly and fairly, hooly and fairly;
O gin my wife wad feast hooly and fairly!

To fairs and to bridals, and preachings and a',
She gangs sae light-hearted and buskit sae braw,   *dressed up*
In ribbons and mantuas that gar me gae barely!
O gin my wife wad spend hooly and fairly!
Hooly and fairly, hooly and fairly;
O gin my wife wad spend hooly and fairly!

I' the kirk sic commotion last Sabbath she made,
Wi' babs o' red roses and breast-knots o'erlaid!
The dominie stickit the psalm very nearly.   *stopped*
O gin my wife wad dress hooly and fairly!
Hooly and fairly, hooly and fairly;
O gin my wife wad dress hooly and fairly!

She's warring and flyting frae morning till e'en;
And if ye gainsay her, her e'en glour sae keen;
Then tongue, nieve, and cudgel she'll lay on ye sairly!   *fist*
O gin my wife wad strike hooly and fairly!
Hooly and fairly, hooly and fairly;
O gin my wife wad strike hooly and fairly!

When tired wi' her cantrips she lies in her bed,   *antics*
The wark a' neglickit, the chaumer unred,   *the room; untidy*
While a' our gude neighbours are stirring sae early.
O gin my wife wad sleep timely and fairly!
Timely and fairly, timely and fairly;
O gin my wife wad sleep timely and fairly!

O word o' gude counsel or grace she'll hear none,
She bardies the elders and mocks at Mess John,   *quarrels with*
While back in his teeth his ain text she flings rarely.
O gin my wife wad speak hooly and fairly!
Hooly and fairly, hooly and fairly!
O gin my wife wad speak hooly and fairly!

I wish I were single, I wish I were freed,
I wish I were doited, I wish I were dead,   *in dotage*
Or she in the mools to dement me nae mairly!   *earth*
What does't avail to cry hooly and fairly?
Hooly and fairly, hooly and fairly;
Wasting my breath to cry hooly and fairly!

Annie Shirer

BURKE'S CONFESSION

William Burke it is my name, in Ireland I was born
I leave a wife behind me, my wretched end to mourn
It was for Scotland I was bound, employment to find
No thought of cruel murder was then into my mind.

I sought and found employment to work in a canal
It was there I met McDugel which proved my downfall
And from my honest labour he caused me to stray
And from our grieving parents we both did run away.

Edinburgh trade being very dull, no work there could be found
We then prepared to leave it was for Glasgow bound
While stopping at a west port, to get refreshments there
I never will forget the hour I met wi' Willie Hare.

We being strangers in the place we thought him very kind
And little knew the hard thoughts that Hare had in his mind
He showed us through his lodging house it was upon our way,
This man he kept poor lodgers and stole their lives away.

To assist in this cruel murder, at first I was afraid
But soon my heart grew hardened and I followed out the trade
Now I do keep a lodging house, supported by this man
And the price the doctors gave for them we murdered many a one.

To keep down suspicion, we went out at a back door,
The doctors always bought them and told us to bring more
To assist in this cruel murder, at first I thought no ill
Till sixty men and women I willingly did kill.

It's nae the murdering of them that caused my disgrace
But the murdering of a little child that smiled into my face
I did not mean to harm it, it was so very mild
But my wife she swore she would discover me if I did not kill that child.

But I am now discovered and landed into jail
I well knew I was guilty so my heart began to fail
It was Hare that ensnared me, and led me astray
But now he's turned King's evidence, and swore my life away.

But now they have discovered him, from his country he must fly
And a harder fate awaits him yet before the day he die
But now the cap's drawn o'er my face, and hides me from all view
My cruel life is at an end and so I bid you all adieu.

JOHNNIE, MY MAN

O Johnnie lad, are ye no thinkin' on risin'?
The day is a' spent, and the night is comin' on;
Ye're sittin' here drinkin', and the stoup is teem before ye   *the tankard is*
                                                                             empty
So rise up, my Johnnie, and come awa' hame.

Oh wha is that there that speaks so kind to me?
It's no my wee wifie called Maggie by name;
Come sit doon beside me a wee while, my dearie,
And I'll rise up contented and gang awa' hame.

O Johnnie lad, the wee-anes is greetin',
Nae meal in the barrel to fill their wee wimes,   *bellies*
While we sit here drinkin' we leave them lamentin',
Oh rise up, my Johnnie, and come awa' hame.

O Maggie lass, when were first acquainted,
Nae hunter nor thirst never troubled our mind;
We spent the lang night among sweet-scented roses,
And never took a thought of gaun awa' hame.

Oh Johnnie lad, that days are forgotten,
That days are awa' and they'll ne'er come again,
We'll think on the present and strive for to mend it,
So gang nae mair to the alehouse nor mak' it your hame.

Johnnie's got up and banged the door open,
Says, Cursed be that alehouse that ever I came,
Singing, Fare ye weel whisky that oft made me tipsy,
Sae fare ye weel whisky, and I'll awa' hame.

Jeannie Robertson
1908-1975

THE TWA BROTHERS

There were twa bretheris at the schuil,
An when they got awa,
For it's 'Will ye play at the stane-chucken,
Or will ye play at the baa.   *ball*
Or will ye gae up tae yon bonnie, green hill,
An there we'll wrastle a faa?'   *fall*

'I will nae play at the stane-chuckin,
Or will I play at the baa,
But I'll gae up tae yon bonnie green hill,
And there we'll wrastle a faa.'

They wrastl't up, they wrastl't down,
Till John fell to the ground,
But a dirk fell out of William's pootch,
Gave John a deadly wound.

For he's taen off his holland sark,   *shirt*
Rived it fraw gair tae gair:
He's stuffed it in the bloody wound,
But it bled mair and mair.

'Oh, lift me, lift me on your back;
Tak me to yon well sae fair,
An wash the blood frae off my wound,
That it may bleed nae mair.'

He's liftit him upon his back,
Taen him to yon well sae fair;
He's washed the blood frae off his wound,
But aye it bled the mair.

'Oh, ye'll take off my holland sark,
Rive it frae gair tae gair,
Ye'll stuff it in the bloody wound,
That it may bleed nae mair.'

'Oh lift me, lift me on your back;
Tak me tae Kirkland fair,
An dig a grave baith wide and deep
And lay my body there.

'Ye'll lay my arrows at my head,
My bent bow at my feet,
My sword an buckler by my side,
As I wes wont tae sleep.'

THE TROOOPER AND THE MAID

Three 'Stralian dragoons coming home from the war,
The night was dark and dreary,
'For I wid know my own soldier-boy
Because I loved him dearly.'

She took his horse by the bridle-head,
An laid it to the stable;
Hay an corn for a pretty soldier's horse,
For to eat while it was able.

She took the lad by the lily-white hand,
An led him tae her chamber;
Cakes an wine for a pretty soldier-boy,
For to eat while he was able.

She went up the stair for to make her bed
Then soft and easy,
For she stript off her lily-white goon
Beside his hat an sabre.
For he stript off his boots and his spurs,
And they both lay down together.

They weren't very long into bed,
When the buglet did sounded,
For the bugle it did play an the trumpet it did say,
'Bonnie lassie, I maun leave you.'

'Oh whan will you come back, my bonnie soldier-boy,
To be the wee thing's daddie?'
'When cockleshells growes in silver bells,
Bonnie lassie, we'll get mairried.'

THE HOBO SONG

Riding on a East-bound freight train,
Speeding through the night,
Hobo Bill, a railroad bum,
Was fighting for his life.
The sadness of his eyes revealed
The torture of his soul.
He raised a weak and wearied hand
To brush away the cold.

Refrain: Bo-ho-ho
Bo-ho-ho, Billie.

No wan li's flickerit roun' him,
No blankets there to fold,
There was nothing but the howling wind
And the driving rain so cold
As the train sped through the darkness
An the raging storm outside.
No one knew that Hobo Bill
Was taking his last ride.

Refrain

Outside the rain was falling
On that lonely buskadoor –
But the little form of Hobo Bill
Lay still upon the floor.
When he heard that whistle blowing
In a dreamy kind of way
The hobo seemed contented
For he smiled there where he lay.

Refrain

It was early in the morning
When they raised the hobo's head.
The smile lingered on his face
But Hobo Bill was dead.
There was no mother's longing
To soothe his wearied soul,
For he was just a railroad bum
Who died out in the cold.

Refrain

Lizzie Higgins
b. 1929

MACCRIMMON'S LAMENT

Round Coolin's peaks the mists is sailin'
The banshee croons her note o' wailin'.
Mil' blue een wi' sorrow is streamin'
For him that shall never return, MacCrimmon.

    No more, no more, no more forever
    Shall love or gold bring back MacCrimmon.
    No more, no more, no more forever
    Shall love or gold bring back MacCrimmon.

The breeze on the braes are mournfully moanin',
The brooks in the hollows are plaintively mournin'.
Mil' blue een wi' sorrow are streamin'
For him that shall never return, MacCrimmon.

    Chorus

MacLeod's wizard flags from the grey castle sallies,
The rowers are unseated, unmoored are the galleys.
Gleams war-axe and broadsword, clang target and quiver
For him that shall never return, MacCrimmon.

    Chorus

FAR OVER THE FORTH

Far over the Forth, I look at the North,
But what is the North, wi' its Highlands tae me?
The South nor the East gie ease to my breast,
It's the far foreign lands o'er the wild rollin' sea.

Ah the lang simmer day, amid the heather and the bracken,
The joy and delight o' hees bonnie blue ee.
I little then kent that the wild westron ocean
Will be rollin' this day 'tween my laddie and me.

Hees father, he frowned on the love of hees boyhood,
And oh hees proud mother looked cauld upon me.
Bit he aye followed me to ma hame in the shielin',
And the hills of Breadalbane rung wild wi' oor glee.

151

We trysted our love on the cairn on the mountains,
The deers and the roe stood bright maidens tae me.
And my love's trying glass was a pure crystal fountain,
What then wis the world tae my laddie and me.

So I look at the West, as I go to my rest,
That happy my dreams and my slumbers may be.
For far in the West, lives the lad I lue best,
He is seekin' a hame, for ma bairnie and me.

THE LASSIE GATHERING NUTS

There wis a lass, an' a bonnie, bonnie lass,
Tae gaither nuts did gang.
She's pu'ed them east, she's pu'ed them west,
She's pu'ed them as they hung.

Tired at last, she laid her doon,
An' slept the wids among,
When by there came three lusty lads,
Three lusty lads an' strang,
Three lusty lads an' strang.

The first o' them, he kissed her mou,
He thocht he did nae wrong.
The second o' them undid her belt
Tied up wi' London whang   *thong*
Tied up wi' London whang.

What the third he did tae her
Is no put in this song,
Bit the lassie risin' tae her feet,
Says, 'I fear I hae sleept too lang',
Says, 'I fear I hae sleept too lang'.

SCOTS AND ANGLO-SCOTS
Mary, Queen of Scots
1542-87

SONNETS FROM THE SILVER CASKET

Still my love grows and, while I live, must grow,
  Because of my great joy in having part –
  Even though it be some corner – of that heart
To which at last my loyal love will show
So luminously that all his doubt shall go.
  For him would I contend with bitterest fate,
  Seek out high honours to enhance his state,
And do for him so much that he will know
How all my hopes of true content or wealth
  Do in obedience and in service lie.
  For him I covet fortune and bright fame;
For him I value mine own life and health;
  For him it is that I do shoot so high:
  And he will find me evermore the same.

My Heart, my Blood, my Soul, my chiefest Care,
  You promised that we two should taste the pleasure
  Of planning the fair future at our leisure;
Yet all night long I lie and languish here
Because my heart is sore beset with fear,
  Seeing that it beats so far off from its treasure.
  At times I am afraid beyond all measure
That you forget me utterly, Most Dear:
Sometimes I dread lest gossip, all-untrue,
  May harden your kind thoughts from love to hate,
Or I am chilled with terror lest some new
  And troublous throw of chance or shaft of fate
May swerve away from me my Dearest Love...
O God, drive Thou all evil omens off!

LAST PRAYER

Oh! my God and my Lord,
  I have trusted in thee;
Oh! Jesus, my love,
  Now liberate me.
In my enemies' power,
In affliction's sad hour
  I languish for thee.
In sorrowing, weeping,
  And bending the knee,
I adore and implore thee
  To liberate me!

153

Elizabeth Melville
fl. 1599

FROM *ANE GODLIE DREAME, COMPYLIT IN SCOTISH METER, BE M. M. GENTLEWOMAN IN CULROS, AT THE REQUEIST OF HER FRIENDS.*

Upon ane day as I did mourne full soir,
With sindrie things quhairwith my saul was greifit,
My greif increasit, and grew moir and moir,
My comfort fled, and could not be releifit;
With heavines my heart was sa mischiefit,
I loathit my lyfe, I could not eit nor drink;
I micht not speik, nor luik to nane that leifit,   *left*
Bot musit alone, and divers things did think.

The wretchit warld did sa molest my mynde,
I thocht upon this fals and iron age;
And how our harts war sa to vice inclynde,
That Sathan seimit maist feirfullie to rage.
Nathing in earth my sorrow could asswage!
I felt my sin maist stranglie to incres;
I grefit my Spreit, that wont to be my pledge;
My saull was drownit into maist deip distres.

All merynes did aggravate my paine,   *merriness*
And earthlie joyes did still incres my wo:
In companie I na wayes could remaine,
Bot fled resort, and so alone did go.
My sillie soull was tossit to and fro
With sindrie thochts, quhilk troublit me full soir;
I preisit to pray, bot sichs overset me so,   *such*
I could do nocht bot sich, and say no moir.

The twinkling teares aboundantlie ran down,
My heart was easit quhen I had mournit my fill;
Than I began my lamentatioun,
And said, 'O Lord! how lang is it thy will
That thy puir Sancts sall be afflictit still?
Allace! how lang sall subtill Sathan rage?
Mak haist, O Lord! thy promeis to fulfill;
Mak haist to end our painefull pilgramage.

'Thy sillie Sancts are tossit to and fro,
Awalk, O Lord! quhy sleipest thou sa lang?
We have na strenth agains our cruell fo,
In sichs and sobbis now changit is our sang:
The warld prevails, our enemies ar strang,
The wickit rage, bot we are puir and waik:
O shaw thy self! with speid revenge our wrang,
Mak short thir days, even for thy chosen's saik.

'Lord Jesus cum and saif thy awin Elect,
For Sathan seiks our simpill sauls to slay;
The wickit warld dois stranglie us infect,
Most monsterous sinnes increasses day be day:
Our luif grows cauld, our zeill is worne away,
Our faith is faillit, and we ar lyke to fall;
The Lyon roares to catch us as his pray,
Mak haist, O Lord! befoir wee perish all.

'Thir ar the dayes, that thow sa lang foretald
Sould cum befoir this wretchit warld sould end;
Now vice abounds, and charitie growes cald,
And evin thine owne most stronglie dois offend:
The Devill prevaillis, his forces he dois bend,
Gif it could be, to wraik thy children deir;
Bot we are thine, thairfoir sum succour send,
Resave our saullis, we irk to wander heir.

'Quhat can wee do? wee cloggit ar with sin,
In filthie vyce our sensles saules ar drownit;
Thocht wee resolve, wee nevir can begin
To mend our lyfes, bot sin dois still abound.
Quhen will thou cum? quehn sall thy trumpet sound?
Quhen sall wee sie that grit and glorious day?
O save us, Lord! out of this pit profound,
And reif us from this loathsum lump of clay!   *remove*

'Thou knaws our hearts, thou seis our haill desyre,
Our secret thochts thay ar not hid fra thee;
Thocht we offend, thou knawis we stranglie tyre
To beir this wecht; our spreit wald faine be free.   *weight*
Allace! O Lord! quhat plesour can it be
To leif in sinne, that sair dois presse us downe?
O give us wings, that we aloft may flie,
And end the fecht, that we may weir the crowne!'   *fight*

155

Befoir the Lord, quhen I had thus complainit,
My mynde grew calme, my heart was at great rest;
Thocht I was faint from fuid yet I refrainit,
And went to bed, becaus I thocht it best:
With heavines my spreit was sa apprest
I fell on sleip, and sa againe me thocht
I maid my mone, and than my greif increst,
And from the Lord, with teares, I succour socht....

MY DEAR BROTHER, WITH COURAGE BEARE THE CROSSE

My dear Brother, with courage beare the crosse,
Joy shall be joyned with all thy sorrow here;
High is thy hope; disdain this earthly drosse!
Once shall you see the wished day appear.
Now it is dark, thy sky cannot be clear,
After the clouds, it shall be calm anone,
Wait on his will whose blood hath bought you dear,
Extoll his name, tho' outward joys be gone.
Look to the Lord, thou art not left alone,
Since he is there, quhat pleasure canst thou take! –
He is at hand, and hears thy heavy moan,
End out thy faught, and suffer for his sake!
    A sight most bright thy soul shall shortly see,
    When store of glore thy rich reward shall be.

Lady Grizel Baillie
1665-1746

WERE NA MY HEART LIGHT I WAD DIE

There was ance a may, and she lo'ed na men,	*maid*
She biggit her bonny bow'r down in yon glen;	*built*
But now she cries dool! and well-a-day!	*woe*
Come down the green gate, and come here away.	
But now she cries dool! etc.	

When bonny young Johnny came o'er the sea,	
He said he saw naething sae lovely as me;	
He hecht me baith rings and mony braw things;	*promised*
And were na my heart light, I wad die.	
He hecht, etc.	

He had a wee titty that lo'ed na me,	*sister*
Because I was twice as bonny as she;	
She rais'd sic a pother 'twixt him and his mother,	
That were na my heart light, I wad die.	
She rais'd, etc.	

The day it was set, and the bridal to be,	
The wife took a dwam, and lay down to die;	*swoon*
She main'd and she grain'd out of dolour and pain,	*moaned and groaned*
Till he vow'd he never wad see me again.	
She main'd, etc.	

His kin was for ane of a higher degree,	
Said, 'What had he to do with the like of me?'	
Albeit I was bonny, I was na for Johnny;	
And were na my heart light, I wad die.	
Albeit I was, etc.	

They said I had neither cow nor calf,	
Nor dribbles of drink rins thro' the draff,	*malt-grain*
Nor pickles of meal rins thro' the mill-eye;	*small amounts*
And were na my heart light, I wad die.	
Nor pickles of, etc.	

His titty she was baith wylie and slee;	*sly*
She spy'd me as I came o'er the lea;	
And then she ran in and made a loud din;	
Believe your ain een, an ye trow na me.	
And then she, etc.	

His bonnet stood ay fu' round on his brow;
His auld ane looks ay as well as some's new:
But now he lets 't wear ony gate it will hing,   *any manner*
And casts himsel dowie upo' the corn-bing.   *dejected*
    But now he, etc.

And now he gaes drooping about the dykes,
And a' he dow do is to hund the tykes;   *dares; hound the dogs*
The live-lang night he ne'er steeks his eye;   *shuts*
And were na my heart light, I wad die.
    The live-lang, etc.

Were I young for thee, as I hae been,
We shou'd hae been galloping down on yon green,
And linking out o'er yon lily-white lea;
And wow gin I were but young for thee.
    And linking, etc.

Jean Adam
1710-1765

THE IMPARTIAL LAW OF GOD IN NATURE

By way of insult thou inquires at me,
Who first it was that gave me wings to fly?
He, who had power to place me on a throne,
Thought fit to place me on a vale alone;
Yet gave me wings, by which I might aspire
To light my lamp at the celestial fire.
Tell thou, my hand it might become a ring,
My neck might seem more graceful by a chain.
Deformity is oft oblig'd to dress,
Paint seems to mend the ruins of a face.
But neither earth nor sea could aught impart,
That e're could raise the ruins of a heart.
All Crœsus' riches could not buy a Muse,
Nor give me inward light fit theme to chuse;
Nor interprizing Cæsar's lot on earth
Could give me cause to boast of heavenly birth.
The law of nature is the same in all,
In such a case a talent is a call.
What do I owe to ought below the sun,
My worth does in a different channel run.
The cause of my creation was as high
As his who does an earthly sceptre sway;
Out of the dust he sprung as well as I,
No more than I can he Atropos fly.
His soul descended from the spotless clime
Of pure etherial substance; so did mine.
One rule of life was given to us both,
As early I engag'd as he by oath.

I am as free as he to gain the prize
Of the unblemisht spotless sacrifice.
No more than he can I with laws dispense,
As much as he do I abhor offence.
The lowest class that is below the sun,
True faith and virtue puts respect upon.
'Tis better to adorn a private lot,
Than be to shining eminence a blot.

THERE'S NAE LUCK ABOUT THE HOUSE

And are ye sure the news is true?
   And are ye sure he's weel?
Is this a time to think o' wark?
   Ye jauds, fling by your wheel.
Is this a time to think o' wark,
   When Colin's at the door?
Rax me my cloak, I'll to the quay,
   And see him come ashore.
     For there's nae luck about the house,
      There's nae luck at a'
     There's little pleasure in the house
      When our gudeman's awa'.

And gie to me my bigonet,   *linen cap*
   My bishop-satin gown;
For I maun tell the baillie's wife
   That Colin's come to town.
My turkey slippers maun gae on,
   My hose o' pearl blue;
It's a' to please my ain gudeman,
For he's baith leal and true.

Rise up and mak a clean fireside,
   Put on the muckle pot;
Gie little Kate her Sunday gown
   And Jock his button coat;
And mak their shoon as black as slaes,
   Their hose as white as snaw;
It's a' to please my ain gudeman,
   For he's been lang awa'.

Since Colin's weel, I'm weel content,
   I hae nae mair to crave:
Could I but live to mak him blest,
   I'm blest aboon the lave: *rest*
And will I see his face again?
   And will I hear him speak?
I'm downricht dizzy wi' the thocht,
   In troth I'm like to greet.   *cry*

There's twa fat hens upo' the bauk,
   They've fed this month and mair,
Mak haste and thraw their necks about,
   That Colin weel may fare;

And spread the table neat and clean,
 Gar ilka thing look braw;   *make everything look fine*
For wha can tell how Colin fared
 When he was far awa'?

Sae true his heart, sae smooth his speech,
 His breath like caller air;   *fresh*
His very foot has music in't
 As he comes up the stair.
And will I see his face again?
 And will I hear him speak?
I'm downricht dizzy wi' the thocht,
 In troth I'm like to greet.
  For there's nae luck, etc.

161

Alison Rutherford (Mrs Cockburn)
1712-94

THE FLOWERS OF THE FOREST

I've seen the smiling of Fortune beguiling,
    I've tasted her favours, and felt her decay:
Sweet is her blessing, and kind her caressing;
    But soon it is fled – it is fled far away.

I've seen the Forest adornéd the foremost
    With flowers of the fairest – most pleasant and gay:
Full sweet was their blooming – their scent the air perfuming;
    But now they are wither'd and a' wede away.

I've seen the morning with gold the hills adorning,
    And the red tempest storming before parting day:
I've seen Tweed's silver streams, glittering in the sunny beams,
    Grow drumly and dark as they roll'd on their way.   *muddy*

O fickle Fortune! why this cruel sporting?
    Why thus perplex us poor sons of a day?
Thy frowns cannot fear me, thy smiles cannot cheer me –
    Since the Flowers of the Forest are a' wede away.

Jean Elliott
1727-1805

THE FLOWERS OF THE FOREST

I've heard the lilting at our yowe-milking,   *ewe*
  Lasses a-lilting before the dawn o' day;
But now they are moaning on ilka green loaning;
  'The Flowers of the Forest are a' wede away.'   *withered*

At buchts, in the morning, nae blythe lads are scorning;   *cattle-pens*
  The lasses are lonely, and dowie, and wae;   *sad*
Nae daffin', nae gabbin', but sighing and sabbing: *dallying, gossiping*
  Ilk ane lifts her leglen, and hies her away.   *stool*

In hairst, at the shearing, nae youths now are jeering,   *harvest*
  The bandsters are lyart, and runkled and grey; *binders, grizzled*
At fair or at preaching, nae wooing, nae fleeching: *coaxing*
  The Flowers of the Forest are a' wede away.

At e'en, in the gloaming, nae swankies are roaming   *young men*
  'Bout stacks wi' the lasses at bogle to play,   *peek-a-boo*
But ilk ane sits drearie, lamenting her dearie:
  The Flowers of the Forest are a' wede away.

Dule and wae for the order sent our lads to the Border;
  The English, for ance, by guile wan the day:
The Flowers of the Forest, that foucht aye the foremost,
  The prime o' our land are cauld in the clay.

Isobel Pagan
1741—1821

CA' THE YOWES TO THE KNOWES

Ca' the yowes to the knowes –
Ca' them whare the heather grows –
Ca' them whare the burnie rows,
 My bonnie dearie!

  Call the ewes to the hills

As I gaed doun the water side,
There I met my shepherd lad;
He rowed me sweetly in his plaid,
 And ca'd me his dearie.

'Will ye gang doun the water side,
And see the waves sae sweetly glide
Beneath the hazels spreading wide?
 The mune it shines fu' clearly.'

'I was bred up at nae sic schule,
My shepherd lad, to play the fule,
And a' the day to sit in dule,
 And naebody to see me.'

  sadness

'Ye shall get gowns and ribbons meet,
Cawf-leather shoon to thy white feet,
And in my arms ye'se lie and sleep,
 And ye shall be my dearie.'

'If ye'll but stand to what ye've said,
I'se gang wi' you, my shepherd lad;
And ye may row me in your plaid,
 And I shall be your dearie.'

'While waters wimple to the sea –
While day blinks i' the lift sae hie –
Till clay-cauld death shall blin my e'e
 Ye aye shall be my dearie!'

  ripple

THE CROOK AND PLAID

Ilk lassie has a laddie she lo'es abune the rest,   *each, above*
Ilk lassie has a laddie, if she like to confess 't,
That is dear unto her bosom, whatever be his trade;
But my lover's aye the laddie that wears the crook and plaid.

Ilk morn he climbs the mountains, his fleecy flocks to view,
And hears the laverocks chanting, new spring frae 'mang the dew; *sky-*
His bonnie wee bit doggie, sae frolicsome and glad,   *lark*
Rins aye before the laddie that wears the crook and plaid.

And when that he is wearied, and lies upon the grass,
What if that in his plaidie he hide a bonnie lass? –
Nae doubt there's a preference due to every trade,
But commend me to the laddie that wears the crook and plaid.

And when in summer weather he is upon the hill,
He reads in books of history that learns him meikle skill;
There's nae sic joyous leisure to be had at ony trade
Save that the laddie follows that wears the crook and plaid.

What though in storms o' winter part o' his flock should die,
My laddie is aye cheery, and why should not I?
The prospect o' the summer can weel mak' us glad;
Contented is the laddie that wears the crook and plaid.

King David was a shepherd while in the prime o' youth,
And following the flocks he pondered upon truth;
And when he came to be a king, and left his former trade,
'Twas an honour to the laddie that wears the crook and plaid.

Anne Hunter
1742-1821

MY MOTHER BIDS ME BIND MY HAIR

My mother bids me bind my hair
  With bands of rosy hue,
Tie up my sleeves with ribbons rare,
  And lace my boddice blue.

'For why,' she cries, 'sit still and weep,
  While others dance and play?'
Alas! I scarce can go or creep
  While Lubin is away.

'Tis sad to think the days are gone
  When those we love were near;
I sit upon this mossy stone
  And sigh when none can hear.

And while I spin my flaxen thread,
  And sing my simple lay,
The village seems asleep or dead,
  Now Lubin is away.

THE LOT OF THOUSANDS

When hope lies dead within the heart,
  By secret sorrow close concealed,
We shrink lest looks or words impart
  What must not be revealed.

Tis hard to smile when one would weep,
  To speak when one would silent be;
To wake when one would wish to sleep,
  And wake to agony.

Yet such the lot by thousands cast,
  Who wander in this world of care,
And bend beneath the bitter blast
  To save them from despair.

But Nature waits, her guests to greet,
  Where disappointments cannot come,
And Time guides with unerring feet
  The weary wanderers home.

Lady Anne Lindsay
1750-1825

AULD ROBIN GRAY

When the sheep are in the fauld, and the kye a' at hame,   *cattle*
When a' the weary warld to sleep are gane,
The waes o' my heart fa' in showers frae my e'e,
While my gudeman lies sound by me.   *husband*

Young Jamie lo'ed me weel, and sought me for his bride;
But saving a croun he had naething else beside.
To mak the croun a pound, my Jamie gaed to sea,
And the croun and the pound, they were baith for me.

He hadna been awa' a week but only twa,
When my mither she fell sick and the cow was stown awa';   *stolen*
My father brak his arm – my Jamie at the sea;
And auld Robin Gray cam a-courtin' me.

My father couldna wark, my mither couldna spin;
I toil'd day and nicht, but their bread I couldna win:
Auld Rob maintain'd them baith, and wi' tears in his e'e,
Said, 'Jeanie, for their sakes, will ye marry me?'

My heart it said na – I look'd for Jamie back;
But the wind it blew hie, and the ship it was a wrack;
His ship it was a wrack – why didna Jamie dee?
And why do I live to cry, Wae's me?

My father urged me sair; my mither didna speak,
But she looked in my face till my heart was like to break.
They gied him my hand – my heart was at the sea;
Sae auld Robin Gray he was gudeman to me.

I hadna been a wife a week but only four,
When, mournfu' as I sat on the stane at the door,
I saw my Jamie's wraith – I couldna think it he,   *image*
Til he said, 'I'm come hame, my love, to marry thee.'

O sair did we greet, and meikle did we say:
We took but ae kiss, and I bade him gang away.
I wish that I were dead, but I'm not like to dee;
And why was I born to say, Wae's me?

I gang like a ghaist, and I carena to spin;
I daurna think o' Jamie, for that wad be a sin.
But I'll do my best a gude wife to be,
For auld Robin Gray, he is kind to me.

Anne Grant
1755-1838

O WHERE, TELL ME WHERE

'O where, tell me where, is your Highland laddie gone?
O where, tell me where, is your Highland laddie gone?'
'He's gone, with streaming banners, where noble deeds are done;
And my sad heart will tremble till he comes safely home.
He's gone, with streaming banners, where noble deeds are done;
And my sad heart will tremble till he comes safely home.'

'O where, tell me where, did your Highland laddie stay?
O where, tell me where, did your Highland laddie stay?'
'He dwelt beneath the holly-trees, beside the rapid Spey;
And many a blessing follow'd him, the day he went away.
He dwelt beneath the holly-trees, beside the rapid Spey;
And many a blessing follow'd him, the day he went away.'

'O what, tell me what, does your Highland laddie wear?
O what, tell me what, does your Highland laddie wear?'
'A bonnet with a lofty plume, the gallant badge of war;
And a plaid across the manly breast, that yet shall wear a star.
A bonnet with a lofty plume, the gallant badge of war;
And a plaid across the manly breast that yet shall wear a star.'

'Suppose, ah! suppose, that some cruel, cruel wound
Should pierce your Highland laddie, and all your hopes confound!'
'The pipe would play a cheering march, the banners round him fly;
The spirit of a Highland chief would lighten in his eye.
The pipe would play a cheering march, the banners round him fly;
And for his king and country dear with pleasure he would die!

'But I will hope to see him yet, in Scotland's bonny bounds;
But I will hope to see him yet, in Scotland's bonny bounds.
His native land of liberty shall nurse his glorious wounds,
While wide, through all our Highland hills, his warlike name resounds.
His native land of liberty shall nurse his glorious wounds,
While wide, through all our Highland hills, his warlike name resounds.'

Jean Glover
1758-1801

O'ER THE MUIR AMANG THE HEATHER

Comin' through the craigs o' Kyle,
  Amang the bonnie bloomin' heather,
There I met a bonnie lassie
  Keepin' her flocks thegither.
      Ower the muir amang the heather,
      Ower the muir amang the heather,
      There I met a bonnie lassie
      Keepin' a' her flocks thegither.

Says I, my dear, where is thy hame?
  In muir or dale, pray tell me whither?
Says she, I tent the fleecy flocks
  That feed amang the bloomin' heather.
      Ower the muir, etc.

We laid us down upon a bank,
  Sae warm and sunnie was the weather;
She left her flocks at large to rove
  Amang the bonnie bloomin' heather.
      Ower the muir, etc.

She charmed my heart, and aye sinsyne   *ever since then*
  I couldna think on ony ither;
By sea and sky! she shall be mine,
  The bonnie lass amang the heather.
      Ower the muir, etc.

Elizabeth Hamilton
1758-1816

MY AIN FIRESIDE

Oh! I hae seen great anes, and sat in great ha's,
'Mong lords and 'mong ladies a' covered wi' braws;   *finery*
At feasts made for princes, wi' princes I've been,
Where the grand shine o' splendour has dazzled my e'en;
But a sight sae delightfu', I trow, I ne'er spied,
As the bonnie blythe blink o' my ain fireside.
My ain fireside, my ain fireside,
O cheery's the blink o' my ain fireside.

    My ain fireside, my ain fireside,
O there's nought to compare wi' my ain fireside.

Ance mair, Gude be praised, round my ain heartsome ingle, *open hearth*
Wi' the friends o' my youth I cordially mingle;
Nae forms to compel me to seem wae or glad,   *sad*
I may laugh when I'm merry, and sigh when I'm sad;
Nae falsehood to dread, and nae malice to fear,
But truth to delight me, and friendship to cheer;
Of a' roads to happiness ever were tried,
There's nane half so sure as ane's ain fireside.

    My ain fireside, my ain fireside,
O there's nought to compare wi' my ain fireside.

When I draw in my stool on my cosy hearthstane,
My heart loups sae light I scarce ken't for my ain;   *leaps*
Care's down on the wind, it is clean out o' sight,
Past troubles they seem but as dreams o' the night.
There but kind voices, kind faces I see,
And mark saft affection glent fond frae ilk e'e;
Nae fleechings o' flattery, nae boastings o' pride,
'Tis heart speaks to heart, at ane's ain fireside.

    My ain fireside, my ain fireside,
O there's nought to compare wi' ane's ain fireside.

Mrs Angus Lyon
1762-1840

NEIL GOW'S FAREWEEL TO WHISKY

Ye've surely heard of famous Neil,
The man who play'd the fiddle weel;
He was a heartsome merry chiel;   *lad*
   And weel he lo'ed the whisky, O!
For since he wore the tartan hose
He dearly liket *Athool Brose*;
And grieved was he, you may suppose,
   To bid 'Fareweel to Whisky', O!

Alas! says Neil, I'm frail and auld,
And whiles my hame is unco cauld;
I think it mak's me blithe and bauld,
   A wee drap Highland whisky, O;
But a' the doctors do agree
That whisky's no' the drink for me;
I'm fley'd they'll gar me tyne my glee,   *afraid, lose*
   By parting me and whisky, O.

But I should mind on 'auld langsyne'
How Paradise our friends did tyne,
Because something ran in their mind –
   Forbit – like Highland whisky, O!
Whilst I can get good wine and ale,
And find my heart and fingers hale,
I'll be content though legs should fail,
   And though forbidden whisky, O!

I'll tak' my fiddle in my hand,
And screw its strings while they can stand,
And mak' a lamentation grand
   For guid auld Highland whisky, O!
Oh! all ye powers of music, come,
For, 'deed, I think I'm mighty glum,
My fiddle strings will hardly hum
   To say, 'Fareweel to Whisky', O!

171

Joanna Baillie
1762-1851

POVERTY PARTS GOOD COMPANY

When my o'erlay was white as the foam o' the lin,   *waterfall*
And siller was chinkin' my pouches within;
When my lambkins were bleatin' on meadow and brae,
As I went to my love in new cleathing sae gay,
    Kind was she, and my friends were free,
    But poverty parts guid company.

How swift pass'd the minutes and hours of delight!
The piper played cheerie, the cruise burn'd bright,   *lamp*
And linked in my hand was the maiden sae dear,
As she footed the floor in her holiday gear!
    Woe's me: and can it then be
    That poverty parts sic company?   *such*

We met at the fair, and we met at the kirk;
We met in the sunshine, we met in the mirk;
And the sound o' her voice and the blinks o' her e'en,
The cheerin' and life of my bosom hae been.
    Leaves frae the tree at Martinmas flee,
    And poverty parts sweet company.

At bridal and infare I've braced me wi' pride,   *housewarming*
The broose I hae won and a kiss o' the bride;   *race*
And loud was the laughter good fellows among,
As I uttered my banter or chorus'd my song.
    Dowie to dree are jestin' and glee,   *hard to beat*
    When poverty spoils guid company.

Wherever I gaed, kindly lasses looked sweet,
And mithers and aunties were unco discreet;
While kebbuck and bicker were set on the board;   *cheese, beaker*
But now they pass by me, and never a word.
    Sae let it be, for the worldly and slee
    Wi' poverty keep nae company.

But the hope o' my love is a cure for its smart,
And the spae-wife has tauld me to keep up my heart;   *fortune teller*
For wi' my last saxpence her loof I hae crost,   *palm*
And the bliss that is fated can never be lost,
    Tho' cruelly we may ilka day see
    How poverty parts dear company.

TAM O' THE LIN

Tam o' the Lin was fu' o' pride,
And his weapon he girt to his valorous side,
A scabbard o' leather wi' de'il-hair't within.
'Attack me wha daur!' quo' Tam o' the Lin.
Tam o' the Lin he bought a mear;
She cost him five shillings, she wasna dear.
Her back stuck up, and her sides fell in.
'A fiery yaud,' quo' Tam o' the Lin.   *old mare*

Tam o' the Lin he courted a May;
She stared at him sourly, and said him nay;
But he stroked down his jerkin and cocked up his chin.
 'She aims at a laird, then,' quo' Tam o' the Lin.
Tam o' the Lin he gaed to the fair,
Yet he looked wi' disdain on the chapman's ware;
Then chucked out a sixpence; the sixpence was tin.
'There's coin for the fiddlers,' quo' Tam o' the Lin.

Tam o' the Lin wad show his lear,   *learning*
And he scann'd o'er the book wi' wise-like stare.
He muttered confusedly, but didna begin.
'This is dominie's business,'quo' Tam o' the Lin.

Tam o' the Lin had a cow wi' ae horn,
That likit to feed on his neighbour's corn.
The stanes he threw at her fell short o' the skin:
'She's a lucky auld reiver,' quo' Tam o' the Lin.   *raider*
Tam o' the Lin he married a wife,
And she was the torment, the plague o' his life;
She lays sae about her, and maks sic a din,
'She frightens the baby,' quo' Tam o' the Lin.

Tam o' the Lin grew dowie and douce,   *dull, quiet*
And he sat on a stane at the end o' his house.
'What ails, auld chield?' He looked haggard and thin.   *old man*
'I'm no very cheery,' quo' Tam o' the Lin.

Tam o' the Lin lay down to die,
And his friends whispered softly and woefully –
'We'll buy you some masses to scour away sin.'
'And drink at my lyke-wake,' quo' Tam o' the Lin.

WOO'D AND MARRIED AND A'

The bride she is winsome and bonny,
  Her hair it is snooded sae sleek,
And faithfu' and kind is her Johnny,
  Yet fast fa' the tears on her cheek,
New pearlins are cause of her sorrow,   *lace trimmings*
  New pearlins and plenishing too;
The bride that has a' to borrow
  Has e'en right mickle ado.
    Woo'd and married and a'!
    Woo'd and married and a'!
    Isna she very weel aff
    To be woo'd and married and a'?

Her mither then hastily spak:
  'The lassie is glaikit wi' pride;   *stupid*
In my pouch I had never a plack   *penny*
  The day that I was a bride.
E'en tak' to your wheel and be clever,
  And draw out your thread in the sun;
The gear that is gifted, it never   *possession*
  Will last like the gear that is won.
    Woo'd and married and a'!'
    Wi' havins and tocher sae sma'!   *silver, dowry*
    I think ye are very weel aff
    To be woo'd and married and a'!'

'Toot! toot!' quo' her grey-headed faither,
  'She's less o' a bride than a bairn;
She's ta'en like a cowt frae the heather,   *foal*
  Wi' sense and discretion to learn.
Half husband, I trow, and half daddy,
  As humour inconstantly leans,
The chiel maun be patient and steady   *man*
  That yokes wi' a mate in her teens.
    A kerchief sae douce and sae neat,
    O'er her locks that the wind used to blaw!
    I'm baith like to laugh and to greet
    When I think o' her married at a'!'

Then out spak the wily bridegroom;
   Weel waled were his wordies I ween: *chosen, guess*
'I'm rich, though my coffer be toom,   *empty*
   Wi' the blink o' your bonny blue e'en.
I'm prouder o' thee by my side,
   Though thy ruffles and ribbons be few,
Than if Kate o' the Craft were my bride,
   Wi' purples and pearlins enou'.
     Dear and dearest of ony!
     Ye're woo'd and buiket and a'!   *registered for marriage*
     And do ye think scorn o' your Johnny,
     And grieve to be married at a'?'

She turn'd, and she blush'd, and she smiled,
   And she lookit sae bashfully down;
The pride o' her heart was beguiled,
   And she play'd wi' the sleeve o' her gown,
She twirled the tag o' her lace,
   And she nippit her boddice sae blue,
Syne blinkit sae sweet in his face,
   And aff like a mawkin she flew.   *hare*
     Woo'd and married and a'!
     Wi' Johnny to roose her and a'!   *arouse*
     She thinks hersel' very weel aff
     To be woo'd and married and a'!

THE SHEPHERD'S SONG (THE LOVER'S WATCH)

The gowan glitters on the sward,   *daisy, turf*
The lav'rock's in the sky,   *lark*
And Collie on my plaid keeps ward,
And time is passing by.
Oh, no! sad an' slow
And lengthen'd on the ground,
The shadow of our trystin' bush,   *meeting place*
It wears sae slowly round!

My sheep-bell tinkles frae the west,
My lambs are bleating near,
But still the sound that I lo'e best,
Alack! I canna hear.
Oh, no! sad an' slow!
The shadow lingers still;
And like a lanely ghaist I stand,
And croon upon the hill.

175

I hear below the water roar,
The mill wi' clackin' din;
And Lucky scolding frae her door,
To ca' the bairnies in.
Oh, no! sad an' slow!
These are nae sounds for me;
The shadow of our trystin' bush,
It creeps sae drearily.

I coft yestreen frae chapman Tam,   *bought*
A snood of bonnie blue,
And promised, when our trystin' cam,
To tie it round her brow.
Oh, no! sad an' slow!
The mark it winna pass;
The shadow of that weary thorn
Is tether'd on the grass.

O now I see her on the way,
She's past the witches' knowe;   *mound*
She's climbin' up the brownie's brae   *fairy*
My heart is in a lowe.   *fire*
Oh, no! 'tis na so!
'Tis glaumrie I ha'e seen: *magic*
The shadow of that hawthorn bush
Will move nae mair till e'en.

My book of grace I'll try to read,
Though conn'd wi' little skill;
When Collie barks I'll raise my head,
And find her on the hill.
Oh, no! sad an' slow!
The time will ne'er be gane;
The shadow of the trystin' bush
Is fix'd like ony stane.

Carolina Oliphant (Lady Nairne)
1766-1845

THE LAIRD O' COCKPEN

The laird o' Cockpen, he's proud an' he's great,
His mind is ta'en up wi' things o' the State;
He wanted a wife, his braw house to keep,
But favour wi' wooin' was fashious to seek.   *troublesome*

Down by the dyke-side a lady did dwell,
At his table head he thought she'd look well,
McClish's ae daughter o' Claverse-ha' Lee,
A penniless lass wi' a lang pedigree.

His wig was weel pouther'd, and as gude as new;
His waistcoat was white, his coat it was blue;
He put on a ring, a sword and cock'd hat,
And wha could refuse the laird wi' a' that?

He took the grey mare, and rade cannily,
An' rapp'd at the yett o' Claverse-ha' Lee;
'Gae tell Mistress Jean to come speedily ben,
She's wanted to speak to the laird o' Cockpen.'

Mistress Jean was makin' the elder-flower wine.
'An' what brings the laird at sic a like time?'
She put off her apron, and on her silk gown,
Her mutch wi'red ribbons, and gaed awa' down.

An' when she cam' ben he bowed fu' low,
An' what was his errand he soon let her know;
Amazed was the laird when the lady said 'Na,'
And wi' a laigh curtsie she turned awa'.

Dumfounder'd he was, nae sigh did he gie,
He mounted his mare – he rade cannily;
And aften he thought, as he gaed thro' the glen,
She's daft to refuse the laird o' Cockpen.

And now that the laird his exit had made,
Mistress Jean she reflected on what she had said;
'Oh, for ane I'll get better, its waur I'll get ten,
I was daft to refuse the Laird o' Cockpen.'

Next time that the laird and the lady were seen,
They were gaun arm-in-arm to the kirk on the green;
Now she sits in the ha' like a weel-tappit hen,   *plump*
But as yet there's nae chickens appear'd at Cockpen.

177

THE ROWAN TREE

Oh! Rowan Tree, Oh! Rowan Tree, thou'lt aye be dear to me,
Intwin'd thou art wi' mony ties o' hame and infancy.
Thy leaves were aye the first o' spring, thy flow'rs the simmer's pride;
There was nae sic bonny tree, in a' the countrie side.
           Oh! Rowan tree.

How fair wert thou in simmer time, wi' a' thy clusters white,
How rich and gay thy autumn dress, wi' berries red and bright;
On thy fair stem were mony names, which now nae mair I see,
But they're engraven on my heart – forgot they ne'er can be!
           Oh! Rowan tree.

We sat aneath thy spreading shade, the bairnies round thee ran,
They pu'd thy bonny berries red, and necklaces they strang;
My mother! oh! I see her still, she smil'd our sports to see,
Wi' little Jeanie on her lap, an' Jamie at her knee!
           Oh! Rowan tree.

Oh! there arose my father's prayer, in holy evening's calm,
How sweet was then my mother's voice, in the Martyr's psalm;
Now a' are gane! we meet nae mair aneath the Rowan tree;
But hallowed thoughts around thee twine o' hame and infancy,
           Oh! Rowan tree.

THE HEIRESS

I'll no be had for naething,
  I'll no be had for naething,
I tell ye, lads, that's ae thing,
  So ye needna follow me.

Oh! the change is most surprising;
  Last year I was Betsy Brown;
Now to my hand they're a' aspiring,
  The fair Eliza I am grown!
    But I'll no, etc.

Oh! the change is most surprising.
  Nane o' them e'er look'd at me;
Now my charms they're a' admiring,
  For my sake they're like to dee!
    But I'll no, etc.

The laird, the shirra, and the doctor,
    And twa-three lords o' high degree;
Wi' heaps o' writers, I could mention,
    Surely, sirs, it is no me!
        But I'll no, etc.

But there is ane, when I had naething,
    A' his heart he gied to me;
And sair he toiled, to mak a wee thing,
    To gie me when he cam frae sea.
        Sae I'll no, etc.

And if e'er I marry ony,
    He will be the lad for me;
For oh, he was baith gude and bonny,
    And he thocht the same o' me.
        Sae I'll no be had for naething,
            I'll no be had for naething,
        I tell ye, lads, that's ae thing,
            So ye needna follow me.

CRADLE SONG

Baloo loo, lammy, now baloo, my dear;
Now, baloo loo, lammy, ain minnie is here:
What ails my sweet bairnie? What ails it this nicht?
What ails my wee lammy? is bairnie no richt?

Baloo loo, lammy, now baloo, my dear,
Does wee lammy ken that its daddie's no here?
Ye're rockn' fu' sweetly on mammie's warm knee,
But daddie's a-rockin' upon the saut sea.

Now hush-a-ba, lammy, now hush-a, my dear;
Now hush-a-ba, lammy; ain minnie is here.

WILL YE NO COME BACK AGAIN?

Bonnie Charlie's now awa,
    Safely owre the friendly main;
Mony a heart will break in twa,
    Should he ne'er come back again.
        Will ye no come back again?
        Will ye no come back again?
        Better lo'ed ye canna be,
        Will ye no come back again?

Ye trusted in your Heiland men,
   They trusted you, dear Charlie;
They kent you hiding in the glen,
   Your cleedin was but barely.   *covering*
      Will ye no, etc.

English bribes were a' in vain,
   An' e'en tho' puirer we may be;
Siller canna buy the heart
   That beats aye for thine and thee.
      Will ye no, etc.

We watched thee in the gloaming hour,
   We watched thee in the morning grey;
Tho' thirty thousand pounds they'd gie,
   Oh there is nane that wad betray.
      Will ye no, etc.

Sweet's the laverock's note and lang,   *lark*
   Lilting wildly up the glen;
But aye to me he sings ae sang,
   Will ye no come back again?
      Will ye no come back again?
      Will ye no come back again?
      Better lo'ed ye canna be,
      Will ye no come back again?

Janet Hamilton
1795-1873

OOR LOCATION

A hunner funnels bleezin', reekin',
Coal an' ironstane, charrin', smeekin';
Navvies, miners, keepers, fillers,
Puddlers, rollers, iron millers;
Reestit, reekit, raggit laddies,
Firemen, enginemen, an' Paddies;
Boatmen, banksmen, rough and rattlin',
'Bout the wecht wi' colliers battlin',   *weight*
Sweatin', swearin', fechtin', drinkin',
Change-house bells an' gill-stoups clinkin', *alehouse; drinking cup*
Police – ready men and willin' –
Aye at han' when stoups are fillin',
Clerks, an' counter-loupers plenty,   *queue-jumpers* [?]
Wi' trim moustache and whiskers dainty –
Chaps that winna staun at trifles,
Min' ye they can han'le rifles.
'Bout the wives in oor location,
An' the lasses' botheration,
Some are decent, some are dandies,
An' a gey wheen drucken randies,   *a few drunken roughs*
Aye to neebors' hooses sailin',
Greetin' bairns ahint them trailin',
Gaun for nouther bread nor butter,
Just to drink an' rin the cutter.   *to smuggle a drink from a bar*
Oh, the dreadfu' curse o' drinkin'!
Men are ill, but tae my thinkin',
Leukin' through the drucken fock,   *drunken folk*
There's a Jenny for ilk Jock.
Oh, the dool an' desolation,
An' the havoc in the nation,
Wrocht by dirty, drucken wives!
Oh, hoo mony bairnies' lives
Lost ilk year through their neglec'!
Like a millstane roun' the neck
O' the strugglin', toilin' masses
Hing drucken wives and wanton lassies.
To see sae mony unwed mithers
I sure a shame that taps a' ithers.
 An' noo I'm fairly set a-gaun,
On baith the whisky-shop and pawn;
I'll speak my min' – and whatfor no?   *why not?*
Frae whence cums misery, want, an' wo,
The ruin, crime, disgrace an' shame,

That quenches a' the lichts o' hame?
Ye needna speer, the feck ot's drawn   *ask, bulk*
Out o' the change-house an' the pawn.
  Sin and death, as poets tell,
On ilk side the doors o' hell
Wait to haurl mortals in;
Death gets a' that's catcht by sin:
There are doors where death an' sin
Draw their tens o' thoosan's in;
Thick and thrang we see them gaun,
First the dram-shop, then the pawn;
Owre a' kin's o' ruination,
Drink's the king in oor location.

A LAY OF THE TAMBOUR FRAME

Bending with straining eyes
  Over the tambour frame,
Never a change in her weary routine –
  Slave in all but the name.
Tambour, ever tambour,
  Tambour the wreathing lines
Of 'broidered silk, till beauty's robe
  In rainbow lustre shines.

There, with colourless cheek;
  There, with her tangling hair;
Still bending low o'er the rickety frame,
  Seek, ye will find her there.
Tambour, ever tambour,
  With fingers cramped and chill; –
The panes are shattered, and cold the wind
  Blows over the eastern hill.

Why quail, my sisters, why,
  As ye were abjects vile,
When begging some haughty brother of earth
  'to give you leave to toil'?
It is tambour you must,
  Naught else you have to do;
Though paupers' dole be of higher amount
  Than pay oft earned by you.

182

No union strikes for you; –
  Unshielded and alone
In the battle of life – a battle it is,
  Where virtue is oft o'erthrown.
O working men! Oh, why
  Pass ye thus careless by,
Nor give to the working woman's complaint
  One word of kind reply?

Selfish, unfeeling men!
  Have ye not had your will?
High pay, short hours; yet your cry, like the leech,
  Is, Give us, give us still.
She who tambours – tambours
  For fifteen hours a day –
Would have shoes on her feet, and dress for church,
  Had she a third of your pay.

Sisters, cousins, and aunts
  Are they; yet, if not so,
Say, are they not sisters by human ties,
  And sympathy's kindly flow?
To them how dear the boon
  From brother's hand that came!
It would warm the heart and brighten the eyes,
  While bending o'er the frame.

Raise ye a fund to aid
  In times of deep distress;
While man helps man, to their sisters in need
  Brothers can do no less.
Still the tambourer bends
  Wearily o'er the frame.
Patterns oft vary, for fashions will change –
  She is ever the same.

THE PLAGUE OF OUR ISLE

It is said, it is sung, it is written, and read,
It sounds in the ear, and it swims in the head,
It booms in the air, it is borne o'er the sea –
'There's a good time coming', but when shall it be?

183

Shall it be when Intemperance, enthroned on the waves
Of a dark sea of ruin, is scooping the graves
Of thousands, while redly the dark current rolls
With the blood of her victims – the slaughter of souls?

A canker is found in the bud, flower, and fruit
Of human progression – a worm at the root
Of social improvement – a fiery simoom
That sweeps o'er the masses to burn and consume.

'Tis found on the heaven-hallow'd day of repose –
Blest haven of rest from our toils and our woes!
That voice of the drunkard, the oath, curse, and brawl,
Are sounds of such frequence, they cease to appal.

We see the grey father, the youth in his prime,
Throw soul, sense, and feeling, health, substance, and time.
In the cup of the drunkard – the mother and wife
Hugs the snake in her bosom that 'venoms her life.

We see the gaunt infant, so feeble and pale,
Crave nature's sweet fluid from fountains that fail;
Or run with hot poison, distill'd from the breast
Of the mother – O monstrous! – a drunkard, a pest!

We've seen, with her bright hair all clotted with blood,
Lie cold on the hearth – where at morning she stood
The wife of a summer – a babe on her breast –
The husband a drunkard – let death tell the rest.

And darker and deeper the horrors that shroud
The brain of the drunkard; what dark phantoms crowd
'The cells of his fancy', his couch of despair
Is empty – the suicide slumbers not there.

O why do we seek, do we hope to bestow
'The colours of heaven on the dwellings of woe'?
'Tis temperance must level the strongholds of crime –
'Tis temperance must herald the 'coming good time'.

Then turn ye! oh, turn ye! for why will ye die?
Ye shrink from the plague when its advent is nigh –
The Indian pestilence, the plague of old Nile –
Less deadly by far than the Plague of our Isle.

Carolina Oliphant (The Younger)
1807-31

OH, NEVER! NO, NEVER!

Oh! never, no, never,
Thou 'lt meet me again!
Thy spirit for ever
Has burst from its chain;
The links thou hast broken
Are all that remain,
For never, oh! never,
Thou 'lt meet me again.

Like the sound of the viol,
That dies on the blast;
Like the shade on the dial,
Thy spirit has pass'd.
The breezes blow round me,
But give back no strain;
The shade on the dial
Returns not again.

When roses enshrined thee,
In light trellis'd shade,
Still hoping to find thee,
How oft have I strayed!
Thy desolate dwelling
I traverse in vain; –
The stillness has whisper'd,
Thou 'lt ne'er come again.

I still haste to meet thee,
When-footsteps I hear;
And start, when to greet me
Thou dost not appear;
Then afresh o'er my spirit
Steals mem'ry of pain; –
For never, oh! never,
Thou 'lt meet me again.

Alicia Anne Spottiswoode (Lady John Scott)
1810-1900

DURRISDEER

We'll meet nae mair at sunset, when the weary day is dune,
Nor wander hame thegither, by the lee licht o' the mune!
I'll hear your step nae longer amang the dewy corn,
For we'll meet nae mair, my bonniest, either at eve or morn.

The yellow broom is waving, abune the sunny brae,
And the rowan berries dancing, where the sparkling waters play.
Tho' a' is bright and bonnie, it's an eerie place to me,
For we'll meet nae mair, my dearest, either by burn or tree.

Far up into the wild hills, there's a kirkyard auld and still,
Where the frosts lie ilka morning, and the mists hang low and chill,
And there ye sleep in silence, while I wander here my lane,
Till we meet ance mair in Heaven, never to part again.

ANNIE LAURIE

Maxwellton braes are bonnie,
Where early fa's the dew,
And it's there that Annie Laurie
Gie'd me her promise true;
Gie'd me her promise true,
That ne'er forgot sall be;
But for bonnie Annie Laurie
I'd lay doun my head and dee.

Her brow is like the snaw-drift,
Her neck is like the swan,
Her face it is the fairest
That e'er the sun shone on,
And dark blue is her e'e;
And for bonnie Annie Laurie
I'd lay doun my head and dee.

Like dew on the gowan lying   *daisy*
Is the fa' o' her fairy feet;
And like winds in simmer sighing,
Her voice is low and sweet,
And she's a' the world to me,
And for bonnie Annie Laurie
I'd lay doun my head and dee.

AFTER CULLODEN

We winna leave thee. Where should we gang ?
  Thou art our King, our life, and our glory.
Trust to us yet, and it shall na be lang
  Ere the dastardly Whigs shall rin trembling before ye.

The bravest and best o' the country lie slain,
  True hearts and bauld wad hae righted ye rarely,
But ye've the mair need o' the few that remain,
  An' in life or in death, we'll stand by ye, Charlie.

Dark though the day be, its clouds will blaw past,
  An' a morrow will come wi' the sun shining fairly,
Up the red steep we will struggle at last,
  An' place the auld crown on your head, Royal Charlie !

We'll never leave thee. Our law is thy will,
  Our heart's blude, our gear, an' our lands are thine fairly,
Lead on ! If ye fa', we'll follow ye still,
  An' dee by your side. We'll hae nae king but Charlie!

Dorothea Maria Ogilvy of Clova
1823-95

THE WEARY SPINNIN O'T

Sittin spinnin, sittin spinnin
  A' the lea-lang day,
Hearin the bit burnie rinnin,
  And the bairns at play.
I'm sweir to get my leg let loose,   *unable*
To do a turn about the hoose;
Oh, amna I a waefu wife
To spin awa my threid of life?
Spinnin, spinnin, ever spinnin,
Never endin, aye beginnin;
Hard at wark wi hand and fuit,
Oh, the weary spinnin o't!

Sittin spinnin, sittin spinnin,
  Vow but I am thrang,   *busy*
My wee pickle siller winnin,
  Croonin some auld sang.
Leese me o my spinnin-wheel,
Gie's us a' oor milk and meal;
Weet or dry, or het or cauld,
I maun spin till I grow auld.   *must*
Spinnin, spinnin, ever spinnin,
Never endin, aye beginnin,
Hard at wark wi hand and fuit
At the weary spinnin o't.

Sittin spinnin, sittin spinnin,
  Sic a wear and tear,
Taps of tow for wabs o linen,
  Till my heid is sair.
Mony a wiselike wab I've spun,
Spreid and sortit i the sun;
Puirtith cauld is ill to bear;   *poverty*
Mony bairns bring mickle care.
Spinnin, spinnin, ever spinnin,
Never endin, aye beginnin,
Hard at wark wi hand and fuit,
Ohl the weary spinnin o't!

Anne Ross Cousin
1824-1906

CHRIST WITHIN THE VEIL

Art can depict for us the Holy Child
  With a sweet majesty of brow and eyes –
A King on 'Mary's' knee – with aureole mild
  Of kindling gold, as when the sun doth rise.

And Art the features marred and dim can trace,
  Seen 'neath the eclipse of Calvary's noontide wan,
Blend love and sorrow in the darkening face,
  And breathe with thrilling power 'Behold the Man'.

Art, too, can picture a dead Christ at rest,
  Discrowned and pale in his majestic sleep;
A son of earth on the great mother's breast,
  While o'er the nail-torn limbs sad women weep.

And Art can body forth the Crucified,
  In risen might still lingering round His grave,
Showing to wistful saints His hands and side,
  Soothing the suppliant to His feet that clave.

But reverence here arrests the noblest flight,
  The purest dream, the subtlest touch of Art;
'Tis faith alone, with pencil of sweet light,
  May trace the Unseen – and only on the heart.

THE DOUBLE SEARCH

There are two gone out in the starless wild –
  Gone out on the desert night;
Earth's sad and weary and homeless child,
  And heaven's fair Lord of Light.

And one is seeking forlorn and blind,
  Can give to his loss no name;
But the other knows well what He stoops to find –
  Knows well what He comes to claim.

Though the hills are dark, though the torrents roll,
  By each must his path be trod;
Both seek, for the Saviour has lost a soul,
  And the soul has lost its God.

189

That piteous cry and that tender call
    Come each from a yearning heart;
Through storm and stillness they rise and fall,
    And they seem not far apart.

I can hear the sound of their nearing feet
    By a sure attraction drawn:
Those night-long seekers shall timely meet,
    As the darkness dies in the dawn.

190

Ellen Johnston

c. 1835-73

THE LAST SARK

Gude guide me, are ye hame again, and hae ye got nae wark?
We've naething noo tae pit awa, unless your auld blue sark.   *shirt*
My heid is rinnin roond aboot, far lichter nor a flee:
What care some gentry if they're weel though a' the puir wad dee?

Our merchants and mill-masters they wad never want a meal
Though a' the banks in Scotland wad for a twalmonth fail;
For some o them hae far mair gowd than ony ane can see.
What care some gentry if they're weel though a' the puir wad dee?

Oor hoose aince bien and cosy, John, oor beds aince snug and warm,
Feels unco cauld and dismal noo, and empty as a barn;
The weans sit greetin in our face, and we hae nocht tae gie.
What care some gentry if they're weel though a' the puir wad dee?

It is the puir man's hard-won cash that fills the rich man's purse;
I'm sure his gowden coffers they are het wi mony a curse.
Were it no for the workin man what wad the rich man be?
What care some gentry if they're weel though a' the puir wad dee?

My head is licht, my heart is weak, my een are growing blin';
The bairn is faen' aff my knee – oh! John, catch haud o' him,
You ken I hinna tasted meat for days far mair than three;
Were it no for my helpless bairns I wadna care to dee.

191

Lydia Falconer Fraser
d. 1876

THOU'RT AWA

Thou'rt awa, awa, from thy mother's side,
    And awa, awa, from thy father's knee;
Thou'rt awa from our blessing, our care, our caressing,
    But awa from our hearts thou'lt never be.

All things, dear child, that were wont to please thee
    Are round thee here in beauty bright, –
There's music rare in the cloudless air,
    And the earth is teeming with living delight.

Thou'rt awa, awa, from the bursting spring time,
    Tho' o'er thy head its green boughs wave;
The lambs are leaving their little footprints
    Upon the turf of thy new-made grave.

And art thou awa, and awa for ever, –
    That little face, – that tender frame, –
That voice which first, in sweetest accents,
    Call'd me the mother's thrilling name, –

That head of nature's finest moulding, –
    Those eyes, the deep night ether's blue,
Where sensibility its shadows
    Of ever-changing meaning threw?

Thy sweetness, patience under suffering,
    All promis'd us an opening day
Most fair, and told that to subdue thee
    Would need but love's most gentle sway.

Ah me! twas here I thought to lead thee,
    And tell thee what are life and death,
And raise thy serious thoughts first waking
    To Him who holds our every breath.

And does my selfish heart then grudge thee,
    That angels are thy teachers now, –
That glory from thy Saviour's presence
    Kindles the crown upon thy brow?

O, no! to me earth must be lonelier,
    Wanting thy voice, thy hand, thy love;
Yet dost thou dawn a star of promise,
    Mild beacon to the world above.

Jane Catherine Lundie
1821-84

PASS AWAY EARTHLY JOY

Pass away earthly joy,
    Jesus is mine;
Break every mortal tie,
    Jesus is mine;
Dark is the wilderness;
Distant the resting-place;
Jesus alone can bless: –
    Jesus is mine.

Tempt not my soul away, –
    Jesus is mine;
Here would I ever stay,
    Jesus is mine;
Perishing things of clay,
Born but for one brief day,
Pass from my heart away,
    Jesus is mine.

Fare ye well, dreams of night,
    Jesus is mine;
Mine is a dawning bright,
    Jesus is mine;
All that my soul has tried
Left but a dismal void,
Jesus has satisfied,
    Jesus is mine.

Farewell mortality,
    Jesus is mine;
Welcome eternity,
    Jesus is mine;
Welcome ye scenes of rest,
Welcome ye mansions blest,
Welcome a Saviour's breast,
    Jesus is mine.

Mary Maxwell Campbell
d. 1886

THE MARCH OF THE CAMERON MEN

There's many a man of the Cameron clan
    That has follow'd his chief to the field;
He has sworn to support him or die by his side,
    For a Cameron never can yield.
        I hear the pibroch sounding, sounding,
            Deep o'er the mountain and glen;
        While light-springing footsteps are trampling the heath,
            'Tis the march of the Cameron men.

Oh, proudly they march, but each Cameron knows
    He may tread on the heather no more;
But boldly he follows his chief to the field,
    Where his laurels were gather'd before.
        I hear the pibroch sounding, etc.

The moon has arisen, it shines on that path
    Now trod by the gallant and true –
High, high are their hopes, for their chieftain has said
    That whatever men dare they can do.
        I hear the pibroch sounding, etc.

THE MOLE AND THE BAT

My friend is a Mole, and I am a Bat,
    Two travellers are we;
And we have gone o'er the wide, wide world,
    To see what we could see.
        But the Mole and I came back again,
            And both of us agree,
        That there's no place in all the world
            So good as our countrie.

And first we went to merry France,
    Where the sun shines warm and bright;
But frogs to eat were no great treat,
    So we only stayed a night,
        So the Mole and I came back again, etc.

And next we went to Holland,
    But 'twas far too damp for me;
'Twas all as flat as the crown of your hat,
    And nothing could we see.
        So the Mole and I came back again, etc.

We then set off to Germany,
  Where they made us understand
That they smoked their pipe and drank their beer
  For the good of their Fatherland.
        So the Mole and I came back again, etc.

We went to Spain and Portugal,
  And thought them pretty places;
But 'twould appear that water's dear,
  For they never wash their faces
        So the Mole and I came back again, etc.

Oh, then we came to Italy,
  Where beggars swarm like bees;
The Mole had to work like any Turk,
  While they sat at their ease.
        So the Mole and I came back again, etc.

Then we went off to Austria,
  Where, much to our surprise,
They tried to shut us up for life,
  And call'd us English spies.
        So the Mole and I came back again, etc.

And next we got to Russia,
  Where we tried to look about;
But we chanced to stare at the Russian Bear,
  And he order'd us the knout
        So the Mole and I came back again, etc.

We started off to America,
  The Land of the Free and the Brave;
But they said the Mole was as black as a coal,
  And they'd sell him for a slave.
        So the Mole and I came back again, etc.

We travell'd off to Africa,
  To see a wondrous lake,
But turned our tail, and made all sail,
  When we met a rattlesnake.
        So the Mole and I came back again, etc.

Then last we went to Scotland,
  Where we met some pleasant fellows,
But every one wore waterproofs,
  And carried large umbrellas.
        So the Mole and I came back again,
            And satisfied are we
        That there's no place in all the world
            So good as our countrie.

Isabella Craig-Knox
1831-1903

TREASURED

Who hath not treasured something of the past,
   The lost, the buried, or the far away,
Twined with those heart affections which outlast
   All save their memories? these outlive decay:
   A broken relic of our childhood's play,
A faded flower that long ago was fair
   Mute token of a love that died untold.
Or silken curl, or lock of silv'ry hair,
   The brows that bore them long since in the mould.
Though these may call up griefs that else had slept,
   Their twilight sadness o'er the soul to bring.
Not every tear in bitterness is wept.
   While they revive the drooping flowers that spring
   Within the heart, and round its ruined altars cling.

OUR HELEN

Is our Helen very fair?
   If you only knew her
You would doubt it not, howe'er
   Stranger eyes may view her.
We who see her day by day
   Through our household moving,
Whether she be fair or nay
   Cannot see for loving.

Oe'r our gentle Helen's face
   No rich hues are bright'ning,
And no smiles of feignèd grace
   From her lips are light'ning;
She hath quiet, smiling eyes,
   Fair hair simply braided,
All as mild as evening skies
   Ere sunlight hath faded.

Our kind, thoughtful Helen loves
  Our approving praises,
But her eye that never roves
  Shrinks from other gazes.
She, so late within her home
  But a child caressing,
Now a woman hath become,
  Ministering, blessing.

All her duty, all her bliss,
  In her home she findeth,
Nor too narrow deemeth this –
  Lowly things she mindeth;
Yet when deeper cares distress,
  She is our adviser;
Reason's rules she needeth less,
  For her heart is wiser.

For the sorrows of the poor
  Her kind spirit bleedeth,
And, because so good and pure,
  For the erring pleadeth.
Is our Helen very fair?
  If you only knew her
You would doubt it not, howe'er
  Stranger eyes may view her.

Mrs Lindsay Carnegie
b. 1844

MY DAUGHTER

She stands in the apple orchard,
Where the flowering branches meet,
And the fragrant shell-like petals
Lie white on the grass at her feet.

In her hands a primrose posy,
In her eyes the dawn of day,
And her curly locks are floating
On the breeze from the fields of hay.

She stands with her shy lips parted,
And the dew in her star-set eyes,
With her trustful face uplifted
To the arch of the grey-blue skies.

The exquisite scent of the lilac,
The buffeting breath of the May,
The fragrance from fields of clover,
Kiss the soul that awakes today.

She stands in here white gown waiting –
'Will he come?' Nay, I cannot say.
She is lovelier than the morning,
Flower-begemmed like her month of May.

Ella Burton
b. 1845

THE TROOPER'S SONG

(FROM THE GERMAN OF HERWEGH)

The anxious night is passed away,
We silent ride in dawn of day;
   We silent ride to death.
The morning winds, how sharp they blow;
Hostess! a glass before we go
   Unto our latest breath.

Alas! young grass so fresh and green,
Like roses red thou'lt soon be seen;
   All red with blood thou'lt lie.
I drink to thee first, sword in hand;
I drink to thee, O Fatherland;
   For thee, for thee I die.

A second draught I drain to thee;
To thee, O Freedom, shall it be –
   This bitter draught to thee.
And what remains to thee I drink,
Christ's Church; oh, mayst thou never sink,
   In death beloved by me.

Unto my love – the wine is gone;
I hear the bullet's whizzing song;
   Bring *her* when here I lie.
Upon the French like storms new born;
Oh, trooper's joy at early morn,
   To die, to die, to die.

Agnes Marshall
b. 1846

LIMPIN' KATE

O Limpin' Kate cam' o'er the lea,   *field*
An' blithesome face, I wow, had she;
Aul' John keeked roon the hoose en' to see   *peeped*
    The lass that got the siller.   *silver*

'If I be auld I hae nae ties,
I'm elder and a laird likewise;
O, lassie, tak' and ne'er despise,
    John o' Girshaw, the miller.'

But Kate laughed oot and said 'Na, na,
An' auld man wud be sune awa';
And micht spend or he gaed it a',
    For nursin' tak's some siller.'

The smith keeked frae the smiddy door –
A thing he never did afore –
Richt after Kate, and then he swore
    He'd put the question till her.

'Na, na,' said Kate, 'I ken your plan,
I little need a thriftless man,
Ye'd let the smiddy fire out whaun
    Ye'd get me an' my siller.'

The weaver rose frae oot his thrums,   *threads*
An' doon to Newton Carse he comes,
Draws in his chair and hechs and hums,
    And glowers as he would kill her.

But Katie was nae feared, no she,
Even when he said, 'Ye maun tak' *me*,
Or I'll blaw oot my brains and dee';
    She thoucht, 'He wants my siller.'

And then she said, 'What's a' your haste?
Ye ne'er thocht I was to your taste?
Ance, when Kate needed help the maist,
    Ye were richt saucy till her.'

O mony a ane cam' coortin' Kate,
But aye she said, 'Ye come ower late;
An' aul' maid's is a blessful state
   When she has got some siller.

'The weaver sune would seal my doom,
The smith would leave my pouches toom;   *empty*
And a' my life would be in gloom,
   If ance I wed the miller.

'Na, I'll just end as I began,
I've gat the wit o' ony man –
I'll tak' the comfort while I can,
   O' my wee bit o' siller.'

Agnes Stuart Mabon (of Jedburgh)

ELECTION RHYME – 1880

The other night I heard a din,
   A tumult and a clatter –
A noise terrific – loud enough
   The strongest nerves to shatter.
Above the hubbub and the strife
   Of voices loud and high,
I yet distinguished now and then
   What seemed a party-cry.

A voice behind me hoarsely bawled,
   'Away with Tory prigs!'
While cries arose on every side,
   'Down with the dirty Whigs!'
I wondered greatly what could thus
   Disturb the people's quiet,
And so resolved to ascertain
   The meaning of the riot.

For information on this point
   I turn'd me to a neighbour,
'Why don't you know that Ben's retir'd
   From Parliament'ry labour?'
For six years he has kept his post
   In fulness and enjoyment,
With ne'er a though of poor old Bill,
   Sick, waiting for employment.

But now 'tis thought that Bill will get
   What he so long has wanted;
For though his body's old and frail,
   His spirit is undaunted.
Poor Benny, too, though quite worn out,
   Must not be underrated,
He'd do – I wonder what he'd not –
   Just to be reinstated.

Says Bill in many a fluent speech,
   And Ben in many a letter,
'The man who votes for *me* does well,'
   'Who votes for *me* does better.'
Ben vows that Bill would smash the Church,
   Upheld by all his backers;
Bill says, 'I'm for Establishment,
   Heed not these idle talkers.'

Old William from the rostrum shouts –
  'My friends, would you be free
From wars and taxes? *now's* your chance;
  Be wise, and vote for me!'
Straight, Benjamin makes this reply –
  'My friends, have you forgotten!
When Billy had the job before,
  You said his work was rotten!'

They both together pledge themselves
  To aid the Temperance cause;
Together vow to modify
  The stringent fishing laws,
And all the little grievances
  That make the people sigh,
We'll do our utmost to redress,
  With one accord they cry.

And then with backers staunch and true
  They each are well provided,
Who promise anything you please
  If you'll by them be guided.
These go about through all the land,
  Each eager for his party,
With 'nods and becks and wreathèd smiles',
  And hand-grips strong and hearty.

O! what an uproar and turmoil
  Electioneering rouses;
Then families are like Parliament –
  Divided in their houses.
Till one or other get the job,
  And have the squabble ended,
People can think of nothing else,
  All business is suspended.

The clerk forsakes his counting-house,
  The merchant shuts his ledger,
The chimney-sweep can't work, nor yet
  The ditcher nor the hedger;
The very clergy, I am told,
  Forget their holy calling,
And hurt their consecrated chests
  With shouting and with bawling.

203

Each party promises so fair
  To give us all we want,
I cannot tell which side to take –
  Upon my life I can't.
I really think I ought to have
  Supporters for my plan,
Then quickly in the proper place
  We'd have the proper man.

The smartest man for such a post
  Is sure to be the best;
And here's the way I would propose
  To put them to the test: –
A wide arena I would clear,
  And have two hoops suspended,
And honestly, in all men's sight,
  The battle should be ended.

Then Ben and Billy should come forth,
  In party-hues bedight,
And back and forwards through the hoops
  Should jump with all their might;
And he who held the longest out
  Should have the much-wish'd job,
And be led forth a victor crowned,
  The darling of the mob!

THE WHIGS ARE IN – APRIL 1880

'Take off yer dusty goon, guid-wife,
  An' thraw yer meal away,
Ye'll never need tae bake again,
  The Whigs hae won the day.
The muckle loaves 'ill fa' like hail,
  The rows like morning dew.' –
'O!' quo' tho wifikie, 'I wish it may be true;
  I wish it may be true,' quo' she,
    'I wish it may be true;
O!' quo' the wifikie, 'I wish it may be true.'

'Ye'll sit and take yer ease, guid-wife,
  I'll cast my coat nae mair;
An' ilka day in Gladstone's reign
  Maist sumptuously we'll fare.
I'll catch the salmon ready boiled,
  An' nane tae sae me nay.' –

'Oh!' quo' the wifikie, 'I wish it may be sae;
 I wish it mae be sae,' quo' she,
  'I wish it mae be sae;
'Oh!' quo' the wifikie, 'I wish it may be sae.'

'The burnies a' 'ill rin wi' milk,
 The public wells wi' wine,
An' legs o' mutton grow on trees;
 O! wull na that be fine?
On rabbits and on hares we'll feast,
 An' muir-fowl not a few.' –
'O!' quo' the wifikie, 'I wish it may be true.'

'The Whigs are in – nae banks 'll break,
 Nae railway brigs 'ill fa',
We'll aye hae peace and plenty now,
 An' no' be taxed ava;
Policemen, lawyers, judges, jails,
 Wull a' be dune away.' –
'O!' quo' the wifikie, 'I wish it may be sae.'

'We'll hae nae mair hard winters now,
 But aye hae weather guid;
Nae mair be fashed wi' scouthrin' heat   *troubled, scorching*
 Or devastatin' flude;
Nae ship 'll foonder oot at sea,
 Wi' cargo or wi' crew.' –
'O!' quo' the wifikie, 'I wish it may be true.'

'We're a' tae luve like brithers now,
 Though how I canna see,
For never since the world began
 Could Whigs and Tories 'gree,
Unless the cannie Whigs could rise
 An' kill the Tory-crew.' –
'O!' quo' the wifikie, 'I wish it may be true.'

'I wish I saw the glorious time
 When Kirk an' State will fa',
And me Protector – wow, guid-wife,
 But I wad busk ye braw;   *dress you well*
O! ye sud hae a gouden coach,
 A' set wi' diamonds clear.' –
'O!' quo' the wifickie, 'I wish that time was here,
 I wish that time was here,' quo' she,
  'I wish that time was here.
O!' quo' the wifikie, 'I wish that time was here.'

205

Flora Maitland MacRae

THE PRISONER'S SLEEP

She lies upon the prison floor
Beside the prisoner's iron door,
Her long, dark hair the pillow makes
Where rests her tired head till she wakes –
Her pale hands folded o'er her breast
Seem waiting for a better rest.
Then who shall go to summon her?
Ah! *who* shall wake the prisoner?
Wake her to die! the sands are run,
Her little day on earth is done.
Wake her! those eyes with tears to steep.
Wake her! away with dreams and sleep!
Wake her to blush o'er sins forgiven!
Wake her to send her prayers to heaven!
Wake her to draw her parting breath,
Wake her to die a felon's death!
Perchance she dreams that she once more
Is playing by the cottage door
That first her childhood's footsteps knew;
Or swinging on the old, loved yew,
Basking beneath the summer sun;
Or chatting when the day was done –
Singing the cattle home at night,
Or telling tales when dim the light.
Dreams she her mother's voice she hears,
Bidding her dry her childhood's tears?
Her father's step, her sister's smile –
Her brother's merry laugh the while –
They all are gone – in dreams alone
Return the days whose light is gone.
Wake her to die! the dismal sound
Her prison wall has rung around,
And must she hear its mournful tone?
Let the poor prisoner dream on!
Oh! must we wake her when her dreams
Are all of better days? She seems
In sleep to turn her large, dark eyes
For help and pardon to the skies.
Yes! she has craved of Heaven to be
Forgiven through eternity.
Wake her to die! no grief, no pain
Can make the captive free again.
The day is come when she must die,

206

No hope for *her* but in the sky.
O ye who bear the Christian name,
Deal kindly with the child of shame;
With those whose crime has brought so low
Be Christ-like, win them in their woe.

Mary Gray
b. 1853

THE VIOLET

(GOETHE: FROM 'ELWIN UND ELMIRE')

It grew upon the lea alane,
Half-hidden, shy, and kent to nane,
   The sweetest wee bit blossom.
There cam' a happy country lass,
Wi' springy step, upon the grass
Blythe liltin' ower the lea;
   A posy at her bosom.

Ah, thocht the violet, could I be
The fairest flooer upon the lea,
   (Waes me, a paltry blossom!)
So micht the bonnie maiden tak' me,
And pairt o' some sweet posy mak' me,
What bliss it were to me
   To lie upon her bosom!

Alas! alas! the heedless maid
Cam' trippin' on and never stayed,
   But trod the wee bit blossom.
It sank, and wi' its fragrant breath.
'Oh, sweet,' it said, 'is sic a death,
Through her, through her I dee.'
   Alack the bonnie blossom!

Mary Inglis

LET THE BAIRNIES PLAY

Oh! let the bairnies play themsels,
  I like to hear their din,
I like to hear each restless foot
  Come trippin' oot and in.
I like to see each face sae bricht,
  And each wee heart sae gay;
They mind me o' my ain young days –
  Oh! let the bairnies play.

Oh! dinna check their sinless mirth,
  Or mak' them dull and wae
Wi' gloomy looks or cankered words,
  But let the bairnies play.
Auld douce wise folks should ne'er forget
  They ance were young as they,
As fu' o' fun and mischief, too –
  Then let the bairnies play.

And never try to set a heid,
  Wi' auld age grim and grey,
Upon a wee saft snawy neck –
  Na! let the bairnies play.
For, oh! there's mony a weary nicht
  And mony a waefu' day
Before them, if God spares their lives –
  Sae let the bairnies play.

Maria Bell
d. 1899

LOSS

My heart to me a garden was
   Where homely flowers had grown,
I chose me none too rare and fine,
   I only watched my own.

Their sweetness was enough for me,
   I wished no brilliant bloom,
They grew and grew, till year by year
   They filled the vacant room.

But passing hands have stooped and torn
   My plants from out their bed,
And now great empty places show
   How far their leaves had spread.

Annie Steel

DREAMS

I dreamt! What was my dream? –
    A dream of love,
And happiness that seemed
    From heaven above.
'If thou shalt dream it thrice,
    Love comes to you.'
I dreamt it only once – it ne'er came true.

I dreamt! What was my dream? –
    A dream of fame,
Of honour, praise, of power,
    And lofty aim.
'If thou shalt dream it thrice,
    Fame comes to you.'
I dreamt it only twice – it ne'er came true.

I dreamt! What was my dream? –
    A dream of woe,
Of anguish, and of pain,
    Of grief. And, lo!
I slept and dreamt it thrice –
    To me came woe.
I've lived, and learned at last 'twas better so.

LOST

Only a light mist floating,
    Gently it comes and goes;
Only a trav'ller hast'ning
    Home ere the daylight's close.

Only a thick fog creeping –
    A stealthy, treach'rous foe;
Only a wand'rer straying
    Far from the plain below.

Only the cruel darkness,
    In it a spirit's flight;
Only the morning brightness
    After the gloom of night.

Hannah Brown MacKenzie

MEMENTOES

Only a ringlet of gold,
  Glossy, and fine, and fair;
A precious relic of days of old,
  Treasured with loving care.

Only a dainty glove
  That a tiny hand once wore;
Picked up, half in jest, and half for love,
  Long ago, from a ball-room floor!

Only a rosebud white,
  Scentless, and withered, and dead!
But it lay, one hour on a summer night,
  'Mid the bands of a golden head.

Only some letters old,
  Tied with a ribbon of blue:
But an old, old tale of love they told,
  And a heart beating strong and true!

Only a memory sweet
  Of a summer long years gone by!
Of the old stone wall where we used to meet,
  Beneath a darkening sky!

Only a sorrowful heart,
  Loveless, and dark with woe!
With a bitter pain, that will ne'er depart,
  For hope vanished long ago!

Only a grass-grown mound,
  And a small white cross at its head!
Where my faded rose sleeps in the cold, cold ground,
  Beyond hope, or woe, or dread!

Annie S. Swan
1859-1943

NAE REST TIL WE WIN HAME

Oor life is but a pilgrimage –
  A long an' dreary road;
Ower mony a stey an' staney brae   *steep and stony hill*
  Ilk ane bears his ain load.   *each one*

Through frosts, an' snaws, an' gatherin' clouds,
  An' mony a rainy day,
Wi' whiles a blink o' simmer sun
  To licht the dreary way –

An' feet grow weary aften whiles,
  An' heids an' hearts the same;
But here there is nae sittin' doon –
  'Nae rest till we win hame.'

For we mann work while shines the day,
  For nicht is comin' sune;
Or what a puir hairst field we'll hae   *harvest*
  To show the Lord abune.

Dear hands slip daily frae oor grasp,
  An' hearts are sundered sair,
An' een grow dim wi' bitter tears
  For them we'll see nae mair.

There's mony a weary burden here
  An' grief we daurna name;
We'll lay them doon in God's ain time,
  'Syne rest when we win hame.'

HARVEST DAYS

The leaves amang the birken shaws   *birch woods*
  Glint yellow in the sun,
An' gently whisper as they fa'
  That summer days are dune.

Thick grow the bonnie clusters red
  Upon the rowan tree,
An' to my een there creeps a mist
  O' tearfu' memory.

An' far an' near in braid hairst-fields
  The reapers are fu' thrang,   *busy*
An' as they hook the gowden grain
  They lilt a blythesome sang.

Oh, bonnie shines the mornin' sun,
  Wi' dew draps in his beam;
An' bonnie shines the harvest mune
  When gloamin' fa 's at e'en.

'Twas in the gowden harvest time
  The Reaper cam' at e'en,
To cut the sheaf o' stannin' corn
  Wi' his dark sickle keen.

Oh! 'twas in love the Master willed
  To tak' His harvest hame,
To bind oor wanderin' hearts abune,
  An' so we daurna blame.

To mind oor time is hastenin' on,
  Sic sorrows here are gien;
But when we've bound oor stent on earth
  We'll meet at hame at e'en.

Agnes H. Begbie

MY LITTLE WORLD

I built me my own little world,
  Not God – but my world was fair;
I perfumed it fragrant with blossoms,
  I hedged it around with care.

And I said, 'It is well; it is quarried
  Strong now, as strong love dare plan;
A home for two hearts it is carven,
  Built by the will of a man.'

I dived the deep depths for its treasures,
  I scaled high the scarrèd height,
And I cried 'Jubilate, O World!
  All perfect, O heart's delight!'

And I looked on my lovely world;
  My blood ran warm as new wine, –
As the hand of a god had fashioned,
  'Twas fair as a thing divine.

And I shouted and sang 'Jubilate!'
  The heart within me was light,
It heard not the brooding footstep
  That bringeth the blinding night.

Jessie Anne Anderson
b. 1861

THE BACK O' HAIRST

It's the Back o' Hairst upon Ythanside,   *harvest time*
  An' the leme o' the rowan's deid   *gleam*
That mindit me i' the mids o' my hairst
  Upon hairt-wrung draps o' bluid.

'Twas a' but a puir, scant hairst that I shore,
  But I gaithered it wi' a will;
Now I rest my hands on his cross, and pray
  Saint Andrew to sain the mill.   *bless*

May never a mealoch o' bitterness fa'   *crumb*
  Frae the mill whaur I grind my corn;
An' may I hain naething o' care or kann
  As I bake my breid the morn.

An' I'll licht a can'le the morn's nicht
  When I gang to sweet Mary's Shrine,
For, although the leme o' the rowan's deid,
  She's lichtit this hairt o' mine.

An' I'll licht anither to God whase grace
  Ga'e strength to win throu' wi' it a';
Though 'twas hungry lan' that I seedit in,
  An' kepit owre miekle snaw.

AT SWEET MARY'S SHRINE

I'll sleep me soun' the nicht while sigh
  The saughs an' tender Ythan: *willows*
They're singin' tae the sairest he'rt
  That e'er Luve aince was blythe in.

Luve broke my he'rt, an' got within –
  He only tried tae pain it: –
How could Luve brak' sae saft a he'rt? –
  I never socht tae hain it.

I tak' the simple, ae-fauld thing
  That's been sae sairly siftit,
An' lay it on sweet Mary's shrine,
  An' leave her grace tae lift it.

Florence Cortis-Stanford

A CROWN OF THORNS

Sad grey woods,
With never a leaf,
Dripping, dripping,
In silence of grief.

November mists
Cling close to the trees,
And move like the bosoms
Of unquiet seas.

Sudden a rift
In the grey cloud grows,
Shot through and through
With blood-red haws.

And instant the grey wood
Springs into flame,
Flinging back to the thorn
Its burden of shame.

For all through the ages
The guilty thorn
Must wear at its dying
That crown of scorn.

TO EMILY BRONTË

The witch-owls call, black shadows fall
   About my lonely way;
The wind sinks down, and ne'er a sound
   Proclaims the passing day.

I am alone, all others gone
   Into the warmth and light,
Again once more, as oft before,
   I hear the voice of night.

For me alone those murmurs come
   From out the rustling woods;
For me alone the sea makes moan
   Beneath his aching floods.

All interwove with jewelled love
   Are beauty, joy and woe;
All one with me, the singing sea,
   The grey sheep as they go.

217

Mary H. Cassady

UNTIL THE DAY BREAK

Fold her hands upon her breast,
Lay her down to take her rest;
Life once was sweet, now sleep is best.

Friends were few, the world was cold,
Her auburn hair had lost its gold,
Her dream of love away had rolled.

Her lover – he was true and tried,
But duty called him from her side;
In his dear country's cause he died.

Gently, gently lay her down,
She bore her cross; maybe the crown
Awaits her in the far Unknown.

Fold her hands upon her breast,
Weary soul that longed for rest;
Life once was sweet, now sleep is best.

Violet Jacob
1863-1946

TAM I' THE KIRK

O Jean, my Jean, when the bell ca's the congregation
O'er valley and hill wi' the ding frae its iron mou',
When a'body's thochts is set on their ain salvation,
    Mine's set on you.

There's a reid rose lies on the Buik o' the Word afore ye
That was growin' braw on its bush at the keek o' day,   *break*
But the lad that pu'd yon flower i' the mornin's glory
    He canna pray.

He canna pray, but there's nane i' the kirk will heed him
Whaur he sits sae still his lane at the side o' the wa',   *alone*
For nane but the reid rose kens what my lassie gied him –
    It and us twa.

He canna sing for the sang that his ain he'rt raises,
He canna see for the mist that's afore his een,
And a voice droons the hale o' the psalms and the paraphrases
    Crying 'Jean! Jean! Jean!'

A CHANGE O' DEILS

'A change o' deils is lichtsome.'
    Scots Proverb

My Grannie spent a merry youth,
    She niver wantit for a joe,   *lover*
An gin she tell't me aye the truth,
    Richt little was't she kent na o'.

An' while afore she gae'd awa'
    To bed her doon below the grass,
Says she, 'Guidmen I've kistit twa,   *coffined*
    But a change o' deils is lichtsome, lass!

Sae dinna think to maister me,
    For Scotland's fu' o' brawlike chiels,
And ablins ither folk ye'll see   *perhaps*
    Are fine an' pleased to change their deils.

Aye, set yer bonnet on yer heid,
   An' cock it up upon yer bree,
O' a' yer tricks ye'll hae some need
   Afore ye get the best o' me!

Sma' wark to fill yer place I'd hae,
   I'll seek a sweethe'rt i' the toon,
Or cast my he'rt across the Spey
   An' tak' some pridefu' Hieland loon.

I ken a man has hoose an' land,
   His arm is stoot, his een are blue,
A ring o' gowd is on his hand,
   An' he's a bonnier man nor you!

But hoose an' gear an' land an' mair,
   He'd gie them a' to get the preen   *pin*
That preened the flowers in till my hair
   Beside the may-bush yestere'en.'

Jist tak' you tent, an' mind forbye,   *care*
   The braw guid sense my Grannie had,
My Grannie's dochter's bairn am I,
   An a change o' deils is lichtsome, lad!

CRAIGO WOODS

Craigo Woods, wi' the splash o' the cauld rain beatin'
   I' the back end o' the year,
When the clouds hang laigh wi' the weicht o' their   *low, weight*
             load o' greetin'   *weeping*
   And the autumn wind's asteer;   *astir*
Ye may stand like ghaists, ye may fa' i' the blast that's cleft ye
   To rot i' the chilly dew,
But when will I mind on aucht since the day I left ye   *anything*
   Like I mind on you – on you?

Craigo Woods, i' the licht o' September sleepin'
   And the saft mist o' the morn,
When the hairst climbs to yer feet, an' the sound o' reapin'   *harvest*
   Comes up frae the stookit corn,   *sheaves*
And the braw reid puddock-stules are like jewels blinkin'   *toadstools*
   And the bramble happs ye baith,   *covers*
O what do I see, i the lang nicht, lyin' an' thinkin'
   As I see yer wraith – yer wraith?

There's a road to a far-aff land, an' the land is yonder
    Whaur a' men's hopes are set;
We dinna ken foo lang we maun hae to wander,   *how*
    But we'll a' win to it yet;
An' gin there's woods o' fir an' the licht atween them,
    I winna speir its name,   *ask*
But I'll lay me doon by the puddock-stules when I've seen them,
    An' I'll cry 'I'm hame – I'm hame!'

PRIDE

Did iver ye see the like o' that?
The warld's fair fashioned to winder at!
Heuch – dinna tell me! Yon's Fishie Pete
That cried the haddies in Ferry Street
Set up wi' his coats an' his grand cigars
In ane o' thae stinkin' motor cars!

I mind the time (an' it's no far past)
When he wasna for fleein' alang sae fast,
An' doon i' the causey his cairt wad stand   *causeway*
As he roared oot 'Haddies!' below his hand;
Ye'd up wi' yer windy an' doon he'd loup   *jump*
Frae the shaft o' the cairt by the sheltie's doup.   *the pony's rump*

Aye, muckle cheenges an' little sense,
A bawbee's wit an' a poond's pretence!   *halfpenny*
For there's him noo wi' his neb to the sky   *nose*
I' yon deil's machinery swiggit by,
An' me, that whiles gied him a piece to eat,
Tramps aye to the kirk on my ain twa feet.

An neebours, mind ye, the warld's agley   *awry*
Or we couldna see what we've seen the day;
Guid fortune's blate whaur she's weel desairv't,   *absent*
The sinner fu' an' the godly stairv't,
An' fowk like me an' my auld guidman
Jist wearied daein' the best we can!

I've kept my lips an' my tongue frae guile
An' kept mysel' to mysel' the while;
Agin a' wastrels I've aye been set
And I'm no for seekin' to thole them yet;   *endure*
A grand example I've been through life,
A righteous liver, a thrifty wife.

But oh! the he'rt o' a body bleeds
For favours sclarried on sinfu' heids.
Wait you a whilie! You needna think   *smeared*
They'll no gang frae him wi' cairds an' drink!
They'll bring nae blessin', they winna bide,
For the warst sin, neebours, is pride, aye, pride!

THE LAST O' THE TINKLER

Lay me in yon place, lad,
    The gloamin's thick wi' nicht;
I canna' see yer face, lad,
    For my een's no richt.

But it's ower late for leein',
    An' I ken fine I'm deein',
Like an auld craw fleein'
    To the last o' the licht.

The kye gang to the byre, lad,   *cows*
    An' the sheep to the fauld,
Ye'll mak' a spunk o' fire, lad,
    For my he'rt's turned cauld;
An' whaur the trees are meetin',
There's a sound like waters beatin',
An' the bird seems near to greetin',
    That was aye singin' bauld.

There's jist the tent to leave, lad,
    I've gaithered little gear,
There's jist yersel' to grieve, lad,
    An' the auld dog here;
An' when the morn comes creepin'
An' the wauk'nin birds are cheipin',
It'll find me lyin' sleepin'
    As I've slept saxty year.

Ye'll rise to meet the sun, lad,
    An' baith be traiv'lin west,
But me that's auld an' done, lad,
    I'll bide an' tak' my rest;
For the grey heid is bendin',
An' the auld shune's needin' mendin',   *shoes*
But the traiv'lin's near its' endin',
    And the end's aye the best.

Mary Symon
1863-1938

THE SOLDIERS' CAIRN

Gie me a hill wi' the heather on't,
　An' a red sun drappin' doon,
Or the mists o' the mornin' risin' saft
　Wi' the reek owre a wee grey toon.
Gie me a howe by the lang Glen road,   *hill*
　For it's there 'mang the whin and fern
(D'ye mind on 't, Will? Are ye hearin', Dod?)
　That we're biggin' the Soldiers' Cairn.   *building*

Far awa is the Flanders land
　Wi' fremmit France atween,   *unfamiliar*
But mony a howe o' them baith the day   *many a hill*
　Has a hap o' the Gordon green.   *covering*
It's them we kent that's lyin' there,
　An' it's nae wi' stane or airn   *stone or iron*
But wi' brakin' hearts, an' mem'ries sair,
　That we're biggin' the Soldiers Cairn.

Doon, laich doon the Dullan sings –   *low*
　An' I ken o' an aul' sauch tree,   *willow*
Where a wee loon's wahnie's hingin' yet   *boys*
　That's dead in Picardy;
An' ilka win' fae the Conval's broo
　Bends aye the buss o' earn,   *clump of fern*
Where aince he futtled a name that noo   *whistled*
　I'll read on the Soldiers' Cairn.

Oh! build it fine and build it fair,
　Till it leaps to the moorland sky –
More, more than death is symbolled there,
　Than tears or triumphs by.
There's the Dream Divine of a starward way
　Our laggard feet would learn –
It's a new earth's corner-stone we'd lay
　As we fashion the Soldiers' Cairn.

Lads in your plaidies lyin' still
　In lands we'll never see.
This lanely cairn on a hameland hill
　Is a' that oor love can dee;
An' fine an' braw we'll mak' it a',
　– *But oh, my Bairn, my Bairn,*
It's a cradle's croon that'll aye blaw doon   *lament*
　To me fae the Soldiers' Cairn.

223

Marion Angus
1866-1946

THE GHOST

The wind that brings
The twilight in
Is musky-scented,
Faint and thin,
When light as dew
On tender herb
A footstep falls
Across the kerb.

Into the street
The children pack,
With, 'Here's the pedlar-
Man come back!
The pedlar with
The red balloons
And flutes that play
The dancing tunes.'

The wind that brings
The twilight home
Is frailer than
The drifted foam,
When light as vapour
On a glass
The footstep falls
Upon the grass.

O Mary, loose
Your cloudy wrap!
The gate is shut,
No timorous tap
Comes on the empty
Window-pane,
To wake your life
To joy again.

'The old wife broods
Beside the fire.
No grief has she,
And no desire.
With puckered lips
And crooked smile
She mutters to
Herself the while.

'A year, or two –
Or maybe three –
And I the pedlar-
Man shall be,
And I the baby
Soft and white
That Mary cries for
In the night,
And I the wind
So faint and thin,
The wind that blows
The twilight in.'

THE TURN OF THE DAY

Under the cauld, green grass
  I hear the waukenin' burn.
    The day's at the turn –
Oh, winter, dinna pass!

Your snaw was white for a bride,
  Your winds were merriage wine.
    Love is fine, fine,
But it doesna bide.

The saft, warm April rain
  An' the clear June day,
    An' floors o' the May –
I'll see them a' my lane.

Under the cauld, green grass,
  Wee waukenin', wanderin' burn,
Sing your ain sang.
  The day's at the turn,
But simmer's lang, lang.

MARY'S SONG

I wad ha'e gi'en him my lips tae kiss,
Had I been his, had I been his;
Barley breid and elder wine,
Had I been his as he is mine.

The wanderin' bee it seeks the rose;
Tae the lochan's bosom the burnie goes;   *loch*
The grey bird cries at evenin's fa',
'My luve, my fair one, come awa'.'

My beloved sall ha'e this he'rt tae break,
Reid, reid wine and the barley cake,
A he'rt tae break, and a mou' tae kiss,
Tho' he be nae mine, as I am his.

ALAS! POOR QUEEN

She was skilled in music and the dance
And the old arts of love
At the court of the poisoned rose
And the perfumed glove,
And gave her beautiful hand
To the pale Dauphin
A triple crown to win –
And she loved little dogs
          And parrots
       And red-legged partridges
And the golden fishes of the Duc de Guise
And a pigeon with a blue ruff
She had from Monsieur d'Elboeuf.

Master John Knox was no friend to her;
She spoke him soft and kind,
Her honeyed words were Satan's lure
The unwary soul to bind.
'Good sir, doth a lissome shape
And a comely face
Offend your God His Grace
Whose Wisdom maketh these
Golden fishes of the Duc de Guise?'

She rode through Liddesdale with a song;
'Ye streams sae wondrous strang,
Oh, mak' me a wrack as I come back
But spare me as I gang.'
While a hill-bird cried and cried
Like a spirit lost
By the grey storm-wind tost.

Consider the way she had to go,
Think of the hungry snare,
The net she herself had woven,
Aware or unaware,
Of the dancing feet grown still,
The blinded eyes –
Queens should be cold and wise,
And she loved little things,
      Parrots
   And red-legged partridges
And the golden fishes of the Duc de Guise
And the pigeon with the blue ruff
She had from Monsieur d'Elboeuf.

Nannie K. Wells
b. 1875

A PRAYER

(WITH ACKNOWLEDGEMENTS TO W. H. AUDEN)

God, give us the grace to hate
our unemancipated state,
and to wipe from Scotland's face
her intellectual disgrace.

The eye that peers forth cannily,
how can it reach the stars on high?
The ear that waits on market price
obeys the voice of cowardice.

The mouth that babbles out 'Ay, ay'
how shall it utter prophecy?
Who on self-interest spends his days
forgets the noble art of praise.

Free us from fear of other folk,
our minds from weight of foreign yoke;
teach us to take our true delight
in things that are our own by right.

The soil that nourished flesh and bones,
the chemistry of Scotland's stones,
in our bodily substance shout
what we ought to be about.

Unmistakable the note
the Northern Wind sings in its throat;
the Highland rivers' sudden rush
raises the authentic blush.

Our mountains that above us tower
alone can judge our 'finest hour';
to clear our word-beclouded minds
we need the Bible of the Winds.

The things for which we ought to die
are plainly written on the sky;
God, now to us the vision give
to know for what we ought to live.

Rachel Annand Taylor
1876-1960

THE PRINCESS OF SCOTLAND

'Who are you that so strangely woke,
  And raised a fine hand?'
Poverty wears a scarlet cloke
  In my land.

'Duchies of dreamland, emerald, rose
  Lie at your command?'
Poverty like a princess goes
  In my land.

'Wherefore the mask of silken lace
  Tied with a golden band?'
Poverty walks with wanton grace
  In my land.

'Why do you softly, richly speak
  Rhythm so sweetly scanned?'
Poverty hath the Gaelic and Greek
  In my land.

'There's a far-off scent about you seems
  Born in Samarkand.'
Poverty hath luxurious dreams
  In my land.

'You have wounds that like passion-flowers you hide:
  I cannot understand.'
Poverty hath one name with Pride
  In my land.

'Oh! Will you draw your last sad breath
  'Mid bitter bent and sand?'
Poverty begs from none but Death
  In my land.

THE DOUBT

I am pure, because of great illuminations
  Of dreamy doctrine caught from poets of old,
Because of delicate imaginations,
  Because I am proud, or subtle, or merely cold.
Natheless my soul's bright passions interchange
  As the red flames in opal drowse and speak:
In beautiful twilight paths the elusive strange
  Phantoms of personality I seek.
If better than the last embraces I
  Love the lit riddles of the eyes, the faint
Appeal of merely courteous fingers, – why,
  Though 'tis a quest of souls, and I acquaint
My heart with spiritual vanities, –
  Is there indeed no bridge twixt me and these?

Edith Anne Robertson
1883-1973

QUEEN MADELINE OF SCOTLAND

Frae her dear France, her dear France
thro' sun-drookit faem
the merry ship carried
the King's bride hame.

Her convoy of princes
daunced in the spray;
but the bairn-queen whispered:–
'I'll rest if I may.'

Her lords and her ladies
who danced in the faem
tost up frae the sea,
have all gone haem.

But around this world
darker seas crawl
and yonder now sailing
she carries her saule.

Ower onbekennt watirs   *unknown*
whaur ilka wave   *each*
hallows and darkens
intil a grave,

She carries her saule
on til its rest, –
bairn, with a white doo
claucht til her breast.

And who can say
what new leed may rise   *language*
ayont the stars
when the auld leed dies;

or if yon fond face
is yet to find
that she grat and grat   *cried*
to leave behind?

THE LAST PURCHASE

Flocks I have owned, and herds,
jewels, and tents, and slaves,
lovely things, but trivial,
even as this body I wear,
or this turban I now unwind.

But there are beatitudes,
not for keeping or losing,
but co-existent with that
which is eternal in me –
the moon, and the stars, and the hills,
the great sun, and the swelling plain,
the ocean wall, hemmed and embroidered with foam.
And a woman's love.

O Sara, Sara,
one with the stars and the wind,
and the mellow plains, and the sea,
ere this my ripe body fall
to the waiting earth, I, the wanderer,
despiser of settled lands, old estates,
seek this once only, one parcel of land,
and buy it with silver and gold;
one small parcel, lovely and unmolested,
to give to thee for a grave.

Helen B. Cruickshank
1886-1975
OVERDUE

O ragin' wind
An' cruel sea,
Ye put the fear
O' daith on me.
I canna sleep,
I canna pray,
But prowl aboot
The docks a' day,
An' pu' my plaid
Aboot me ticht,
'Nae news yet, mistress!' –
Ae mair nicht!   *one more night*

THERE WAS A SANG

There was a sang
That aye I wad be singin';
There was a star,
An' clear it used tae shine;
An' liltin' in the starlicht
Thro' the shadows
I gaed lang syne.

There was a sang;
But noo, I canna mind it.
There was a star;
But noo, it disna shine.
There was a luve that led me
Thro' the shadows –
And it *was* mine.

SPRING IN THE MEARNS

(FOR LEWIS GRASSIC GIBBON, 23 FEBRUARY 1935)

Clouds of smoke on the hill
where the whin is burning,   *gorse*
staining the clear cold sky
as the sun goes down.
Brighter the fire leaps up
as night grows darker;
wild and lovely the light
of the flaming whin.

233

Blackened the stubborn bush;
no more the golden
nut-sweet blossom shall lure
the wandering bee.
Twisted branches sink
to a sullen smoulder
where the small stonechat clinked
contentedly.

Come again when the rains
have carried the ashes
into the hungry soil
and lo! the green
Earth that was seared by fire
has now begotten
tender herbage for tough,
and grain for whin.

Body of man to death,
flesh to ashes,
muscle and tissue and bone
to dust are come.
Ah, but the spirit leaps
from the cindered fibre,
living, laughs at death
that is but a name.

Life goes on for ever;
the body smoulders,
dies in the heat of the pace,
is laid in earth.
Life goes on; the spirit
endures for ever,
wresting from death in earth
a brave new birth.

He who set the flame
of his native genius
under the cumbering whin
of the untilled field
lit a fire in the Mearns
that illumines Scotland,
clearing her sullen soil
for a richer yield.

GLENSKENNO WOOD

Under an arch o' bramble
  Saftly she goes,
Dark broon een like velvet,
  Cheeks like the rose.

Ae lang branch o' the bramble
  Dips ere she pass,
Tethers wi' thorns the hair
  O' the little lass.

Ripe black fruit, an' blossom
  White on the spray,
Leaves o' russet an' crimson,
  What wad ye say?

What wad ye say to the bairn
  That ye catch her snood,
Haudin' her there i' the hush
  O' Glenskenno Wood?

What wad ye say? The autumn
  O' life draws near.
Still she waits, an' listens,
  But canna hear.

SHY GEORDIE

Up the Noran Water
In by Inglismaddy,
Annie's got a bairnie
That hasna got a daddy.
Some say it's Tammas's,
An' some say it's Chay's;
An' naebody expec'it it,
Wi Annie's quiet ways.

Up the Noran Water
The bonny little mannie
Is dandled an' cuddled close
By Inglismaddy's Annie.
Wha the bairnie's daddy is
The lassie never says:
But some think its Tammas's,
An' some think it's Chay's.

235

Up the Noran Water
The country folk are kind;
An' wha the bairnie's daddy is
They dinna muckle mind.
But oh! the bairn at Annie's breist,
The love in Annie's e'e –
They mak' me wish wi' a' my micht
The lucky lad was me!

Bessie J. B. MacArthur
b. 1889

LAST LEAVE

O I remember you so lithe and gay,
   yet with a wistfulness you could not hide;
clear eyes that questioned in some subtle way,
   and would not be denied.

So young you seemed in battle-dress of blue,
   almost a radiance shone about your head;
such delicate awareness filtering through,
   I cannot dream you dead.

Vanished perchance, with spirit strong and wise,
   none left the tale of valour to unfold;
only the echo of your brave emprise
   for memory to hold.

Vanished perchance, yet with familiar grace,
   when sudden silence falls across the room,
smiling you steal to your accustomed place
   and know yourself at home.

NOCHT O' MORTAL SICHT – 1942

A' day aboot the hoose I work,
My hands are rouch, my banes are sair,   *rough, sore*
Though it's a ghaist comes doon at daw,   *dawn*
A ghaist at nicht that clims the stair.

For nocht o' mortal sicht I see –
But warrin tanks on ilka hand,
And twistit men that lie sae still
And sma', upon the desert sand.

And nocht I hear the leelang day
But skirl o' shell and growl o' gun,
And owre my heid the bombers roar
Reid-hot aneath the Libyan sun.

But when the licht is on the wane,
And antrin winds gae whinnerin by,   *strange, whizzing*
It's snaw comes swirlin round my feet
And drifts in cluds across the sky.   *clouds*

And syne it's straikit owre wi' bluid,   *soon, streaked*
And syne the wind is hairse wi' cries,
And syne abune the Russian snaws   *above*
I see the Kremlin towers rise.

While round the city, mile on mile,
The grim battalions tak their stand,
And deid men streik from aff the grund   *stretch*
To grup their comrades by the hand.

And sae it haps that ilka day   *happens, every*
Frae mornin' licht to gloamin' fa',
It is a ghaist that walks the hoose
And casts its shadow on the wa'.

THE COLLADY-STANE

O Truth's a braw collady-stane,   *quartz*
   sae fu' o licht
it leams, a muckle siller stern,   *gleams, star*
   athort the nicht.

But some wad hae it reid as bluid,
   some gowd, or green,
and some they canna see't for mist
   afore their een.

Bur aye they ettle to be richt,   *reckon*
   theirsels – or nane –
gin they but get an orra glisk   *odd glimpse*
   o yon braw stane.

O green, or gowd, or cramasie,   *crimson*
   or siller licht –
which will you hae to traivel wi
   athort the nicht?

Isobel Wylie Hutchison
b. 1889

FOR THOSE AT SEA

The shining starfish and the inspirèd weed
Shall clamber in your fingers unafraid.
Your bright astonished eyes shall take their meed
Of Leviathan and the treasure that is laid
On the floors of ocean. Ye shall never see
Through the green arteries of the watery deep
The tedious growth of earth, yet shall ye be
Changed in her change, and lapped in Protean sleep
Your sympathetic hands shall softly move
With the music of her tides in their ebb and flow.
Ye shall be part of all that ye did love,   ·
Mid strange new-fangled dreams lulled to and fro
In the wake of moons and stars outnumberèd,
Until the unplumbed sea restore her dead.

THE GHOST-SHIP

Fast frozen in the solid pack
    She rides the sheeted tide
And follows on an unknown track
    Steered by a secret Guide.

A wistful driven captive she,
    Poised on her icy floe,
Chained to the currents of the sea
    That waft her to and fro.

Sometimes with longing heart she seems
    To steer again for home,
Following with the southward streams
    Towards Bering Strait and Nome.

In vain! Caught by relentless grip
    Of forces scarcely guessed,
The veering winds blow back and clip
    Her fast in ice-cold breast.

Ride On! Ride Out! We meet no more,
    Sad captive of the wave,
Thy bourne some far forgotten shore,
    The polar night thy grave.

239

ESKIMO FOLK-SONG

(from a dance-song of the Aivilik-folk, trans. from the Eskimo of Dr Knud Rasmussen)

Hard times, famine
Afflicted us all,
Gaunt were the maws of men,
Empty stood meat-casks,
Aj-ja – japapé.

Do you see yonder?
Menfolk are coming
Dragging of seals there
Into our dwelling.
Aj-ja – japapé.

Plenty there is now
One more amongst us,
Times when rich banquetings
Bring us together,
Aj-ja – japapé.

Knowest thou savour
Of pots on the boil?
And blubber that ripples
On border of side-bench?
Aj-ja-japapé
Hu-hué! Joyful
Welcome we those
Who brought to us well-being!

Wendy Wood
1892-1981

MERLIN

Hands of twigs hindered my course,
Emerald leaves were a million eyes,
The past year's foliage at my feet
Whispered surprise.

Through airy deeps no wood-bird called,
Only the quiet swayed to and fro;
The light was strange, as if the moon
Gave after-glow.

In robes of misty amethyst,
With eyes of green and limbs of tree,
Stood old Merlin, entangled still
In his philosophy.

WHY

Some stars are breenging
Towards us,
And some are streeling agley
So why should we plod
A monotonous god
On a straight and narrow way?

Some comets go shooting
Beside us,
Meteors dropping athud,
Why should our minds be static,
Why should we act the dud?

Surely the stars that
Are in us
Should orbit our minds with flings
Far from the dubbie ditches   *dirty*
Of demure and conservative things?

Nan Shepherd
1893-1981

CAUL' CAUL' AS THE WALL

Caul', caul' as the wall
That rins frae under the snaw
On Ben a' Bhuird,
And fierce, and bricht,
This water's nae for ilka mou',   *every*
But him that's had a waucht or noo,   *draught*
Nae wersh auld waters o' the plain   *tasteless*
Can sloke again,   *slake*
But aye he clim's the weary heicht
To fin' the wall that loups like licht,   *leaps*
Caulder than mou' can thole, and aye   *suffer*
The warld cries oot on him for fey.

O, LICHT AMO' THE HILLS

O, licht amo' the hills,
S'uld ye gang oot.
To what na dark the warld'll fa'.

Nae mair the thochts o' men
'll traivel 'yont the warld
Frae aff some shinin' Ben.

Nae mair the glint o' snaw
Oot ower the warld's wa'
'll mak men doot
Gin they've their e'en or na.

O, licht amo' the hills!

Naomi Mitchison
b. 1897

REMEMBERING 1926

Knock hard on the door
Of the comfortable place,
Watch his face, her face
Hearing behind the door
How, in the Strike, that May,
Suddenly some boys' hearts
Flared up in a rage of war,
Like when people say:
Drums and trumpets to the fray,
Our day, our day, our day, all foes to slay!
So from friend, friend parts
To see no more,
Oh no more home, mother, cows, pigs, ducks, hens clucking
    in the loose hay!
If they'd been at Oxford
They'd have broken a window,
Lighted a bonner
With some don's books,
Might and main
Satisfied honour!
But all these Smiths and Cooks
Who had no advantages,
They wanted to wreck a train
And kill some people.

Let us admit, oh yes, admit the crime,
The whole dreadful intent:
If the driver had not checked his engine in time
The horror it would have meant
To strangers innocent.

If they had this in their minds, could hear or see
Screamings, breakings and pain,
One could only think, devils that they must be!
Aghast at the hand and the brain
Vision could not constrain.

But they did not see it, could not have, no more
Than men in the trenches knew
With their whole hearts the foul content of war,
So for these young strikers too
Obscuring banners blew.

But trains are things
We ought to care about.
We have sat calmly in trains
With wise eyes looking out.
As the world sways and swings
Past shut, thick window panes.
An easy picture to make:
Ourselves in the wrecked train,
Pinned down – burning – for Christ's sake
Get me out of it!
Suppose it had been that…
Trains solid, real, like England, property, law, oh yes, no doubt of it,
Part of the Thing one prizes.
So the Judges came from London
And held their Assizes.

'They put us into Quod,
Damn their eyes, damn their eyes,
They were God, they were God
Making speeches,
On Judgement Day.
Oh you'ld be frightened too, you'ld tell lies!
Oh it's not so easy even if you do know how!
Then our mates split on us, no use yelling fair play,
It's no game now.'

They won't see the Ties played
They won't see the whippet races.
They won't hear the odds laid.
They won't feel sun or shade.
They won't see their girls' faces.

244

A bitter cup to drink of!
In the silence there they will think of
The roaring, glorious crowds as the ball tops the goal:
They will miss the singing
As the cage leaps down the shaft, bringing
Them and their young mates to the hidden seams of coal:
Lamps at the face blinking,
The great picks jarring and clinking,
The soft, harsh sliding of the coal loosened at last:
The sense of something brewing,
The intense stress of thinking and doing
When the capped flame shows danger and things happen fast:
The strength of working power
Hardened and changed at the sharp conscious hour
To plain, lovely courage, and a life given for friends:
Or not that, but only
Coming up from a darkness lonely
Into pale, clean dawn and bird song when the night shift ends:
Their Sundays of love-making
When the young buds that Spring were breaking,
When the warm breezes were sweet and through the grasses stirred:
They have lost all this, they have lost it,
Oh away, careless, they have tossed it,
For the sake of something unknown, an idea, a sudden word!

So they were put in there, alone, alone, alone,
Till it sank into the stilling blood, the dulled bone.
There the sick brain of a lad,
Full of queer, twisted longings, would turn rotten, go bad,
Thin worms biting body and brain,
Girls unkissed, untouched, drinks missed, that un-wrecked train,
And a bitter youth wasting, passing that would never come again!
Ellison, Sanderson, Harbottle, Baker
English lads from the North Countree
Stick to the Land, lads, never forsake her!
Oh the oak and the ash and the bonny gallows tree.
Stephenson, Wilson, Roberts, Muckle,
Laugh as the clean-limbed English do!
Pull in your belt and snick the buckle,
What's six years when you're twenty-two?

They were convicted and sentenced: there art ends
And in its place is
The thing one never knew,
Jumping out on its friends,
Saying to me and you
And the comfortable faces,
Look what our laws can do,
Look how well we can hate!
Give them four years in prison, six years, eight –
We, standing apart,
Secure in our possessions,
The stuff of science and art,
We watching oppressions,
Letting Judges reply for us
With a bloody Assize again,
Letting them cry for us,
In vain, in vain, in vain!
And all because we're afraid
Of something happening
To the nice world we know,
The world that has been made
Out of order and comfort and slow
Changes that never bring
Hurt to us or our friends,
The world that gently pretends
That everything must be all right that has always been so!

So we curse it, well and good,
But while cursing, but while hating,
Have we truly understood
All the content we are stating?
Did we notice where we stood?

THE HOUSE OF THE HARE

At the time I was four years old
I went to glean with the women,
Working the way they told;
My eyes were blue like blue-bells,
Lighter than oats my hair;
I came from the house of the Haldanes
Of work and thinking and prayer
To the God who is crowned with thorn,
The friend of the Boar and the Bear,
But oh when I went from there,
In the corn, in the corn, in the corn,
I was married young to a hare!

246

We went to kirk on the Sunday
And the Haldanes did not see
That a Haldane had been born
To run from the Boar and the Bear,
And the thing had happened to me
The day that I went with the gleaners,
The day that I built the corn-house,
That is not built with prayer.
For oh I was clean set free,
In the corn, in the corn, in the corn,
I had lived three days with the hare!

FROM *THE BULL CALVES*

CLEMENCY EALASAID

July 1940

Mi ritrovai in una selva oscura
  Blindly, gingerly, beginning to grope through the prickly future,
  With only thorns left on my white rose
  To jag and tear at the heart suddenly,
  Hands out, I move.
  Knowing that inside those shut drawers, the woolly coats and the
      vests,
  The cuddly shawls and the flannels, all, all, wait cold and folded.
  When I go down to the room I left last, in pain and happy,
  They will come and put them away, sorry for me, hoping I may have
      forgotten,
  As though forgetting were possible.
  Having imagined beforehand, very precisely and very gently,
  The white cot by my bed, the old cot with the new green blankets,
  The new dark soft head, the faint breathing, the warmth and love,
  The ghost of the cot is still there when I turn to my right.
  And when I turn to my left, there is the sea, there is Carradale Bay,
      and sea-deep,
  Dark and alone where the Cluaran dropped her, my dear, my
      daughter,
  Not in my arms, not in my womb: in the box Angus made, a small
      weight.

Round about, says the Boyg
Thinking of these things, wrongly, archaically, personally,
I must retract, I must say to myself
She was not yet human, not individual, cannot be lonely,
It is only my projection of love onto her,
Only the months of bearing, the pains of labour interpreted
And interpreted wrongly.
Because I had touched her, kissed her, been happy for a few hours,
I had built up a structure of love and vanity, my pride, my youngest.
That was irrational, and, because irrational, wrong.
Peer Gynt, for ever projecting and protruding his self onto the world,
Symbol of the individual, of capitalism, of commercial progress,
He is finished. But the Boyg in the Dovrefeld
Still remains above half-starved, half-beaten Norway,
And will remain.

You said to me: Come back, come back, mother – knowing
That I was not wholly here, but half pulled down, half drowned in
    the sea tangle,
Beside my baby, where the waves covered, in the wake of the
    Cluaran.
I must, I will, come back.
These twenty centuries of bourgeois bargaining,
Since Jesus, himself a Jew, saw through it, saw there must be
No scales of corn-growing justice, but only love,
Have left their mark on me.
Now I am trying to bargain, to say take her death, my grief,
But save me the others, from bombs, shells, from pandemic
Disease, save me children and husband, save Ruth, Dick, Taggy and
    all of them,
Clutching out for lives on the spread bargain counter, clutching them
    to my heart,
But looking up I see
No bargainer on the far side of the counter, nothing: only another
    projection:
Round about, says the Boyg.

Roll up the map of Europe

Should we try to make sense of a senseless situation?
Over-simplifying, after the habit of the orthodox,
Catholic or Marxist. Shall we try to make sense of Oran?
Try to make sense of inevitable hatred
From mothers of French sailors, babies who had lived
Through the years of hope and pride and delight, boyhood and
    manhood,
Now murdered by the Ally, perfide Albion?
How make a bargain on that? Roll up the map of Europe.
The lights have gone out: the concentration camps are full: the men
    and women
Who thought themselves safe have been betrayed to the vultures,
To Himmler, Goering, Franco, to those whose faces
Express Satanic possession. Paris is dead.
Only the bones remain. Paris of the Commune
Dead as the sailors at Oran. This winter we hope to starve
France, Belgium, Holland, Denmark, Norway, Poland:
Harvest of dead babies, disease, hatred: no sense.
My breasts tingle and stab with milk that no one wants,
Surplus as American wheat, surplus and senseless.
Not her soft kind mouth groping for me. Useless, senseless.
If my baby had been starved by England, would I ever forgive?
Roll up the map of Europe.

Carradale

This was to have been a binding between me and Carradale.
Weeper of Carradale Glen, fairy hare, cleft rock, did none of you
    speak?
How shall I stay here, how go on with the little things,
How not hate Carradale, the flowery betrayer,
Dagger in fist?
How be crushed into such humility as can continue
The daily work, alleviation of meals and sleep and slight laughter?
How, having known happiness, not see it anywhere?
I should have been happy before, in Highland May
Of blossom and bird-song. Ah, how not be happy
When one could not foresee?

Time and the hour runs through the roughest day

The roughest day is not yet. This was a rough day
For me and perhaps for Carradale. But the roughest day,
The day lived through by Macbeth who had been king,
Some say a good king, and by Gruach, my ancestors,
Hangs now in the future, the unturned page, the history book;
So far unwritten, and we, single-sighted,
Not having seen the ghost funeral nor identified the bearers,

249

Imagine it next week or next month, Ragnarok, the doomday.
Who knows what each shall lose? Who knows the issue?
Will there be another birth, a fair one, or is West Europe
Too old, too old for that, as I shall be too old
For another bearing
Before the roughest day is past: as I am now
Unable to imagine the new times, because of the blackness
Steadily ahead of me, the still curtain
Over my dancing daughter, my innocent, my small one.
Ah darkness of the spirit, lift, lift, let the hour run through you!
The roughest day is to come. We shall perhaps
Live through it, or others will. In a hundred years
Things may be seen in order, making sense, drawing a new map:
Human endeavour going roundabout, unselfishly,
May, arriving suddenly on the Dovrefeld, see ahead, make fresh
     ski-tracks.
In a hundred years
The French sailors at Oran, the Scottish dead at Abbeville,
The tortured in the concentration camps and all the leaders,
The ones who thought themselves godlike, forgetting the Boyg,
And I, and my children, and all the people of Carradale,
We shall be dead, at last out of the running of events and hours.
     The page will have been turned,
The history written, and we, anonymous,
Shall be condemned or not condemned, gently upbraided
For folly of not foreseeing, for dithered watching of hours
While the roughest day runs by.
But the trees I planted in the heavy months, carrying you,
Thinking you would see them grown, they will be tall and lovely:
Red oak and beech and tsuga, grey alder and douglas:
But not for you or your children. What will it matter then, forgotten
     daughter,
Forgotten as I shall be forgotten in the running of time,
Maybe a name in an index, but not me, not remembered
As I alone remember, with what tears yet, the first kiss, the faint
     warmth and stirring?
The waves will cover us all diving into darkness out of the bodies of
     death,
Vanishing as the wake of a boat in a strong current.
The hot tears will be cooled and the despair of the middle-aged,
     rolling up their map,
Will be forgotten, with other evil things, will be interpreted,
Will be forgiven at last.

Alice V. Stuart
b.1899

SIMULACRUM

LINES ON AN EARLY PHOTOGRAPH

This is a self I have forgot,
   A self of years gone by.
This pensive girl the camera caught
In mould of cheek, and mode of thought,
   This was, but is not, I.

Strange revenant, I confront her here
   Set in her narrow frame
Cherished by you. Alas, my dear,
Harbour no ghost of a bygone year,
   I am not still the same.

Static she is, serene and fair,
   Soft lip and candid brow
Of trustful girlhood, dreaming where
No harsh breath from our outer air
   Blows on her timeless Now.

Her irised hopes I have left behind,
   Her fragile innocence too.
You have lived with a ghost, and will not find
The mortal woman to your mind
   Whom life has shaped anew.

Say then farewell to her, or me.
   Keep dreams inviolate
Or banish them. We would not be
Like those who dwell with a fantasy
   Grafting it on their mate.

THE CLOCK IN THE SICK-ROOM

The room was shrouded from the sun;
Outside, the birds' rejoicing din
Mocked the uneasy peace within,
Where slow-drawn breaths came one by one.
More vitally, it seemed, than they,
The quick clock ticked the livelong day:
Tick-ticked, tick-ticked, the livelong day.

251

The groping fingers nerveless dropped,
Silent the fretful breathing ran,
The mechanism that was man
For ever with the heart-beat stopped.
The metal case of cunning springs,
Man-made, outlasted man's decay;
Instinct with life beside the clay,
Tick-tick, tick-tick, the soulless thing
Reiterated all the day,
Tick-tick, tick-tick, the livelong day.

THE UNQUIET TIDE

As the long reaches of the tide
draw out, draw out, even so subside
the unquiet urges of my heart
poured to some infinite apart.

But when the strong tide makes again
flung in its fury shorewards, then
with what vexed thoughts and wildering woe
tossed 'gainst this world of men I go !

Could that strange moon my spirit draws
flung shoreward, seaward by its laws
stand still in heaven, and let me be
a tranquil and a tideless sea.

Only, perhaps, with severing breath
in the large benison of death
shall my vexed heart, that unquiet tide
stand silver-calm and sanctified.

Flora Garry
b. 1900

TO SUFFIE, LAST OF THE BUCHAN FISHWIVES

A fish creel wi a wife aneth't
Steed at wir kitchen door.
A sma' quine grat at the wild-like shape   *girl, cried*
She'd nivver seen afore.

Ye cam fae anidder warl, Suffie,
Amo' hiz lan'ward folk,   *us*
The sough o the sea in the vera soun'   *sighing*
O the words ye spoke.

Oor wyes warna yours, we nivver vrocht   *ways, worked*
Wi net nor line
Nor guttin knife, nor fan on haggert thoom   *found on a cut thumb*
The stang o the brine.

We niver hid to flee demintit
Tull the pier-heid,
Nor harken tull the heerican at midnicht,
Caul' wi dreid.

Spring efter Spring, or the teuchat's storm wis past   *winter's*
Ye wannert the road,
Heid tull the sleepy win' an boo't two-faal,   *bent double*
Shoodrin yer load.

Simmer parks war kin'lier tull yer feet
Gin steens an styoo.   *stones and dust*
Bit fyles the stirkies chase't ye.   *bullocks*
Fa wis feart? Them or you?

Yon bricht that wis eence yer hair   *tousled bush*
Is grizzl't noo,
An ower lang scannin o the sea his bleach't
Yer een's blue.

Wark an dule an widder sharpit yer face   *woe*
Tull skin ower been,
As the tides tormint an futtle   *whittle*
A sma' fite steen.   *white stone*

253

Weel, umman, noo it's lowsin-time, we wuss	*loosening-time*
For you a fylie's ease;	*while's*
Syne, at the hinmost wa'gyaan,	*waygoing*
Quaet seas.	

AE MAIR HAIRST

She promised weel aneuch—a heavy crap.	*enough, crop*
Bit a dull, mochy Simmer it wis, wi afa little drooth.	
Some o's, ye'll min', gey forcey, cuttit ower green,	*warm*
An syne the widder broke.	
Caul', roch shooers drave doon on a nor'east win'.	
The cattle oot on the girss	
Wannert wi their backs up roun' the dykes,	
Nivver ristin'.	
Aye the onding, aye the clorty dubs.	*muddy pools*
I' the howe o Ythan week efter weary week	
The stooks steed tasht an water-loggit.	
Mornin efter mornin yon fite haar	*white mist*
Cam' blawin in fae the coast.	
Bit ae foreneen the win' swang roun' to the west,	
The cloods were heich an licht,	
The sky wis blue-er gin we'd seen't a Simmer.	
The howes firmt up. The strae began to reeshle.	*straw, rustle*
Shaef efter shaef, we turn't the stooks wi wir han's	
In tull the face o a strong sunshiny breeze	
I' the cornyards, the smell o the ripened grain.	
We workit hard, fyles by the licht o the meen,	
Fyles on the Sabbath day,	
An we got aff the grun', ae mair hairst!	*one more harvest*
An noo fae Mormond Hill as far's Bennachie,	
The raikit stibble parks lie teem an quaet,	*empty and quiet*
Wytin' for the ploo.	

Marion Lochhead
1902-85

FIDDLER'S BIDDING

Och, gin ye come to our toun,
    to our toun, to our toun,
Och, gin ye come to our town,
    play up a rantin air.

Play like the verra deil, lad,
    be bauld, lad be daft, lad;
steer up the verra deil, lad,
    and fleg us aa sair.

For we're aa deid in our toun,
    in our town, in or toun;
we're deid and damned in our toun,
    and neither ken nor care.

DAFT MEG'S SONG

There's Tibbie merriet on the grieve,   *married*
    An' Kate on Tam the miller,
An' Jean hes routh o' suitors; she's   *plenty*
    Na braw, but she hes siller.   *silver*

Noo I hae neither man nor gear;
    'Puir silly Meg' they ca' me; –
But, aince atween the mirk an' licht   *dark*
    I went, whaur nae een saw me.   *eye*

An' there I met a braw, braw lad
    Wha fleeched, an' said he loo'ed me;   *flattered*
He decked my hair wi' gowden kaims,   *combs*
    Wi' braws an' kisses wooed me.   *finery*

He's brither to the Elfin Queen;
    He'll come richt sune to wed me.
Can I tak' thocht for man or gear,
    Wha'll hae a Prince to bed me?

MAN O' GRACE

Rab's a man o' unco grace;   *uncommon*
  Nae saunt o' a' the human race   *saint*
Cud tak' his heigh an' haly place
  Sae near the Lord!
Sic awesome unction lichts his face,
  An' thrills his word.

Gin Rab were God, puir men wad be
Sair hauden doun in penaltie,
For ilka sin oor weird we'd dree;   *our fate we'd endure*
  Nae grace wad fa'
Frae Mercy-seat; but damned we'd be,
  Puir sinners a'.

Och, Guid be thankit, Rab's but dust!
Wi' ither sons o' airth he must
Fa' to Deith's dour an' auncient lust'
  Ane day he'll be
'Mang the unrighteous an' unjust.
  Puir Rab maun dee!   *die*

Margaret Winefride Simpson

VILLANELLE

O winter wind, lat grievin be,
Lat grievin be, and murn nae mair: *mourn no more*
Simmer sall set thy sorrow free.

New hurt the heavy hert sall dree;   *shall endure*
Thy weariness awa sall wear:
O winter wind, lat grievin be.

Wi a' the waes the warld sall see   *woes*
What wae hast thou that can compare?
Simmer sall set thy sorrow free,

Yet what delicht sall puirtith pree   *poverty try*
When time sall solace thy despair?
O winter wind, lat grievin be.

What fear onkent can trouble thee,
What misery that nane can share?
Simmer sall set thy sorrow free,

But man in dule doth live and dee;
A birn mair brief is thine to bear: *burden*
O winter wind, lat grievin be:

Simmer sall set thy sorrow free!

THE WAUKRIFE WIN'

The waukrife win' gangs back an' fore   *wakeful*
   Thro' the teem, mirk ha's o' Nicht,   *empty, dark*
An' the blinterin' starnies winner an' glower,   *blinking stars*
   Wae at the sorrowfu' sicht –
For lang sall he watch or he sees oot-bye
   The grey face o' Daylight:

An' lang sall he wait or he hears the Dawn
   Come tirlin' at the pin...
Troth, there's little content when a cankert carle   *angry man*
   Is neither to haud nor bin',
An' the heich, black wa's o' Midnicht dirl
   Wi' the wail o' the waukrife win'!

257

Dorothy Margaret Paulin
b. 1904

SAID THE SPAEWIFE

Said the auld spaewife to me –
  'Never be humble!
Lads'll tak' the rough o' your tongue
  An' never grumble;
But the thing nae man can bide,
  An' he be human,
Is that mim-moothed snivellin' fule,   *affected*
  A fushionless woman.'   *dull*

PRAYER ON GOOD FRIDAY

We were in the frenzied mob, you and I,
When they shouted: 'Crucify Him! Crucify...'

Once we'd realised The Way, it was we
Who, frightened, turned aside from Calvary.

We were the nation's counsellors who saw
In Him discord, and danger to the Law.

We are the timid common folk who choose
Seeming security; who compromise – and lose.

And ours the unlovely sins of self; the pride,
The heedlessness – neglect of Him who died.

Still, year by year, His passion we renew
And darken Love with death. O, grant us too,

Father, forgiveness. Send to our hearts a sword –
Not peace – till we shall know Thy Word.

Maimie A. Richardson

THE HULK

Last night I dreamed that the sea cradled me;
That round my bows the salt waves foamed and dashed,
That shrieking winds flung high the insolent spume
Over my deck to drench my bellying sails;
And as I heaved and trembled to the swell,
My ancient heart remembered, and was glad.
When from among the driving, flying clouds,
An Autumn moon hung low and full and red
Till all my spars stood clear beneath her light –
Then my old heart grew fine again and brave,
And I forgot the mudflats and my shame.

Dorothy Seward Walton

MURDERER

No one guessed his secret
how he nursed and nurtured
that devil-baby curled hard as a fist
clenched into itself and caged
inside his ribs. It was
his one companion, his own creature
for his heart
forever starved, purse-pinched
was bankrupt, had possessed
no currency and could not give
to anyone nor pay a creditor.

By day and night he fed it pabulum
of poison pap; it swelled, waxed fat,
raged for release: –

In the split second when it burst out blind
beating for freedom at a clouded shape,
a hated obstacle, he knew
a terrible, an orgiastic joy, the towering power
of Lucifer before
falling.

Then his opened eyes
saw the sick emptiness the devastation death –
cold: he heard silence filling up with fear,
the rustling wings from unseen distances, the slow
gathering of the dark
vultures, the avenging sleuths.

RHYME OF A JOURNEY FROM LONDON TO EDINBURGH (1914)

Farewell to one city
at dawning of light
and hail to another
at fall of the night.

On to the North steams
triumphant the train
ceaselessly grinding
a rhythmic refrain.

Meadows fly past and
a luminous sheet
of wind-rippled water,
a grimy back street.

Stark rows of houses
break up the pale sky,
a jangle of coal-trucks,
a station passed by.

Cast the old thoughts that
troubled your mind
to drown in that river
left gleaming behind,

new ones come stirring
with live young wings
from rhythmical power
and swift-running things.

There's a cathedral
in mist: as a dream
it has vanished, and slowly
we slacken and steam
into that station
whose girders of might
curve upwards, transfigured
in columns of light.

No stopping! No staying!
mad demons of speed
have boarded the engine
are hissing their greed.

Sudden lurch forward
and once more away
and see, we are racing
the dying of day!

A bridge we are crossing
with thunderous swerve;
left and right flashes
a river's gold curve;

Glittering windows
rise tier upon tier:
held steeped in the sunset
what city is here?

To twilight, to darkness
and night has begun.
The miles of our journey
are nearly outrun.

Waken, wan travellers,
Look! Very high
There stands the great castle
Along the dark sky.

HOSPITAL WARD (1)

Our sheeted shapes in twenty beds aligned
are now conjoined in unforeseen alliance
arranged in ordered neatness for the long
night. But we wander in and out of sleep of pain
    fretting the air with fevered sounds
pressures of thoughts suppressed
which deny arrangement, are disordered.

Beyond the windows a faint crayoned moon
a tree-branch inked on a torn
page of cloud are merely pictures from a book
    do not belong here:
we stare at our own sky of white gloss paint
our lit electric moon that lends
a nimbus to the calm head of a nurse.
Through the dark hours she stays as our assurance
for we float in limbo, in suspension
    of time and known realities
    in this strange microcosm
waiting to be freed as did those tranced ones
held in their palace in the fairy tale.

HOSPITAL WARD (2)

With dedicated care
she was anaesthetised incised repaired
and stitched up deftly.

From the deep drowned peace
from under the dead weight of years
her heart, old blind retainer, brought her back.

Now she must show similitude of life:
two nurses walk her up and down the ward
between them, worn rag doll with dragging feet
an infant's tears
trickling her cheeks.

In the startled night
she suddenly screams, it is a desperate sound,
a child lost in a labyrinth of fright
thrashing for exit round and round
the mulberry bush, the dense dark-rooted shape
of immemorial fears.

Release her soon
you faithful servants of the flesh
hand in your resignation, let
her spirit rest.

Kathleen Raine
b. 1908

FROM *EILEANN CHANAIDH*
(ISLE OF CANNA, INNER HEBRIDES)

THE ANCIENT SPEECH

A Gaelic bard they praise who in fourteen adjectives
Named the one indivisible soul of his glen;
For what are the bens and the glens but manifold qualities,
Immeasurable complexities of soul?
What are these isles but a song sung by island voices?
The herdsman sings ancestral memories
And the song makes the singer wise,
But only while he sings
Songs that were old when the old themselves were young,
Songs of these hills only, and of no isles but these.
For other hills and isles this language has no words.

The mountains are like manna, for one day given,
To each his own:
Strangers have crossed the sound, but not the sound of the dark oarsmen
Or the golden-haired sons of kings,
Strangers whose thought is not formed to the cadence of waves,
Rhythm of the sickle, oar and milking pail,
Whose words make loved things strange and small,
Emptied of all that made them heart-felt or bright.
Our words keep no faith with the soul of the world.

HIGHLAND GRAVEYARD

Today a fine old face has gone under the soil;
For generations past women hereabouts have borne
Her same name and stamp of feature.
Her brief identity was not her own
But theirs who formed and sent her out
To wear the proud bones of her clan, and live its story,
Who now receive back into the ground
Worn features of ancestral mould.

A dry-stone wall bounds off the dislimned clay
Of many an old face forgotten and young face gone
From boundless nature, sea and sky.
A wind-withered escalonia like a song
Of ancient tenderness lives on
Some woman's living fingers set as shelter for the dead, to tell
In evergreen unwritten leaves,
In scent of leaves in western rain
That one remembered who is herself forgotten.

Many songs they knew who now are silent.
Into their memories the dead are gone
Who haunt the living in an ancient tongue
Sung by old voices to the young,
Telling of sea and isles, of boat and byre and glen;
And from their music the living are reborn
Into a remembered land,
To call ancestral memories home
And all that ancient grief and love our own.

ISIS WANDERER

This too is an experience of the soul
The dismembered world that once was the whole god
Whose unbroken fragments now lie dead.
The passing of reality itself is real.

Gathering under my black cloak the remnants of life
That lie dishonoured among people and places
I search the twofold desert of my solitude,
The outward perished world, and the barren mind.

Once he was present, numinous, in the house of the world,
Wearing day like a garment, his beauty manifest
In corn and man as he journeyed down the fertile river.
With love he filled my distances of night.

I trace the contour of his hand fading upon a cloud,
And this his blood flows from a dying soldier's wound,
In broken fields his body is scattered and his limbs lie
Spreadeagled like wrecked fuselage in the sand.

His skull is a dead cathedral, and his crown's rays
Glitter from worthless tins and broken glass.
His blue eyes are reflected from pools in the gutter,
And his strength is the desolate stone of fallen cities.

265

Oh in the kitchen-midden of my dreams
Turning over the potsherds of past days
Shall I uncover his loved desecrated face?
Are the unfathomed depths of sleep his grave?

Beyond the looming dangerous end of night
Beneath the vaults of fear do his bones lie,
And does the maze of nightmare lead to the power within?
Do menacing nether waters cover the fish king?

I piece the divine fragments into the mandala
Whose centre is the lost creative power,
The sun, the heart of God, the lotus, the electron
That pulses world upon world, ray upon ray
That he who lived on the first may rise on the last day.

HEIRLOOM

She gave me childhood's flowers,
Heather and wild thyme,
Eyebright and tormentil,
Lichen's mealy cup
Dry on wind-scored stone,
The corbies on the rock,
The rowan by the burn.

Sea-marvels a child beheld
Out in the fisherman's boad,
Fringed pulsing violet
Medusa, sea gooseberries,
Starfish on the sea-floor,
Cowries and rainbow-shells
From pools on a rocky shore,

Gave me her memories,
But kept her last treasure:
'When I was a lass,' she said,
'Sitting among the heather,
'Suddenly I saw
'That all the moor was alive!
'I have told no one before.'

That was my mother's tale.
Seventy years had gone
Since she saw the living skein
Of which the world is woven,
And having seen, knew all;
Through long indifferent years
Treasuring the priceless pearl.

MOON

Sailing by night on the dark Adriatic in the moon's eye
I slept upon the watery flood where only spirits walk
In the womb of archaic night between deeps and skies;
And in my sleep sublunary saw the moon disclose
Her other face that only dreamers and the dead may see,
That seemed or was more real than moon over mast or funnel
Of the throbbing ship that traced my wake towards Piraeus.

Then I, unable to be elsewhere than in my dream
Fear-stricken like a hare must gaze and could not stir
As the revolving moon destructive from its orbit tore
Appalling as it grew and grew
Until it hit the ground and came on in giant bounds.
I struggled to rise, and with my downflung body
Shielded my daughter; survived, as the hurtling moon traversed
    my terror.

What dread, nameless and pre-human, imprinted upon time's
    memory the moon I dreamed?
With what glazed reptilian eye then gazed archaic earth?
What falling moon rebounded from Alps Andes and Cordillera?
What Palaeozoic dragon-whelp's ancestral life transmitted
Image indelible of antediluvian cataclysm
Whose terror from dream to dream, dreamer to dreamer, hunts
    life down?

The seer of Patmost by these same heaving waters born
Where on the sea of glass a mineral dragon sprawls its peninsula
Saw in his caverned sleep moon turn to blood and the stars fall.
Plutarch beheld the dead drawn into that dread nocturnal face
Blake saw plucked from the socket of night by the mortal hand of Time.
The lost Book of Moonlight we in our dreams may read
Where past and future are mirrored predestined woes
Of all the children of Gea, that stony dragon's brood.

Olive Fraser
1909-77

THE VIKINGS

King Haro's navy met on St Laurence Wake in 1263 at Ronaldsvo under the leadership of his great ship Brimvald

I saw the dead upon St Laurence Wake
   Sailing in beautiful Brimvald. They were young,
Younger than death and life, with a sweet tongue
   I have heard in my blood before,
Dreaming it was the wild gannets that make
   Their comment upon Sulna-stapa shore.
I cried upon the dead, 'Why is your face
   So beautiful in the regretless place?

'Surely among the dead there is no will
   For dragon-necks of gold and for straight sails,
And Brimvald with the silver bitterns' tails
   Is quiet under dark skerries now.'
'O we are loved among the living still,
   We are forgiven among the dead. We plough
In the old narrows of the spirit. We
   Have woven our wealth into your mystery.'

And I remembered words that I had heard
   And never heard. And vessels that I knew
And thought were visions. The mute swans that flew
   Over grey islands were like these
And yet were nothing. Once at Herlesferd
   I saw a ship whose path on the green seas
Made joy to brindled sea-birds, and my breath
   Was dangerous and scant, bitter like death.

'O if you died upon St Laurence Wake
   Why are you beautiful and young,' I cried
'Like dreams of you I saw on a great tide
   Lovelier and more young than I?
Even when I heard the wild white eagles take
   Over the earth with their cruel minstrelsy
You were more light than I have ever been.'
   They said, 'We are your Soul that you have seen.'

A GOSSIP SILENCED

THE THRUSH AND THE EAGLE

'I keep the machair where   *land*
The burnies gae.'
'I keep the mountain, bare
O' a' but snae.'

'I see the rush steikin'   *piercing*
My bonny nest.'
'I see the ray seekin'
The amethyst.'

'I have a muckle pea
Inside my crap.'   *stomach*
'I hae two maukins wi'   *maggots*
A grouse on tap.'

'I hear the worms below
The mole's bings.'   *mounds*
'I hear the whisprin' o'
The aungels' wings.'

'I sit wi' merles a' day,   *blackbirds*
An' crack, an' a'.'   *talk*
'I sit wi' cloods and say
Naethin' ava.'

'I coont the lasses in
The simmer leas.'   *summer meadows*
'I ken the Lord coontin'   *know*
The centuries.'

LINES WRITTEN AFTER A NERVOUS BREAKDOWN. I

I have forgotten how to be
A bird upon a dawn-lit tree,
A happy bird that has no care
Beyond the leaf, the golden air.
I have forgotten moon and sun,
And songs concluded and undone,
And hope and ruth and all things save
The broken wit, the waiting grave.

269

Where is that mountain I must climb
To gain again some common time,
Not this stayed clock-hand that must be
Some foretaste of eternity?
Where is that task or terror that
Will wake a slow magnificat
From this dead sense, from these dull eyes,
That see no more to Paradise?

There is no night so deep as this
Inevitable mind's abyss,
Where I now dwell with foes alone.
Feather and wing and breathing bone
And blessèd creatures come not here,
But the long dead, the aguish fear
Of never breaking from this hold,
Encapsuled, rapt, and eras old.

There is no second of escape.
As with some forest-wandering ape
Whose sad intelligence may go
So far and nevermore may grow,
I am enchained most subtly by
A thousand dendrons 'til I die,
Or find my mountain, storm and shock
This graven hour and start the clock.

September 1964

LINES WRITTEN AFTER A NERVOUS BREAKDOWN. II

Come, lamefoot brain, and dance and be
A merry carnival for me.
We are alive in spite of all
Hobgoblins who our wits did call.
With ghosts and gallowsbirds we went
Hundreds of leagues 'til, fiercely spent,
We laid ourselves to weep and cry
Beyond the house of memory.

We have been lepers, and now run
To sit again within the sun,
And smile upon some country fair
With Punch and poor dog Toby there.
We, who did only think to die,
Now laugh and mock the revelry.
Up, barefoot brain, and fill your hall
With flags as for a festival.

Yet you are poor and slow to do
The blessed things I ask of you.
Haunting with spectres still and still
Remembering your dungeon's chill.
Where you did cower and aye did grow
A frenzied circus for your foe,
Who sought you in the blood's dim arc,
And in the night-time, in the dark.

Peace, friend, and think how we are here
Through dangers, desolations, fear.
We two alone, now all is o'er,
Will never move from pleasure more.
We two will sit like birds i' the sun
And preen and pipe while others run
And straddle in the world's proud play.
We have been night, who now are day.

October 1964

THE DEFENCE OF LADY JONET DOUGLAS

*In July 1537 Lady Jonet Douglas was charged in the Court of Session in
Edinburgh, with treason, and conspiring the king's death by poison; and
also assisting and fortifying her brothers and uncles all of whom had been
put to the king's horn as traitors and rebels, and expelled from Scotland.
She was found guilty, strangled, and burned at the stake. False witnesses
appear to have been hired and their evidence was secretly cut out of the
Record, which otherwise gives a full report of the proceedings.*

THE DEFENCE

Regard poison, I am not guilty:
Anent the second charge
I follow the instincts of my heart
Which admit neither of violence
Nor of inhospitality. If that is guilt I am guilty.
I never showed kindness to my people
For gain, nor seeking their praise,
But just because I love them
As sisters and brothers do.
Family loyaltie, and clan loyaltie
Are part of our life, I think;
Woven into the pattern of our life.
I saw they were enduring hardship;

271

Cold, and hungry, and wearie,
And if I had happened to ask them
While they sat wolfing the pies,
And the home-farm cheeses, laid
On the fair Tantallon china;
And quaffing the hot ale
From great silver tankards
That now rest elsewhere:
If I had happened to ask them
Why they endured such hardships
(A thing I never asked)
They would have cried, I know,
'For the love and service of our country!'
Loving them I should have thought them mistaken
But on what is nearest to our hearts
We can speak but seldom, and then
Our words may flow unbid
From some knowledge we had not known
Till we heard them fall from our lips.

But it has now become plain to me,
Those who hate my brother
Are furious that he's not in their power
Nor fallen a victim to their spite.
So they sing out their malisons on me,
They look to sup their vengeance
From the coggie of my blood
And charge me with crimes,
Which, if I had wrought them,
Would have taken their lawings
In the currency of Death.
But it belongs to no judge on earth
To punish man – or woman –
For sins committed by others.
There must be clear proof
That the prisoner is the offender.
Therefore you have no right to punish
In me the deeds of another
However blameworthy these might be.

Above all it is your aucht to deem
The things I am accused of
Have some likeness to the truth:
The weightiest evidents
Of the guilt or of the innocence
Of an impeached person –
Is it not their former conduct?

272

And what such faults hitherto
Could anyone lay to my charge?
Did ever anyone reproach me
With one single item of scandal?
Examine my way of life –
And if you can find nothing
Reproachable in my conduct
What way syne can ye believe
I am come all of a sudden
To contrive this murder?
This very height and perfection
Of all that is pitiless?

I witness before you all
I would not willingly hurt
The most despicable wretch alive;
How then could I murder my sovereign,
Him I have aye held in reverence
Him never did me wrong,
How could I light on him
My maiden smack of crime?

Is it feckless of me to mind you
That no normal person is capable
Of such a damnable and unnatural deed
Saving in some fell clutch
Of Fate, or saving they are pressed
Into plots by rewards or revenge?
My birth, my invironment,
Has sheltered me from the former:
As for the latter, since the King
Has never wrought me any wrong,
And since it is my instinct
To love rather than to hate,
How could I be suspect
Of thirsting for revenge?

And to make my pretended crime
Appear the more frightful
It is forby given out
The way was to be by poison.
Is it a man or a devil
Charges me with such wickedness?
I never saw any poison,
Nor saw aucht of its preparation.
Let them tell me where I coft it,
Or who procured it for me.

Further even tho' I had it,
How was I to use it
Since I never come near the Palace;
For it is common knowledge
That we bide in the country
At a great distance from the Court.
What opportunity could I have
For to poison the King?

Those things must make plain to you
To show I am innocent
Of the crimes I am charged with:
And the office of you Judges
Is it not to protect injured innocence?
But if the malice and power of my enemies
Be such, that, guilty or innocent,
I must be condemned –
Well, I shall die cheerfully
For I have the witness of a good conscience,
This mysterious Voice within:
Can the great Pope in Rome tell us
If this is the Voice of God?...
Anyhow I know no other
In this solemn hour,
And equally I know
Hatred is of no use.

Why should there be one loyalty
To your family, and another to your King?
For we are all one family.
When we say our *Paternoster*,
If waygoing, I beg you from my heart
Let me be the sole sufferer!
Let those other innocent ones
Not suffer with me,
Seeing I am here solely
For that I am a Douglas:
My husband, my son, my cousin
Are none of them of that name or family.
I would end my life less uncomforted
If I knew you had absolved them.
As for you, sirs, the more of us who thole   *suffer*
Your unjust justiciary
The greater must be your sin,
The more awful your damnation
When on the Lang Day

You thole the Grand Assize
Under an impartial Judge.

Am I not old before my time
Through the discipline of those years,
Like thousands in this sore harried land?
On one side husband and son endangered,
On the other, my own brothers in need;
And within, yon proud Olympus
Divine Law sits unmoved, telling me
That if I am condemned to death
That is a small thing.
And to have been inhospitable
To my own kith and kin
That would have been a crime.
For I owe a longer allegiance
To the dead than to the living
A darker, though not a more passionate
Allegiance. My noble ancestors
Would far overflow this Courthouse,
Like a great sea, and each one –
If each one not good, was noble,
Good at war with evil
In his heart, as in my heart.
And in my pulses their pulses beat.

Janet Caird
b. 1913

TRAITOR

We were from the beginning close partners,
worked well together,
saw eye to eye.
He went out, brought in material, made the contacts:
I had the ideas, laid down policy,
was, I thought, the dominant element,
tactfully now and then letting him think he had control.
    At first I made excuses,
pretended not to notice,
overlooked the small rebellions
ignored the subtle underminings
until the truth was unavoidable.
    We do not face each other across a table of deadlocked
negotiations:
the relationship is sidelong.
I do not admit,
he does not assert,
that he is boss
and will some day apply
the final ineluctable sanction.

THE QUILT

A girl, she began the quilt,
dove-tailing the colours
into a kaleidoscope.
They said: It's a waste of time.
What you want, they said,
is stuff to boil and wash
and hang on the line
and use again and again.
But she finished the quilt
and laid it away in the drawer.
    Came age;
    went house, possessions, all;
    came the high iron bed,
    came kindly alien care.
    The old woman took out her quilt.
    Her hands moved over it
    reading the textures,
    the silk, the velvet, the mourning serge, the taffeta.
    She draped it round her shoulders
    and sat in peace.

276

But time's rag-picker fingers
found her quilt,
loosened the stitches,
undid the seams,
scattered the pieces on the bed-spread
and left her shivering.

FAITH

How enviable they whose hands uplifted pluck
their apple from a tree
well-tended, well-established;
shapely fruit and ripe,
lustrous rind, satisfying flesh,
to chew strolling in the garden,
or munch for consolation
while rain batters the tool-shed.
Some apples fall to ground,
bruised by rough air,
mined by wasps,
ravaged by birds,
half-fruit and pitiable –
yet worth the picking.
These sorry things are apple still
and at the core
are small black seeds alive.

LET THE SNOW COVER HER

Let the snow cover her.
She is too old to follow the sledge
and her fingers too stiff
to hold the bone-needle and stitch
the silk-soft sealskin.
It is years and years since she bore her children
in the warm snow-house on the ice-floe.
Here in the hollow
the down of the snow-drift
the silence and cold
will lull her to sleep.
Let the snow cover her.

MILD NOVEMBER

Too mild, too mild November:
ageing roses meeting early summer's aubrieta;
birdsong too,
and puzzled rooks prospecting
their windy tenements.
The birds disdain the pauper menu
of mouldy cheese and crumbled biscuit
charitably scattered on the window-sill.
They guzzle
yewberries hollyberries cotoneaster,
feast on windfalls
and frail transparent skins
scatter the grass as if
sloughed from small rotund reptiles.
But the sun, relentless mathematician,
draws out the shadows;
his compass diminishes, diminishes
the curve of rising and descent,
and the inexorable comes
like a thief in the night.
The birds are clamorous mendicants,
the trees wear frosty shrouds,
premature and geriatric flowerings shrivel.
It is
the wise aconites and wary snowdrops,
resisting blandishments,
obeying the compass
who in due time
will lead the great revival.

THE ROSE SOLILOQUIZES

Such lies they told!
Wait, they said, wait.
You must be patient.
We – they said with quiet arrogance –
we grow quietly; no rushing round,
no clawing for food, no gabbling,
no squeaks, squeals, hootings – all that noise.
No. Roots, deep roots,
drawing life directly from the earth;
leaves drawing life directly from the sun –
that is our way.
So you must be patient.
First a swelling on the stalk,
a small green shoot, leaves and then
you will start to grow –
the flower, the crowning, carrying
the honour, the responsibility,
of fruit to come –
not without the reward of pleasure –
yes, pleasure.
On a day of sun, of heat,
your petals will unfurl into light, into warmth.
Insects will throng; flirtatious butterflies,
earnest worker bees, urgent in busy-ness,
portly bumble-bees, dark, fuzzy,
pollen bags yellow on their thighs.
They will uncurl a long proboscis
to tap the nectar secreted in your heart,
and pay with quickening pollen.
   Oh! Such lies!
   There never was light sun heat.
   Tight-clenched against the brutal wind, the battering rain,
   leeched of colour, fragrance,
   my petals, plopped to earth,
   re-cycle into humus.

Ann Scott-Moncrieff
1914-43

A NIGHT IN THE COUNTRY

Oh, what a glister's to the wintry night!
Whan aa the company are gleg and bien.   *merry, cosy*
In the fank o silence made by mountains
They're birlan wi an oorie quean.   *whirling round with a strange woman*

They're birlan doon a yellow wine
Far glintier nor her hair,
And aye their sauls are gashant wi laughter.   *loud*
And aye she laughs the mair.

Oh, whativer maks the anaphrodisiacal
Wine sae sig and warm?
Tyned fleurs gie their deemless pouer
Wi lees o love for barm.

Up raves the fire more roary than the host,
It rouchles in the lum, and   *roars in the chimney*
Glims in gawsy glass, and luely in their een
Mid brash and bummand!   *swanking and boasting*

DIRGE

Now words are a' tae smoosh
And argument's in bruck,
The way you kent was best
To raise us oot o' muck,

By is the spirting tears:
The ree-raa cries instead,
Waaly feet walk the street,
'Plane dirls for the dead.

Now for a while sib
To your daithless flesh we haud,
The biding bairn, the high-sky loon,
And man made like to God.

A' slidders: owrehaillet we   *overtaken*
Catch inklan o' the word and see
The upstair 'room, the famyous supper spread,
By Christ Jesus wi' wine and bread.

LINES WRITTEN IN AUTUMN 1940

Split, heart, split, like the gowk chestnut,
Cast off the nylded spottered shell,
Those spongey barbs that you know well
Were never yet received, but
Grow interiorly from vanity.
Green, splumed-out, surface-deep,
Sad stucco growths! You yet must threep
Real agony to reach reality.
The shelter of those splaying leaves
Won't last you long
Though now they seem so strong
Streaked by the wind, a giant's neaves.
So leap, heart, leap, split and bound,
Splairge on this new autumn stoney frosted ground.
Break, heart, break.. for skinkling store   *small*
Of pebble-truth within, for seed,
The brown bright bairnie's bead,
The smooth infinity of core.

Jessie Kesson
b. 1916

SPELL-BINDERS

I miss the ancient mariners
the tellers of tall tales
who cluttered up the close-mouth
of my childhood
and cornered me
reluctant to set but *one* believer free.

I miss the sound of Verily
their vows that proved it so
     As sure as *Death!*
         As God's my Judge!
the ebb and flow
the tides of talk receding in their sighs
     You're far owre young tae ken
        the way it was
           the things that happened
              then.

Yet.
Youth was no impediment.
'Twas then I knew
a tale is *still* a tale
be it false – or true.

ELEGY

I did not know that you were dead
A granite tomb-stone told me so
Verified that Evelyn Mary
Died long years ago.
Too young for wine for broken bread
Barred from Communion with the Host
We were released set free to go
When voices rose to paraphrase
… 'Twas on that night when doomed to know'.
We *didn't* then
Yet. We were familiar with the dead.
We knew each name carved out in stone.
Played hide and seek amongst their tombs
While others mourned to atone.
     I've chanced upon your 'Hidie' Place
     But cannot find you.

Rhoda Bulter
b. 1929

HERTACHE

Is it thunder I hear idda distance?
Is it onnly cloods darkenin da sky?
Is it lightening at flashes ahint da hill?
Is it juist wid an tang flottin by?
Sometimes I feel at a presence
Skurts me tight, till I herdly can spaek,
Whin I staand oot mesel idda mirknin,   *darkness*
An da wind oobs aboot da yerd daek.
An I hear a deep yaag fae da ocean,
Watter swittles as it rins doon da shore,
An me hert wid spleet if I hedna da feet
Ta kerry me in trow da door.

Vera Rich

AT THE RING OF BRODGAR...

At the Ring of Brodgar
The unfledged heather nestles round the stones,
Half fronded over
The tormentil glints flashing yellow eyes,
Stones, stained with lichen,
Stand, wind-swept clean against a wind-swept sky,
And high, high over,
The oyster-catchers clamour through the air,
Or settle, poising
Atop the stones, bold in brief silhouette
Like Chinese paintings.

IN THE CATHEDRAL OF ST MAGNUS

Here, like a grove of God,
Strong arches bend stone branches in a tall
Paean of polychrome; like jagged leaves,
Dog-toothing fringes arcs of majesty.
Dark forest shadows flit across a floor
Flowered with changing light, while, like the beat
Of a far cataract, the organ thrills;
        Now like the peal
            Of a high lark, it soars,
        Now like a shower
            Of summer rain, it pours,
        Now like a wind-tossed sea
            Pounding the shores...
        Now like the thunder-chariot of God
            It roars
Its tempests on the soul, the primal joy
Of elemental worship caught, distilled
By hands, God-blessed with skill,
Into the clarity of sun and rain
And silence...
            I lean back against the stones,
Red-shadowed, strong as prayer and cool as time.

Margaret Reynolds
b. 1937

SEVENTY

FOR MY FATHER

The fire and brimstone have been modified;
sermons that raged have calmed to fireside

talks. Though assumptions still control response
somehow the answers fit the faith that once

stretched tighter than the drumskin; now it deeps
in hollows that give comfort when he sleeps

and when he wakes closely yet loosely guards
his gestures and his words.

ERUPTION

Before she left she took a jug of wine
and placed it in the centre of the table
beside a dish of olives and some bread
and for an instant heard the sounds of laughter

of sons and daughters. Close the terror pressed;
it forced her on to find a ritual
to circumscribe the moment and contain
its nature in a ceremony. Then

she closed the door. The golden lava poured;
she watched the house as long as she was able,
filling the scorching air with all her prayers,
but her belief was widowed of all hope.

POVERTY

Thread
without cloth
to sew upon,

Leaf
without branch
to grow on,

Foot
without land
to walk upon,

Life
without love,
and so on.

Tessa Ransford
b. 1938

MY TROY

I am my own Cassandra and foresee
the fall of my own Troy –
   murder of the heroes
   destruction of her children
   women taken as spoils.

None can save Troy now – the very gods
are scuttling in retreat.
   She brought the dummy horse
   within her sacred space –
   it spilled out all its spite.

She was deceived and ransacked utterly
by Greek aggrandisement.
   her altars now are fallen
   golden treasures stolen
   palaces in flames.

Helen now has lost her queenliness
her beauty and her youth.
   She lives to end her life.
   The brutal brothers both
   now lord it over us.

Cressida has been flung to and fro
between opposing warriors
   who mock her now, since she
   preferred their manhood
   to the cause they fought.

Your victory Achilles shall be short
but Troy's defeat eternal.
   Her suffering shall be sung
   whenever human worth
   is slain and trampled on.

I am my own Cassandra and foresee
my death in Mycenae.
   No place for the displaced.
   We dwell within our sorrow
   in every earthly kingdom.

ALCHEMICAL SONNET

As that fanatical bird-singing morn
To elixir of enchantment responded,
Amazed in half-light of uncertain dawn
We lay in crazy alchemy enbonded.

The nugget of our hard-won self had melted,
A softening-unto-death and yet sublime,
But a more precious metal still unsmelted
Demanded mettle unimpaired by time.

Our hay-day soon descended into night,
Buried the fond treasure of our promise,
Unpractised our impracticable rite
Leaving ashen memories for solace.

Such ores refined in pain may lastly prove
Gold – in the alembic of our love.

LOVE GAINSAID

What we write is easily deleted
Crossed, blotted out; for now we see
It makes no sense: This tragedy
Misunderstood by fools, was not completed.
Heretic to Plato's real ideas
You swallowed your own words, destroying them
As thoroughly as you concocted them –
Those vows, bestowals, poems, letters, tears.

How can I, unaided, keep our treasure
Heavy behind locked lips in strongroom heart,
If you decide it was but dross and lead?
There is no thought nor whisper that can measure –
No song, no symphony, nor any art –
The destitution of a love gainsaid.

FROM *SHADOWS FROM THE GREATER HILL*

MARCH 15TH

The Ides of March blew white
blew horizontal
cut at every level,
routed out a resting place
on abraded ledges of the ruined chapel,
reduced to what endures
on its promontory.

Young trees:
ash, sycamore, beech, wild cherry,
plucked from their nurseries
in Armadale or Perthshire,
lifted with that soil still
mingled in their roots and
dipped in rich earth
to form a slender grove across the park.

Those young trees
stand
black, slim, sharp
at brave attention
on this their first trial.

Each reveals the code it carries
for shaping stillness
patterning sky.

Stand slight sentinels.
Guard new positions.
Draw yourselves up
to attain your height.
Now's no time for leaning,
for generosity.
The warm spring sun that fed your first days
and blessed your new placement with balmy pretences
has withdrawn today.

You must explore the dignity you dwell in,
hold to purpose
keep direction.
It will pass
this injustice –
and you will have grown.

DECEMBER 24TH

Apollo winters here:
strings his lyre like stars
through clouds, like swans
brightened in the wind:
practises his geometries
scaled to our particulars,
arcs, crags, promontories.

A coiled, constricted formula
translated into sections of our landscape,
our city-weathered hill:
reduced yet refined
from Delphic drama, grandeur
or golden Minoan harmony;
his circles here, triangles,
his proportions are coded
in our alpha rock,
our liquid sky, diagonal,
and huge, cold, omega, winter nights.

Alison Fell
b. 1944

FOR MYSELF

In her
thirty-three year old
long grown
prime,
still the gnarled
changeling
peeks from her
cot,
ugly as a turnip
sheep-gnawed,
little sprout
which grew
in the dark
lives hardy through
frost,
etched
with a breadknife,
lonely as
black Hallowe'en,
fire hungers
in her lantern
eyes

SIGNIFICANT FEVERS

A January night. Moonlight
strikes the window. Six sweaters
heaped on the chair,
two pairs of jeans each
containing crumpled knickers.

Proper little girls don't lose their clothes,
the text in the head goes; they fold them
the night before, they dream of piles
of linen neat as new exercise books.

Hot-head, scaly-skinned,
feeble and feverish,
I toss under the weight of quilts.

Liz rings up miserable,
comes round with lemons and whisky.
Her blouse has an ironed crease
down the outside of each sleeve.

Lévi-Strauss if I understand him right
says that women disrupt the man-made
opposition between nature and culture.

We nod and drink whisky. The
significance of the fever mounts.

There's no word for the feeling women
have of being in the wrong before
they even open their mouths,
Dale Spender says.

Provisional love. Too much of nothing
can make a woman ill-at-ease.
I'm feeling – *warren*,
hollowburnt. I object to this
set-up, let it be said.

The pale princess on her timid
bed never talks back.
She's dying, but
terribly pleased you asked.

Life is short as a shoelace,
but who knows it?
'68' I say, 'the politics of desire –
will we see it again?'
Liz says she wants everything *now*,
everything on offer.
Both of us agree that what we
would most relish at the moment
is to be madly desired. We feel
in the wrong about this too.

Lonelyhearts, Classified:
John, 34, interests publishing, astrology,
walking. Own car, limited income.
Seeks intelligent feminist 20-40,
Box Y288.

I disagree with Liz: No,
they can't all be creeps.
I'm feeling – *oldmould, grabbited*.

In the West, much was made
of killing dragons. St George
and the other heroes with all
their hardware, littering
the ley lines with sites
of slaughter and canonisation.

In the structures of fever,
never a dull moment.
(The spiral round the stone,
the spiral deep in the storm)

In the East they bound
women's feet and believed
in the harmony of man and landscape,
paths of wind, water and dragons,
forces which must not be impeded
by rails, tramways, television aerials.

Sweat stains the sheets. I
have boils, Liz has cold sores:
energies seeking escape routes.

Clean neckties of news announcers,
rescuing us from dragons.
Clean underpants. A consensus.
Under the newsdesk their toes
manipulate electric trainsets.

Proper little girls don't lose their clothes,
the text in the dream goes.
I'm feeling – *ragbitter,
hellworthy*.

The nuclear train which is found
on no timetables sidles
through London in the night,
containing dead hearts blazing:
an energy which has been eaten
and will eat.

Watching the commercials, we note
the speed of the assault, messages
addressed to envy and ego.
We toast each other, high-heeled monsters,
and no country we can name.

'What is good and bad taste is very subjective',
an ITV executive explains,
of ads shown during a play about women in Auschwitz.
'Of course we ruled out several categories
immediately – no food or vitamins,
hair preparations, holiday camps,
or gas products of any kind.'
His smile oils the screen.

Clawing at the pillows and the heaped
quilts, *High time*, I say, that the
dragon took hands with the pale princess –
shadow victim defended (sometimes) by
men and lances and smiling
back, always smiling –
first strike in a
quest selfish and long
negative to positive
(I never knew her name)

Take   eat   speak   act

(The spiral deep in the storm,
the world turning over)

knife

knife my warm handle knife my clasp tight knife my
stroke easy knife my warm cheek my cool blade knife
my flat of the hand knife my slap my safe knife my
finger and thumb no slice i am trim knife my good eye
knife my fly straight knife i am i am my good eye daddy
girl knife my don't cry my see it fly knife my throw my
show it off knife do you like i am my slice my rasp
knife my pink i am i am my dare my red will come knife
my daddy eye good girl knife see it i am i am my blood
my brave my rasp see it my pink pith knife dare do you
like me do you like my gash.

THE HALLOWE'EN WITCH

(FOR THE WIRE-CUTTERS AT GREENHAM COMMON, 31 OCTOBER 1983)

She who slips out
of doors in the hour
between blindness
and enchantment
must be flotsam or
trouble

After the moon goes down
and the cameras are asleep
she does butterfly-balance
on the turn of the night
where the weathers set sail

Safer than shuttered houses
in the space she waits
while soldiers in their muttering beds
suckle like cats at the blankets
and dream of a long eye entering,
the wall open wide

Only in the morning
she is busy and small and
they will not know her
as she wipes the scattered
sun like dust from her
black clothes
and hides in the city's
grinding eye

BORDER RAIDS

(FOR MY GRANDMOTHER)

Fierce pins plough her hair
You can tell by the angry drag
of the net
that once she was beautiful,
envied and glad of it
The nightingale of the county,
electrifying the village halls

She told me she wore winged hats
tall as gladioli,
and the hanging moon sang with her,
and how they clapped and horded
at her doors

When she went,
she went like the old bunch, cursing,
blue as smoke,
you could almost smell the burning
(Oh, they were a wild lot, the Johnstones,
border raiders,
horse stealers, setting the Kirk alight
and all their enemies inside)

With her heart tattered
as a tyre on the road
she begged for morphine
and to be done with it,
to be gone among the gliding dead

She glints now in the gooseberry bushes,
her broom hisses out at low-dashing cats
In the night she slaps up her window
and hurls hairbrushes

I've been thinking
If I could go back,
stealing up the cemetery hill
to borrow back her bones,
I'd give her to the merry gods
of the midsummer garden
who dance among the columbines
who fib and fart
and I'd tell them to trumpet her out

Sheena Blackhall
b. 1947

HEDGEHOGS

A bourich o preens	*bundle, pins*
That's quick tae fleg;	*take fright*
Twa bitticks o' een	*two spots of eyes*
An a wee, wee neb;	*nose*
Come scooshlin oot, wi the starry mune	*crawling*
Fin whins are dark an the walks are teem.	*when, bushes, empty*

Far they come frae, naebody kens,	*where*
Jinkin awa frae the sicht o men	*dodging*
An for their coortin', I maun suppose,	
They rub their snoots like Eskimos!	

HEN'S LAMENT

It's nae delight tae be a hen,
Wi' clooks an claws an caimb.
Reestin wi the rottans
In a hen-hoose for a hame.

Nae suner div I sattle doon,	
My clutch o' bairns tae hatch;	
The fairm-wife comes – a scraunin' pest –	
She cowps me aff ma cosy nest	*tips*
A tarry-fingered vratch.	*wretch*

Jist lately, though, she's changed her tune –
Ma platie's piled wi corn,
'Sup up, ma bonnie quine,' says she,
'We're haein broth the morn!'

GLOAMIN

There's a hole i the sky, at the back o the day	
Tae gang til't, naebody daurs	
For there, like a bar-fit bairn, stauns nicht	*bare-foot*
Wi his neive stap-fu o stars.	*packed full*

The day creeps oot, wi a hirplin gait	*limping*
A gomeril, spent, an dane	*simpleton*
Its lowe burned grey, as a ghaistie's goun	*flame*
An the gloamin glint, in its een.	

An ben yon chink, at the back o the cloud
Far the settin sun sits reid   *where*
Fleerichin up, till an unkent hame   *sparking*
Are the souls o the newly deid.

There's a hole i the sky, at the back o the day
A place far naebody's been
Till Daith, the lanely leerie man
Cams steekin their waukrife een.   *shutting sleepless eyes*

Liz Lochhead
b. 1947

DREAMING FRANKENSTEIN

FOR LYS HANSEN, JACKI PARRY AND JUNE REDFERN

She said she
woke up with him in
her head, in her bed.
Her mother-tongue clung to her mouth's roof
in terror, dumbing her, and he came with a name
that was none of her making.

No maidservant ever
in her narrow attic, combing
out her hair in the midnight mirror
on Hallowe'en (having eaten
that egg with its yolk hollowed out
then filled with salt)
– oh never one had such success as this
she had not courted.
The amazed flesh of her
neck and shoulders nettled
at his apparition.

Later, stark staring awake to everything
(the room, the dark parquet, the white high Alps beyond)
all normal in the moonlight
and him gone, save a ton-weight sensation,
the marks fading visibly where
his buttons had bit into her and
the rough serge of his suiting had chafed her sex,
she knew – oh that was not how –
but he'd entered her utterly.

This was the penetration
of seven swallowed apple pips.
Or else he'd slipped like a silver dagger
between her ribs and healed her up secretly
again. Anyway
he was inside her
and getting him out again
would be agony fit to quarter her,
unstitching everything.

Eyes on those high peaks
in the reasonable sun of the morning,
she dressed in damped muslin
and sat down to quill and ink
and icy paper.

AN ABORTION

The first inkling I had of the beast's agony
was the something not right
of her scrabbling, scrabbling
to still not quite find
all four feet.
Sunk again, her cow-tongue lolled
then spiked the sky, she rolled
great gape-mouth, neck distended
in a Guernica of distress.
That got through to me all right
behind glass as I was
a whole flat field away.
It took an emblem-bellow
to drag me from my labour
at the barbed words on my desk top.

Close to, green foam flecked her muzzle
and drizzled between big bared brown teeth.
Spasms, strong, primeval
as the pulsing locomotion of some
terrible underwater creature,
rippled down her flank
and her groan was the more awesome
for being drier, no louder than a cough.
When she tried to rise again
I saw it.
Membrane wrapped, the head of a calf
hung out and the wrong-looking bundle
of a knuckle. Then her rope-tail dropped
and she fell back on it, steamrollering it
under her.

When the summoned men came,
buttoning blue coveralls over
the Sunday lunches and good-suit waistcoats,
the wound string around one man's knuckles
meant business and the
curt thank-you-very-much of the other
dismissed me.

Shamed voyeur, back at my notebooks again
my peeled eyes caught the quick hoick
of the string loop, the dead thing flopping
to the grass, the cow on her knees and
up again, the men leaving, one
laughing at some punchline.

The thing is this. Left alone,
that cow licking at those lollop limbs
which had not formed properly
with her long tongue,
that strong tongue
which is a match for thistles
and salt-lick coarse as pumice stone
tenderly over and over again at
what has come out of her and she is responsible for
as if she can not believe it will not
come alive,
not if she licks long enough.

Outside she is still licking, licking
till in the blue dusk
the men in blue come back again
and she turns, goes quietly with them
as if they were policemen
and she knew exactly what she were guilty of.

REVELATION

I remember once being shown the black bull
when a child at the farm for eggs and milk.
They called him Bob – as though perhaps
you could reduce a monster
with the charm of a friendly name.
At the threshold of his outhouse, someone
held my hand and let me peer inside.
At first, only black
and the hot reek of him. Then he was immense,
his edges merging with the darkness, just
a big bulk and a roar to be really scared of,
a trampling, and a clanking tense with the chain's jerk.
His eyes swivelled in the great wedge of his tossed head.
He roared his rage. His nostrils gaped like wounds.

And in the yard outside,
oblivious hens picked their way about.
The faint and rather festive tinkling
behind the mellow stone and hasp was all they knew
of that Black Mass, straining at his chains.
I had always half-known he existed –
this antidote and Anti-Christ his anarchy
threatening the eggs, well rounded, self-contained –
and the placidity of milk.

I ran, my pigtails thumping alien on my back in fear,
past the big boys in the farm lane
who pulled the wings from butterflies and
blew up frogs with straws.
Past thorned hedge and harried nest,
scared of the eggs shattering –
only my small and shaking hand on the jug's rim
in case the milk should spill.

PAGE FROM A BIOGRAPHY

When she was seventeen she left home, secretly,
and lived rough amid the Axminster:
became clever as Caliban at knowing the most
nourishing morsels among the jewel-berries she filched
        from the chintz.
Left alone she'd sample every tipple in the drinks cupboard
(topping up the junglejuice with tapwater).
She learned to name her poison
and know her true enemies.

She'd left no note but as they
did not seem to notice she'd gone she never
heard the deejay appeal for her return
or at least a postcard, no need for an address,
to set their minds at rest.

As for the weasel, well there was no sign of one
and this family wasn't cocktail cabinet class
but occasionally she thought she glimpsed
something furry and honey coloured with Christknows
what kind of jaws and teeth slink behind the radiogram
and lie there limp as a draught excluder.

She poked the odd clandestine crust at it
flattering herself that Trouble was her Middle Name.

302

ST VALENTINE'S DAY HEART CATALOGUE

(Rap)

1. hearts are always red and shiny
2. hearts come in all colours
3. hearts are made of padded satin
4. hearts can be candystriped
5. hearts make neat pincushions
6. hearts take long slow cooking but with care and the right sauce they rival liver braincheese or sweetbreads any day.
7. Heartbroken Doctor Tells Court How Gorilla Played Cupid (Globe and Mail)
8. 'Ave a 'eart 'Arry she panted and 'ang on a tick! (Cockney porn-novel)
9. King's Road's Mary Quant told the conference that with the advent of the miniskirt in the sixties the crotch had been redefined as the new erogenous zone. Ms. Quant confided to delegates that she often jollied Plunkett (her husband, entrepreneur Alexander Plunkett-Green) into helping her dye her pubic hair some fantasy shade, or to trim it to a neat heart shape. (New Statesman.)
10. Hearts will definitely not be worn on sleeves this season (Harpers)
11. My Husband Had A Heart Transplant And Now He Loves The Donor's Wife (Confession Magazine)
12. The Heart is just another pumping muscle (Doctor Christian Barnard)
13. Having asked for directions from a friendly policeman, here she was en route to his heart, via his stomach. With a half-shudder, she left the lower bowel and set off gingerly along the rather treacherous surface of the greater intestine which coiled before her – a tunnel she wasn't too sure she saw the light at the end of. She wondered if she would have let herself get involved had she known in advance that it entailed so much messing with entrails. However, it was too late to think of that now. She loved him. She was in it, up to here.
14. Heartbreak Hotel offers cheap, out of season rates for Winterbreak Weekends.
15. Heartsease makes a sweet Victorian posy. Combined in a nosegay with love-that-lies-bleeding and a sprig of maidenhair fern, spring brides should find it a piquant bouquet.
16. Heartshaped pastrycutters can make candykisses of common or garden cookiemix. When cool, sprinkle with a little cinnamon and powdered rhinohorn.
17. How the heartshaped sunglasses and the lollipop of Lolita catapulted lovely Sue Lyons to stardom.
18. There are all manner of betrothals, and any are blessed as long as the heart be true.
19. Nowt up with the ticker, any trouble with the waterworks?
20. The heart is a lonely hunter.

21. My heart's in the Highlands.
22. Half a heart is better than no.
23. Remember, don't take any wooden
    Hearts.

AFTER A WARRANT SALE

I watched her go,
Ann-next-door
(dry-eyed,
as dignified
as could be expected)
the day after they came,
sheriff's men
with the politeness of strangers
impersonally
to rip her home apart –
to tear her life along the dotted line
officially.

On the sideboard that went for fifteen bob,
a photograph.
Wedding-day Walter and
Ann: her hair was lightened,
and her heart.
No-one really knows
when it began to show –
trouble, dark roots.

It was common knowledge
there were faults on both sides,
and the blame –
whether it was over drink
or debt no-one seems to know,
or what was owing to exactly whom.
Just in the end the warrant sale,
and Ann's leaving.

But what seemed strange:
I wondered why,
having stayed long past the death of love
and the ashes of hope,
why pack it up and go
over some sticks of furniture
and the loss of one's only partially
paid-for washing machine?

Those who are older tell me,
after a married year or two
the comforts start to matter
more than the comforting.
But I am very young,
expecting not too much of love –
just that it should completely solve me.
And I can't understand.

Valerie Gillies
b. 1948

FOR A SON'S FIRST BIRTHDAY

You were a Moses striking rock.
I let out the life
that wanted to come.

What I forget
is that restiveness:
there was the true childbed.

I watched the back of your head come:
that much form
let me know you were a son.

No bald pate, but a full head of hair;
the appearance of your scalp unfolding
the reality of a new mind within.

Born wringing wet as the moorlands,
you were blue
as blaeberry behind their leaves.

Your first breath
blew you up so pink
you were ragged robin in the marshes.

What I forget
is your first sound:
loud, brilliant and reedy.

ROADGANG WOMEN

Here come the stonebreakers,
these little skeletons of the roadgang women
with their long strands of hair
knotted high at the back of their skulls.

They take a moment
to wipe sweat from around their eyes
with a corner of torn sari.
The road waits for their hands.

306

They carry stones in baskets on their heads,
like apricots marked by a bird's beak,
wizened and bruised:
both heads and stones.

A raised track on a country without limit.
A big sun beating off any shade.
A woman stitches a piece of shadow
with an upright stick and sacking.

She breaks stones below it.
Once, she eats from a shallow tin dish
with not much in it;
some steamed riceflour cake.

Old women of thirty
work in the day's quickforge.
Nobody can work like them,
though they pause to quarrel or laugh.

They must find fire nourishing,
as the salamander does, who is meant
to live in the flames,
where others would die, she lives happily.

FELLOW PASSENGER

Mister B. Rajan, diamond buyer,
crystallises from this travelling companion.
He goes by rail, it seems, by criss
and cross, Hyderabad to Bangalore
to Madras, Madras, Madras,
seeking the industrial diamond.

He brings new orient gems from hiding.
Himself, he wears goldwealthy rings
of ruby, and, for fortune,
another of God Venkateswaran.
His smile is a drillpoint diamond's,
incisive his kindness.

Sparrowboned, he walks unstable passageways,
living on boiled eggs and lady's-fingers
with noggins of whisky to follow.
He dreams of his house, the shrineroom picture
of Sai Baba, corkscrew-haired young saint.
And he has at home beautiful hidden daughters.

TRICK OF MEMORY

Three years north
of the tropic of cancer
have changed me.
I no longer put oil on my head
or sew jasmine, to sleep with it in my hair.
I pinch shut the letters from India:
their language seems wrinkled
as the features of cholera.
It is difficult to picture their writer,
crosslegged on a teak swing indoors.

I used to long for a pair
of the silver toe-rings worn by women
married into the princely family.
Now their faint sound would seem
unattainable as a skein of geese.
I used to love the royal blue
of the two-tone sun-and-shade
silk sari worn by the mothers
of pretty boys named Dilip or Ajoy.
Now that blue would seem
remote as a piece of sky.
I do not care to remember
what husband might entitle me to toe-rings,
or what son would have sent me peacock saris.

THE TIGER TAKES ALL

This tiger passed your house
near dawn, as out we stumbled, calling dogs
from their frenzy by our shouts
while all the guns were cocked.

And there the tiger glowed,
still springing handsomest beneath the stars.
Had our eyes, too, its tawny yellow
in one of our avatars?

Houseguest among your daughters,
arranging my sari by the heavy wooden screens,
   my bedcover is skinned fur:
     I blink tigerish dreams.

   Now do we not recall
our smiles were virtuosities for two
   yet lonely as the morning growl
     of tiger at an altitude?

   Well they might be, those looks
that say goodbye in stripes and brights;
   the square frilled head which took
     its leave of sharp light.

   For there you, Shivé, glow
without the black streaks or white belly;
   only the naked exercise of power
     is tiger in your valley.

Catherine Lucy Czerkawska
b. 1950

BEING ME

Roughly once a month
The leaves framed by my
Kitchen window crawl
Over the sky.
They are black
Like currants
Or (more menacingly) insects perhaps
And there are shiny gaps
Where the light comes between.
I perceive how we
Talk in metaphors mostly
And hardly know that
We and all our days
Consist of them.

Roughly once a month
The world and its straight ways
Aggravates.
Instead there is this
Ill-at-easiness with things,
This crookedness of things.
Odd details of shape
And colour and sound intrude,
Odd connections that the mind makes,
Odd affinities it knows.
Things are other and the same at once.
Anything is possible.

Roughly once a month
I think that maybe
I could put
This faculty to some good use
Being me.
As long as I am reassured that
You will not hedge it with
Fearful rationality
And call it madness.
Well I will defy you:
Not insane but sometimes seeing.

THE FOX

The fox walked through an autumn dark
His skin alert, his nose involved
In a hundred scents
All shifting towards decay.
His flesh cried for flesh.
In a little pool
Fringed with mist
Flat and thick dark he
Saw a perfect moon reflected.

Her beauty quickened his heart
Plump as a cherry
To bite and suck.
His head full of the moon
The fox's eyes flew right and left.
Now he would have her
Deftly and like a scragged chicken
By the neck –
Chicken or cherry was all one
To itching teeth.

The fox pounced.

But the deceitful moon sailed on
And the lunatic fox dripped home
Hungry.

THE OTHER SIDE OF THE STORY

I am no pale princess out of fairy tale.
I would have my skin too thick to feel
The pea through my piled feather beds.
There is no prince charming enough
To dare my Rapunzel tower
Nor bring me a glass slipper
Nor weave me a rose encrusted bower.

But I will be malicious Morgan
Who wished fair Guinevere dead
Or Blodeuedd who was created flowers
And for her lack of faith
Became the hunting owl instead.

311

And I will be the wicked queen
Who cuts off her suitors' heads
One by gory one,
Who carries fatal apples
And a poisoned spindle
And dances to her death
Beneath the blazing sun.

Dilys Rose
b. 1954

DREAM FEAST

Like pie-dogs, they cower at the tail end
of every interminable queue, alert to nothing
but the sudden movement of a foot. They pick
and scratch at the periphery, unseeing,
distractedly drawing uncertain circles in the dirt.
They're etched on the scenery. They'll not desert
for richer dunghills but spend a lifetime
praying for windfalls, rotting morsels.
The last lean moon convinced them
they'd be mad to stray. So they linger,
the ugly unlovable glut of dull-eyed waifs
clutching the filthy hem of the world's skirt.

They sleep a lot: their dreams are crammed
with sides of beef, mountains of rice.

Kate Y.A. Bone

SOME GHAISTS HAUNT HOOSES

Some ghaists haunt hooses, this ane haunts my hert,
An' aye I harken for its lichtlie step
That gars a stound gan thru' me. Ilka pairt
Is rugged tae mind what aince this meant tae me.
Nae skeleton I see; this ghaist is busked in flesh,
An' a' my thochts are hidden in the bluid
That feels the dule, but disna bode tae tell   *grief, stay*
What aince I felt but noo I maun forbear.
Some ghaists haunt hooses, this ane haunts my hert.

Morelle Smith

THIS MORNING, THE WINDOW WAS DARKENED

This morning, the window was darkened
By huge wings beating against the pane.
You remarked how cloudy it was today.
I could have told you but –
You had to go to post a letter,
And there really wasn't time.
Maybe .... sometime.
But down the road they came so close
I had to beat them off
And, tripping over a stone, a hand came out to help me –
It could have been the beginning of another story
Lasting a lifetime and a glance
But his eyes were bright and ticked like clocks
And his briefcase was packed so full
I was afraid it would burst open any minute.
The wild woods are no place to go before the moon is up
And I couldn't trust these signposts in another language.
All the people walking round with placards on lapels.
I tried to piece the words together,
But somehow they never made sense.

You turned the room upside down yesterday,
Looking for a summer that you lost last year
Muttering, it must be here somewhere.
I wondered if you'd gone to the wild woods to look for it,
But afraid to say it,
In case you found it there.
Coming back through the streets flowing like rivers,
I only just made the door in time
And had to recite the magic word, over and over,
To stop the walls caving in.
And I can still hear them outside,
Fainter now, spasmodic but insistent.
The birds are singing well tonight you said
When you came in. Did you make that phone call?
I could have told you why not but –
You had to meet a friend for tea
And there really wasn't time.

THE CAMEL-DRIVER'S STORY

Some laughed at him
As he set out to climb the high mountain
Saying it did not exist
For they had never seen it
And pointed to what he was leaving behind.
But he put their mouths in a cradle
And left it to rock in the valley.

On his way some asked him to stay with them
Enjoying the pleasures of life.
They dismissed his arguments as fig-leaves
And burst an apple in his face.

Some asked him to stay with them
To tell them of his wisdom.
When he refused
They chewed his tongue
And flung it far away
But nursed an itch inside their bones
To talk about him with their friends
And mystify their children.

Some asked him to stay with them
To help them build houses and grow food
But he saw the houses were built on a river
And the crops grew by themselves.
So they littered his way with hammers and shovels
Dug holes in his silence
And drank from the tears in his eyes.

When he left
He found the mountain-top
Where he had been all the time
And all the people he had passed were there as well
But surging past him
Like the striving bubbles from beneath a waterfall
Gasping to be free
But so intent on swimming
That they didn't notice him.

Only then could he turn back
Into their vision
And help them to be free.

THE STAR-REAPER

In the city, it was cold, but dry,
Not wild and snow-laden like here.
Another world, of buses, noise,
Traffic-lights and passing people.
Grey skies and mists
But pavements dry,
And telling nothing of this world
Of snow, deep ice and freezing wind,
Waves of snow,
Drifting in the wind,
Across the roads,
Across the trees,
Deep, buried, sleeping trees,
Sleeping in the snow,
Their buried summer dreams.

I miss you now, wood-elf,
With your dreams of deer,
Your eyes of snow, and stars
And buried moonlight,
Leaping up the years and tears and fallen pines,
Star-leaping,
Buried in sky-forests,
Orion, sky-reaper,
Through the diamond fields, to meet me.
Your name sky-hunter
Echoes in the darkened side of Venus,
Through bright Saturn's ring
And the scattered plains of Sirius,
The hunter's friend.

Cold, the city,
With your sleeping sun bright in some other sky,
Your sun bright in a day of white earth, and white sky,
Tears from some ice-hearted god.
And you among the trees,
Deep in the frozen tracks of some elusive stag,
Heart of fire,
Spirit of earth,
It moves somewhere among the pines,
Somewhere in front of you,
Frozen footprints cast in the stone snow.
I see the star-reaper,
Moon-sister,
Sunfire in snow forest,
Earth-lover and sun-born.

Sally Evans

SILLY QUESTION TO A POET

Why didn't you use the word *halcyon*
instead of *kingfisher*?
Consider, will you
how kingly are kingfishers
and how very blue.
The beautiful word *halcyon*
shimmering in a dictionary
flutters its glory,
shelters in papery shade
while the direct river narrowly
ripples with alternative meanings
and drains in blue clarity
of kingfisher days.
The hyacinth halcyon
whistles querulous
over swamped pasture
in fresh but trivial tone
hollow as an osier,
pastel streaked with rust.
I say the kingfisher's a must
in my vocabulary,
streams in my mind
stocked with shining fishes
winding through Hardy's novels
read for the first time at sixteen
when lovers under oak trees
had a mystery they have lost.
The peace in the oxbow,
the solitary water,
the small bird's weather eye upon a bough
are more important now,
and to impress by whispering *halcyon*
is to try to gild the gold
hidden ready to gleam, already made
by artists mingling blue and brown and cream
adding and mixing in a dream
to make a flowerlike form with beady eye
upon a bush
that wings down to the ripple, a flash
for food, a rare, mysterious
and delicate magician in a wood.

Christine Quarrell
THE CLOSE MOUTH

Weans greeting
Folk meeting
Toilets flushing
Lassies gushing
Wives talking
Men walking
Dogs running
Sills sunning
Middens clattering
Smells battering
Senses thrilling
Stairhead sobbing
Tenements throbbing
Couples winching
Doughballs mincing.
     EAST
     WEST
     NORTH
     SOUTH
All life began at
the close mouth.

Jenny Robertson

JOURNEY NEAR THE BORDER. POLAND 1986

Our bus lurched on.
I saw a sign: Treblinka.

The black road ran between frozen fields.
We were thirty kilometres from death.

A hundred thousand ghosts,
thin and white as snowflakes
melted into mud.

Bundled in bulky wrappings
people pushed out at their destinations.

Ours was an unheated building
where, with repentance and prostrations
the Orthodox began their Lent.

Six weeks later,
instead of Resurrection,
their cries of mercy mingled
with a cloud of radiation.

No feast now for those who fasted.
Ploughed fields spring green with sickness.

Barbed wire shuts nothing out.

Sue Gutteridge

FOR EILEEN

You said
'I like the shape of our friendship'.
True, it had a definite beginning.
The accidental meeting at the formal luncheon
Was instant joyful connection.
We were the last to leave. Drunk at 4 p.m.,
You thanked our host for coming.

But its beginning, like its end, was out of character.
For the most part it was a married female friendship
Conducted Monday to Friday, nine to five.
No all nighters.
No no-holds-barred drunken confidences.
No weekends.
Married female friendship –
An art form, bred of constrictions
Which are the stuff of it.
Fitted in the spaces between the children.
Half sentences thrown across the noise of playing
Or fighting.
Patrick kicked me.
I want the doll's pram.
Clara's cut herself – there's *blood*.
I want a biscuit.
Anyway, it's time to go.
The men are coming home.

Was it death that did it.
Gave the friendship its shape.
Hot-housed it.
Gave it the lovers' mode
Of precious, planned-for time
Stolen from children, men, work.

Long journeys for brief meetings
Rich with significance.
Mutual, pleasurable self-analysis when you said,
'I like the shape of our friendship'.

Angela McSeveney

ULTRASONIC SCAN

In a standard issue one size shift
I present myself as a votive offering.

I am laid out
and warm oil poured
across my body.

Cold metal skims along my skin
and makes invisible incisions.

I can't read the omens
as my insides flicker
on a black screen.

Ellie MacDonald

BITTER HAIRST

Nae stars i the lift
juist a croodlin wund tae be my jo,
an daurkness straikit out
ayont eternity.

Ahent my een
I ken o emptier places lost tae licht,
an endless ghaists that aince
were you an me.

sky
crooning, lover
stretched

Alison Smith
b. 1962

SECRET ANNEXE

Prinsengracht
in Amsterdam
and in among the houses
there is one
where tourists clump
where soldiers thumped
and clumped
and gutted
and the shock
appears in eyes
of those who feel the fear
still hidden here
and a little girl
look
dressed in red
skips singing
throwing shadows
right across the page
and someone shaves her hair
and strips her bare
and sews a star into her skin
but she commands
the audience's full attention
with her song
and suddenly a fiction's tangible
words speak the truth
throw shadows
on the flickering film
of frightened people
with their shaven
flickering eyes
behind barbed wire
the celluloid
a naked yellow image
of our own humanity
and holidaying we
who fear to feel
in comfy numbness
pay our money
at the door
and clump the stairs –
the secret's out –
and black cracks web this houses floor

BUDDY CAN YOU SPARE A

time?
It's twenty five past
bloody
three
kids playing
on the tip
and nothing coming
through the
post or in the
paper or the
pub more likely
well
why don't you
bloody
look instead of
watching programmes
for the kids
out playing
        circus owners
        nurses
        doctors
        teachers
        tailors
        soldiers
        sailors
        rich men
        poor men
        cops and
rubbish
for the
bloody
tea
I told you
twenty five past
bloody
three

Kathleen Jamie
b. 1962

SKEINS O GEESE

Skeins o geese write a word
across the sky. A word
struck lik a gong
afore I wis born.
The sky moves like cattle, lowin.

I'm as emty as stane, as fields
ploo'd but not sown, naked
an blin as a stane. Blin
tae the word, blin
tae a' soon but geese ca'ing.

Wire twists lik archaic script
roon a gate. The barbs
sign tae the wind as though
it was deef. The word whistles
ower high for ma senses. Awa.

No' lik the past which lies
strewn aroun. Nor sudden death.
No' like a lover we'll ken
an connect wi forever.
The hem of its goin drags across the sky.

Whit dae birds write on the dusk?
A word niver spoken or read.
The skeins turn hame,
on the wind's dumb moan, a soun,
maybe human, bereft.

SHIPS/ROOMS

Though I love this travelling life and yearn
like ships docked, I long
for rooms to open with my bare hands,
and there discover the wonderful, say
a ship's prow rearing, and a ladder
of rope thrown down.
Though young, I'm weary:
I'm all rooms at present, all doors
fastened against me;
but once admitted I crave
and swell for a fine, listing ocean-going prow
no man in creation can build me.

WEE WIFEY

I have a demon and her name is
> WEE WIFEY
I caught her in a demon trap, the household of my skull.
I pinched her by her heel throughout her wily transformations
until
> she confessed
>> her name indeed to be WEE WIFEY
and she was out to do me ill.

So I made great gestures like Jehova: dividing
land from sea, sea from sky,
> my own self for wee wifey
(*There*, she says, *that's tidy!*)

Now I watch her like a dolly
keep an eye,
> and mourn her;
for she and I are angry/cry
> because we love each other dearly.

It's sad to note
> that without
>> WEE WIFEY

I shall live long and lonely as a tossing cork.

Madeline Munro

THE FLY CATCHERS

I

They grew around the edges of the bog
and by the old Drum road, well overgrown
by then, the leaf-curled butterwort, fly catchers,
unsocial little flowers, not just as rare
as the scented orchids we might want
to press, but always their violet innocence
flawed by those specks of irksome flies,
motes in the eye.
              Two-tiny-faced insectivore,
no one had told us of your acid baths, your
rosette appetite—though in the orchards
you and your Venus friends have taught sharp
gardeners yet another trick. Out-timing bees
they shower the hoodwinked trees with phantom
sex, and smile as seedless apples swell.

II

Set in typical pose on a final
favoured perch behind museum
glass, Spotted Flycatcher. Little
Artful Dodger, filching flies from the air
with a snap of that flat beak trap.
He does without the showy garb. His aerobatic
shocks outshine Collared and Pied,
Tyrant and painted Paradise.

And how absurd to speculate for long
on that skilled savagery. Outside
the city seethes with plundering
need. The multitudes who, too, must feed
push by – and would not see, even before
their eyes, on the green farms,
those darkened buildings, unholy, summerless,
that hold the prey of tyrant sapiens.

DEATHS

Sometimes a cow lost
All the strength to rise, day
Upon day returning adamant
To her damp misery until
We, too, accepted there would be
No miracle.
         And then the other
Stricken days the knackery
Arrived, lorry with pulley
And rope, grey merchant in death
To take away a mare, still
Young, the dreaded fever caught
In the summer grass.
         And
Stuck in my head, one stifling
Day, the pass stuffy with smells
Of last year's straw, old sacks,
And lack of air, watching
A hen, caught in the throes
Of something like the staggers;
Cruel burlesque of rise and fall;
Lesson in death – the slow,
Indifferent struggle, the squeezing out
Of life, wrung to the last half jerk.

Elise McKay

UNRAVELLING KNOTS

He was good
at unravelling knots.
Fingers, blunt but purposeful,
slowly and surely,
followed the string's clue —
in, over, through and out —
unknitting the world's distress.

Tangles were handed to him
to undo. Strangers brought
him their tensions.
And smiling a little,
secretly,
he made things straight.

Why then the tangled life?
Did he not see the net he wove
around himself
until too late,
or did he think he could undo it —
given time?

The shears were too swift
that snipped the knot,
and left the ends to dangle;
uselessly, remote.

MIGRANTS

Waxwings on cotoneaster,
mirror imaged, side by side;
what cold wind blew them here, to find
in this grey land their Africa?
Fleeing a barren waste, they settled
for red berries on a rain-swept bough
and called it paradise.
Our giddy swallows chitter south;
each to its necessary place.
But we, with broken instinct trailing
in the snow, can only peck the scraps
cold fortune flings, or else, despairing,
fly too near the sun, and melt the wax
from stiff and unaccustomed wings.

THE AMMONITE

He took the fossil gingerly
and held it in his hand.
It was too hard
for his ten years to comprehend.
I thought he'd ask, how old?
Instead, 'What was it like – alive?'
I tell him 'It was curled and soft,
could feel, like you.'

His hand in answer tightens round the stone
as though he tried to force the meaning through.
No use; his grasp uncurls,
he loses interest, hands it back.
But I have seen the fossil imprint
on his palm. Three million years
to make this one soft mark.

Margaret Gillies-Brown

EMIGRANT JOURNEY

There was the comfort and the all mod-con of home
With its recognisable dangers;
There was the journey,
The endless coming on of the same wave,
The no-land time of ocean and high hopes
Until the icebergs rose
Like crystal palaces...

There was the moving days
And weary nights of train-hours overland,
The trees, the lakes, the straight and rolling plains
Until time stopped in sheer fantasy
Of a pre-dawn winter morning –
Gloved hand swinging the iron-hard handle
Of a frozen water pump
At the edge of a bark-rough cabin;
Above, the sky, moving strange magnificence,
Voile curtains of colour
Changing, shifting imperceptibly;
Below, the star sparkled snow –
A virgin's looking glass
Where spruce trees shot the only shadows
That made no movement –
Silence, immensity of silence,
Oil fires were burning brands
Reaching for chiffon robes
Of an aurora of dancers
Repeating dream sequences...

I tried to wake from unreality,
Felt my spine freeze,
heard coyotes howling down the night.

LAND OF THE COYOTE

Born again
Into fresh experience.
Time stops a moment
Beside these wood-shingled walls
Of this small shack
In my new wilderness:
Lets me catch up.

From a brazen sky
A cutout bluebird drops,
Flies overhead,
A stray thought pulses the mind –
Colour must deepen with proximity;
Straggling cottonwoods,
With bark on spindle-trunks
Smooth, silver-white
And ragged at the edges,
Give small pattern to this extensive plain,
The straight-snake train
Slides past the tall grain tower,
That apostrophe's the vast near-empty page,
And blows the world's most hollow sound:
All else is silent – still
Except for pale gold coyote
That lopes along like large Alsatian dog
And turns with curiosity
To watch a stranger species
Lonely in *his* land.

OPPOSITE SIDES OF THE MOON

Full moon
To Anne is
White light on night fields,
Strangeness through the orchard,
Glory on magnolia,
Loveliness over Loch Ard,
Silver calmness on the river ...

But to Jane
A fierce pulling of the tide,
Towering waves within her,
Storm in the brain,
Unreasonable rage,
The crash of crockery,
Disturbance in an empty room –
A lunatic arrangement.

JUNG AT BOLLINGEN

He chose to place on a pedestal
The stone the builder rejected;
Strange and significant, he thought,
That the accurate Swiss
Should have cut this rock corner wrongly:
He set it facing the lake,
Sat looking at it long
In sunshine and rain
Trying to absorb its different nature,
Feel its inscape;
Then, with love, he began to carve
Keeping true to line and texture,
The whirl and whorl of it –
First the all seeing eye
Facing the terrace of his tower –
And for the rest, mostly
The sculpture of words
Borrowed from alchemy and ancients,
Intuitive symbols flowing to finger-ends
Showing the whole –
The long rolling round of life.

Later in his green garden
He must often have looked at it,
Watched as it imperceptibly gathered patina,
Felt quiet satisfaction in this –
His orison.

STRONTIUM 90

How can it be
That this rambling river,
This hill-clasped village
Gave you your name?
Just now splashed with the brilliance of broom
Deep in a dream of bluebells,
Heady with scent of hawthorn.

Yet, climb out of this valley a little
And it becomes more possible.
These stark mountains,
Hard outlines on the sky,
Turbulent outcrop of rock
Cloud grey, moonscaped,
The harsh heather, dark,
Lacking all promise of purple
The rubble-rounded holes,
Gashed ground,
This miner's ruined home;
A single rowan tree
Planted to ward off evil
Now marks the spot.

Here no bird sings.

Notes

p. 19 *Tàladh Dhòmhnaill Ghuirm (Donald Gorm's Lullaby)*
The song was composed for the infant, Donald Gorm of Sleat (in Skye), by his nurse. The nurse praises the baby as he will be in manhood; the celebration of the martial and domestic prestige she wishes for her charge is clearly drawn from professional praise poetry. The text given here is collated from several different versions and it is unlikely that any one performance of the song would have been this long. The song uses the earliest form of folksong metre in which the lines of stanzas of irregular length are linked by the assonance of the final stressed syllable (in this case the penultimate syllable). The song opens and closes with a complicated refrain and each half-line is followed alternately by the refrain *Nàile bho ho hò* and *Naile bho ho hì.*

Naile: the refrain should probably be regarded as meaningless vocables, but Ronald Black of the Department of Celtic at Edinburgh University holds that the refrain may originally have been an invocation to St Naile, a disciple of Colum Cille at Iona.

beatings with slippers: a reference to the traditional forfeit in cards of six strokes of the slipper on the palm of the hand.

the land of MacSween and MacKay as well: that is, north west Scotland and Gigha.

Cù Chulainn: the hero of the Old Irish Ulster cycle, he inherited magical powers from his father, the god Lugh, and was thus able to defend Ulster single-handedly from her enemies.

fiana: bands of warriors whose exploits are recounted in the Middle Irish Fenian Cycle.

Ossian and valorous Oscar: Finn mac Cumhaill was the leader of the most celebrated band of Fenians. His son was Ossian, famed for his musical abilities; his grandson was Oscar.

p. 25 *Bothan Airigh am Bràigh Raithneach (The Sheiling in Brae Rannoch)*
Because of the location, it can be assumed that it was a young MacGregor woman who composed this song. It is remarkable for the vigorous and confident way she describes her husband's ability to provide for her by cattle-lifting, and for her delight in the sheiling way of life when cattle were taken to higher ground for summer pasture. The metre is syllabic with seven syllables in each line. The final words of every couplet rhyme throughout the song, so the couplets may be sung in quatrains, the second couplet of one quatrain becoming the first couplet of the next.

hair fillet; kertch: a woman's marital status was shown in traditional Gaelic dress by the form of her head-dress, the hair fillet (*stiomag*) being worn before marriage, and the kerchief (*bréid*) being worn after marriage.

Mearns; Caithness: Caithness and the Mearns had been part of Gaelic territory and the cattle there were still regarded by the Gaels as legitimate quarry.

p. 29 *Craobh an Iubhair (The Yew Tree)*

The song is composed to the MacKay chief of the Rinns of Islay. It is typical of waulking songs in the way in which it mixes traditional forms of praise from the learned tradition with unlearned incantations for the man's safety and frank evocations of courtship. The composite authorship is evident in the sharp changes of matter and mood. Tree imagery has its origins in pagan beliefs and is used here as a metaphor for the young man's virility and fruitfulness. The metre is common in waulking songs: each line is sung twice, first as the second line of the couplet, then as the first.

penny of fortune: this was kept as a charm which was turned three times at the new moon.

p. 33 *'S fliuch an oidhche 'n nochd 's gur fuar i (Wet the night is)*

This waulking song demonstrates two common themes abruptly juxtaposed: the first is the celebration of good seamanship; the second describes the plight of a young woman who is abandoned by the father of her child because of the difference in their social status.

with no drinking from saucer: this is a reference to celebrations in the chief's drinking-hall, from which she is now excluded.

p. 35 *Dh'éirich mise moch Di-Dòmhnaich (I rose early on Sunday morning)*

The song tells of rape, pregnancy and subsequent ostracization. In referring to her head-dress, she explains her unmarried status and the man's failure to act honourably. With a frankness characteristic of the unlearned tradition, the song names the man who is the offender.

p. 39 *Clann Ghriogair air Fògradh (Clan Gregor in Exile)*

The MacGregors were the most famous of the dispossessed clans. As the clan of Glenorchy they came under Campbell dominance in the late thirteenth century when the MacGregor heiress, Mariota, married a Campbell and died without progeny. From that time on the Campbells treated the MacGregors as illegal squatters and tried to remove them from their hereditary lands. Matters became worse after 1604 when James VI issued a letter of fire and sword against the MacGregors for their aggression against the Colquhouns of Luss. Further acts of 1607 and 1633 abolished the name of MacGregor, prohibited their meeting or baptism and allowed for their extermination as vermin. These measures were not repealed until 1775.

The song is said to have been composed by a MacGregor woman who was harbouring fugitives in her house. When the enemy approached she went outside to attend to some task and sang this song to mislead them about the fugitives' whereabouts.

Panegyric elements of learned poetry exist alongside the peculiarly fresh diction of folk poetry in the details given of her own position by the road, the images of the murdered man in the bog and of her own pain like an arrow in her thigh. The metre is stressed and the couplets sung in continuation quatrains.

Straths: St Fillans, Loch Earn.

Handsome John: John Drummond, the king's deputy forester, was killed by the MacDonalds of Glencoe in 1589. The MacGregors themselves were not involved, but at the time they were the allies of the MacDonalds.

the Loops of the Lyon: the spot where the river meanders below Loch Lyon.

p. 43 *Nach fhreagair thu, Chairistiana? (Won't you answer, Cairistiona?)*

The core of the song was composed by the foster-mother of Cairistiona who watches as the boat carrying the girl's coffin approaches. The lament follows a waulking song metre; one line is sung at a time, followed by the chorus of three lines.

the King's Court: the court of the Lord of the Isles in Islay?

in order to wed you: changing from the third to the second person, and back again to the third, is a common feature of all Gaelic poetry.

p. 45 *An T-Eudach (The Jealous One)*

This song is often ascribed to Màiri Nighean Alasdair Ruaidh, but this is not certain. In any case the song has been adapted as an art song of its genre. The mention of the poet seeing Fiunary on the Morvern coast suggests it may have been composed by Màiri while exiled on Mull. Accounts of jealousy are not uncommon in the folksong tradition. The couplets are sung as continuation quatrains with the following chorus: *Hìrirì ohù robhó/Roho ì ohì o.*

p. 47 *Ailein Duinn, o hò hì, shiubhlainn leat (Brown-haired Allan, I'd go with you)*

The song was composed for the poet's lover, Allan Morrison of Lewis, who was drowned on his way to their wedding. The poem is a very late example of folksong metre where lines are linked by end rhyme only into stanzas of irregular length.

the wetness of your clothing: this method of defining grief by what it is not (known as 'emphatic antithesis') is a common feature of Gaelic folksong.

English schooling: the Statutes of Iona of 1609 sought to undermine Gaelic culture by insisting that clan chiefs send their eldest sons and daughters to the Lowlands for their education.

the place where you are: Anna's prayer not to be buried on land but in the place where Allan drowned appears to have been granted. It was reported that when she died of a broken heart shortly after composing this song, the crew carrying her coffin over to Harris had to throw it overboard because of the roughness of the seas. The coffin was seen to go against the direction of the current and to sink in the same spot that Allan's boat went down. The sea then became calm and the crew returned home safely.

your breast's blood: the drinking of the beloved's blood was part of the mourning ritual from pagan times.

p. 51 *Luinneag Anna Nic Ealair (Anna Nic Ealair's Song)*

This is an ecstatic (and even erotic) love-song to Christ, based on the Song of Solomon. Donald Meek of the Celtic Department, Edinburgh University, suggests that the work was composed after 1807 when the Old Testament became available in Gaelic. Meek believes that the song demonstrates the influence of Gaelic folksong on the Gaelic hymns of the evangelical movement. He also suggests that the reference to illness in verse one may refer to the outbreaks of cholera in Argyllshire at that time. The stanzas consist of two couplets which are linked by end-rhyme; the lines of each couplet have two stresses and are linked by *aicill* in which the last stress of the first line rhymes with a word in the second line.

p. 53 *A Phaidrín do dhúisg mo dhéar (Oh Rosary that woke my tears)*

The work is a lament in the classical style for her husband, Niall Og MacNéill, Constable of Castle Sween, Knapdale. The metre is *rannaigheacht mhór*, a syllabic metre used by professional poets, requiring each line to have seven syllables and to end with a monosyllable, and for *aicill* to exist in each couplet.

lion of Mull: kennings are an ancient feature of praise poetry; in stressing his nobility, a chief is saluted as some animal, plant, hill, geographical location, etc.

Dùn an Oir: a place in south-west Ireland. The distance poet bands would travel to attend a chief's court was a measure of the chief's influence and munificence.

Sliabh Gaoil: a hill in Knapdale.

Sanas: Machrihanish in Kintyre.

Dùn Suibhne: Castle Sween on the island of Gigha.

the cluster of nuts on the tree: reference to chiefs as nuts, apples or saplings were used to give a sense of the chief's fertility and promise.

p. 57 *Cumha Ghriogair MhicGhriogair Ghlinn Sreith (Lament for MacGregor of Glenstrae)*

The poem was composed by an aristocratic Campbell woman whose husband was beheaded by her own father in April 1570 (according to the chronicle of the vicar of Fortingall). The metre is *séadna*, a syllabic metre requiring a count of eight syllables ending with a disyllable in the first line of each couplet, and seven syllables ending with a monosyllable in the second line of the couplet. The monosyllables at the end of each couplet must rhyme. The song is still sung as a lullaby in the Hebrides, and is known by the title *Griogal Cridhe*.

latha Lùnasd (Lammas morning): Derick Thomson has shown that *latha Lùnasd* (1st August) is probably a mistake for *Latha Tùrnais* (Palm Sunday) as it is unlikely that MacGregor would have been detained after his capture in August until the following April before being beheaded (*see Scottish Gaelic Studies*, 10, p. 68).

a curse on nobles and relations: the poet curses her own father who captured her husband.

I'd have drunk my fill: the drinking of the beloved's blood, the beating of palms and the tearing of hair were all part of ritualized mourning.

Grey Colin: Ruthven's daughter: Colin Campbell of Glenorchy was married to Ruthven's daughter.

Campbell in Taymouth: MacGregor was executed at Taymouth Castle.

without apples: again, the tree/fruit imagery is part of the evocation of the fertility of the chief (for an interesting discussion of the pagan tree-cult, see John MacInnes in *Sar Ghàidheal: Essays in Memory of Rory MacLean* (An Comann Gaidhealach, 1986)).

Baron of Dull: whom her parents had wished her to marry.

p. 61 *Atà fleásgach ar mo thí (There's a young man in pursuit of me)*; *Is mairg dà ngalar an grádh (Woe to the one whose sickness is love)*

These short poems show the influence of the courtly tradition which was spread to Scotland and Ireland by visiting clerics. Invariably, the theme is about clandestine or unrequited love in which love as a sickness is a common metaphor. The metre is *rannaigheacht mhór*, that is, seven syllables per line, end rhyme link the two couplets and *aicill* within the couplets.

p. 63 *An talla am bu ghnàth le Mac Leòid (The Hall of MacLeod)*

The poet is reputed to have composed this work on the spot when she was asked by Sir Norman MacLeod of Berneray what sort of eulogy she would make for him when he died. The poem follows the panegyric code very closely in describing the chief in his drinking hall, in hunting deer and in his character and appearance, but the metre differs noticeably from the classical form. This metre can be described as 'strophic'. Each verse reads as three lines, the first two having two stresses, and the third three. The first two lines are a stroph each; the third line is one and a half strophes. The final word of each stroph in the verse rhyme with each other; the final word of the half stroph rhymes with all the other words in that position in the poem.

Fenian Warriors: see note to *Tàladh Dhòmhnaill Ghuirm (Donald Gorm's Lullaby)*.

p.67 *Cumha do Sheumas MacGillean (Lament for her husband James MacLean)*

The poet was born on Coll and composed eulogies to several of the MacLean chiefs. This lament for her husband has elements of classical panegyric in the controlled praise she gives to her husband, but it also has strong elements of folksong in the account she gives of her own emotions, particularly in her sense of threatening insanity in the wake of her grief, and in the sense of immediacy given by such details as his empty seat being the cue for her song, or his death taking place the previous Monday.

an arrow in my liver: again, a concrete image of the poet's pain.

Body white as bog cotton: white skin conformed with the ideal of beauty; it is often compared with bog cotton, foam, chalk or swan's down.

the narrow bed of deal-boards: this common euphemism for a coffin, and the description of the body turning black in the grave, are derived from mediaeval religious poems on death.

Maol Ciarain: 'the tonsured one of St Ciaran' referring to a follower of St Ciaran (d. 549), apparently famed for his sufferings.

p. 73 *Alasdair a Gleanna Garadh (Alasdair of Glengarry)*

This is a formal elegy (as opposed to the lament of the preceding poem) composed by the poet on the death of Alastair Dubh, the eleventh MacDonald of Glengarry who died in 1721 or 1724. The poem is remarkable for the near-incantatory use made of kennings (in verses five to seven) to give a sense of the dead man's former nobility, bounty and ferocity. The poem is syllabic and contains eight syllables per line with penultimate stress.

wounds again torn open: a possible reference to the poet's recent loss of her husband and daughter.

our tallest oak trees: another tree image of the chief's strength and virility.

Sir Donald, his son and brother: three MacDonald chiefs of Sleat died within three years of one another.

capercailzie: the wood-grouse, from *capull-coille,* 'horse of the wood'.

without finishing the matter: a possible reference to the risings of 1715 and 1719 in support of James Francis Edward Stuart, the Old Pretender.

you were the oak ... you had no connection with the lime tree: ancient learning (common to Ireland and Scotland) believed certain trees to be noble while others were servile.

your son in your position: the chief was succeeded by his son, John, who lived until 1754.

p. 77 *Comhairle air na Nigheanan Oga (Advice to Young Girls)*

This poem belongs to a certain genre of moralistic poems which warn against the dangers of premarital intimacy. Another poem, *An aghaidh na h-obair nodha (Against the New Work),* was composed in response to *An obair-nogha (The New Work)* in which the poet, George MacKenzie, celebrated a degree of sexual licence. Sileas' poems insist on caution before a promise of marriage, rather than marriage itself, an attitude which perhaps reflects the traditional practice in Scotland of a couple marrying once the match had proven itself fruitful. The eight-line stanza is made up of four couplets each with two pairs of internal rhymes; the couplets are linked by end rhyme on the final syllable.

With your smooth tongue ... into the grave: the notion of love as a sickness or wound was a tradition of courtly love and is used here to demonstrate the artificiality of a young man's declarations in his attempts to deceive a young woman.

however hard his knee: 'knee' is a literal translation of the Gaelic. I do not know whether the image is that of wrestling, or whether it is a euphemism for the man's sexual arousal.

p. 81 *Do Rìgh Seumas (To King James)*

This is a Jacobite song designed to raise support for James Francis Edward Stuart who claimed the throne after the death of Queen Anne in

August 1714. Anne had named George, Elector of Saxony, her heir, but when he acceded as George I, James declared his intent to oppose George by freeing Scotland from the Union. The subsequent Jacobite Rising did not begin for nearly a year when supporters of the Stuarts gathered at Braemar in 1715, but James did not come to Scotland until December of that year when the Rising was almost over. The poet's assertion, then, that King James was on the water (verse 1) should not be taken literally, but should be understood as a rousing call to his supporters. The song is based on an existing tune and chorus. Each stanza consists of five two-stressed lines which are linked by end rhyme.

his powerful fleet of vessels: James had hoped that Louis XIV would support his cause and supply him with troops and vessels. However, Louis died in September 1715, and his successor, the Duke of Orleans, did not offer any help because he did not want to antagonize George I.

tyrant Whigs: the Whigs supported the Union and the House of Hanover.

a pig in the saddle's no horseman: Colm Ó Baoill, the editor of Sileas's poetry, knows of no such proverb, but knows of other instances of the Hanoverian monarchs being referred to as pigs by the Jacobites.

they bought off you with a coinage: this probably refers to the government's attempt to buy the peace of the Highland chiefs with an annual sum of £360.

a poisoned onion: this is a pun on the Gaelic for 'union', *uinein*, and the word for 'onion', *uinnean*.

(The above details are from Colm Ó Baoill's *Bàrdachd Shilis na Ceapaich*.)

p. 85 *An Iarraidh Dhiomhain (The Vain Search)*

This is based on the common mediaeval themes of contempt for the world and its pleasures. It asserts that all glory must end in death and that lasting peace can only be found in God. The metre is four stresses per line in four-line stanzas. The lines have internal rhyme and end rhyme between lines one and two, and between lines three and four. The poem does not have the rhythmic subtlety associated with earlier Gaelic poetry.

p. 89 *Nuair Bha Mi Og (When I was Young)*

This is one of the best examples of the type of nostalgic songs composed for exiled Gaels; it evokes the beauty of the place the Gaels had been forced to leave, for economic, if not for legal, reasons. The communal way of life is remembered and compared with the ruined villages which are one of the few reminders of those who once lived there. The singer now returns to her native place only as a summer visitor. The exaggerated sentiment of these songs, designed for mass appeal, is very different from the taut presentation of emotion found in many of the earlier poems of this anthology. The lack of subtlety of thought is reflected in a lack of rhythmic subtlety.

p. 91 *Brosnachadh nan Gàidheal (Incitement of the Gaels)*

The poem is a campaigning song for the candidates put forward by the

Highland Land Law Reform Association for the elections of December 1885 to counter the laws of land tenure which threatened the welfare of the Highland crofters.

Put up Charles ...: the candidates mentioned in this verse are Charles Fraser MacIntosh who was returned for Inverness-shire; Donald MacFarlane who was returned for Argyll; Angus Sutherland who failed to be returned in Sutherland.

the Courier: *The Inverness Courier* supported Sir Kenneth MacKenzie and waged a campaign against MacIntosh.

a fleet of battleships ...: In November 1884 Sheriff Ivory sailed into Uig in Skye and proceeded to Staffin and Valtos with a company of soldiers to put down unrest among the crofters.

by the landowners ...: the Commissioners of Supply in Inverness cooperated with Ivory by sending policemen to Skye to put down the unrest.

the accursed angels: Ivory referred to himself and his troops as 'Satan and his angels'.

the Braes: the 'Battle of the Braes' took place on 17 April 1882 when Ivory and his policemen were attacked by the women and men of the Braes (in Skye) after arresting the leaders of the unrest there. In 1881, the crofters of the Braes had refused to pay their rents as a protest against the loss of their traditional grazing rights to Ben Lee in favour of a large sheep farmer. When notices of eviction were sent to them, the crofters retaliated by burning the notices. Ivory was then sent to round up the ringleaders. In the ensuing 'battle' seven women of the Braes and twelve policemen were wounded.

Who went with books: books and broadsheets were circulated, often sponsored by the landlords, to persuade the crofters to emigrate. The pictures of opportunities for emigrants were often falsely optimistic and many Highlanders felt they had been deceived.

(The above details are courtesy of Màiri Mhór's editor, Donald Meek.)

THE BALLAD TRADITION

Although some of the ballads can be dated by identifying historical events, etc., no systematic attempt has been made here to date individual works. The earliest written forms of the ballad date to 1650, but because these works are part of an oral tradition, they are clearly of much earlier origin. There is a huge corpus of works in the tradition and those presented here are but a representative sample. Spelling is phonetic, and often inconsistent, in the texts used here. The source of the text is identified after the title.

p. 114 *The Bonny Hyn* (F. J. Child, *English and Scottish Ballads*, 50)

This text is originally from Herd's *Scottish Songs* (1776) where there is a note stating that the ballad was copied from the mouth of a milkmaid in 1771. The narrative is that of a young girl who is seduced by a young lord whom she discovers is her estranged brother. She kills herself by putting a knife through her heart and is buried by her brother beneath a holly tree.

He tells his father that a beautiful hind is buried there and that is why he cannot leave the place.

p. 115 *The Gypsy Laddie* (*Child*, 200A)
Gypsies cast a spell over a lady and lure her from her castle. Her husband pursues her with a band of fifteen men, but fails to win her back.

p. 116 *Lady Daisy* (*Child*, 269A)
The text is originally from Aytoun's *Ballads of Scotland* where it is recorded that the song was 'from the recollection of a lady residing in Kirkcaldy'. Lady Daisy falls in love with the handsome kitchen boy and becomes pregnant by him. When her father finds out he kills the boy and delivers his heart in a cup of gold to Lady Daisy. Moved by his daughter's grief, the father repents his hasty action.

p. 118 *The Wylie Wife of the Hie Toun Hie* (*Child*, 290A)
In material collected for Scott's *Minstrelsy*, this song is recorded as being from 'the recitation of a female friend, who sang it to a lively air'. A group of men are drinking in an inn and talking about women. One says he would like to seduce a beautiful young girl who lives in town. The innkeeper's wife entices the girl to the inn, locks her in a room, and invites one of the men to seduce her. She has a child and two years later he returns to marrry her.

p. 119 *Get Up and Bar the Door* (*Child*, 275A)
A housewife is busy at her work when a cold wind blows in the house. Her husband bids her bar the door, but she will not. They agree that whoever speaks first will do it. Two travellers come, but getting no reply to their questions, begin to eat and drink all in sight. One of the travellers proposes to take the husband's beard off, while the other plans to seduce the wife. Only then does the husband speak and has to bar the door. References to this song suggest that it was much bawdier in the original.

p. 121 *The Four Marys* (*The Greig-Duncan Folk Song Collection*, 195B)
There are many versions of this ballad and several interpretations of this particular event. In general, it is agreed that the reference is to one of Mary, Queen of Scots' maids-of-honour who was executed for the murder of her newborn infant. Under Scots law, infanticide was a crime punishable by death until 1803. The girl's lover, the queen's apothecary, was also executed, but in some versions, Darnley (the king) is implicated.

p. 122 *Jamie Douglas* (*Andrew Crawfurd's Collection of Ballads and Songs*, 61);
This tale about unfaithfulness stems from an incident in the eighteenth century, when Colonel William McDowall of Lochwinnoch, returning home from the West Indies, brought back a negro servant, the 'blackemoor' of the poem.

p. 123 *Jock T' Leg and the Merry Merchant* (Crawfurd, 59)
This work belongs to the Robin Hood group of ballads. Jock and the Merchant put up at a tavern and order a meal. Jock tries to get the merchant to pay for it, he refuses, and they go 'dutch'. Jock gets up in the

night and tries to persuade the Merchant to make an early start on the road. The Merchant wants to wait until daybreak because he fears Jock will try to steal his money, but Jock promises to see him through safely. Once on the road, Jock reveals that he is the famous robber, Jock the Leg. He whistles and his armed men appear and Jock promises safe passage in return for money. But the merchant still refuses to pay up.

p. 125 *Bonnie Belleen* (Crawfurd, 64)
A beautiful young girl is sitting at the window when a young man passes by and declares his love. He marries her and takes her to his castle, but she longs to return home. He becomes enamoured of another woman and marries her. In response, Bonnie Belleen kills herself by jumping from the Castle tower and drowning in the waters below.

p. 127 *The Twa Sisters* (Child, 10B)
This famous old ballad is a story of jealousy between two sisters. In this version, the older sister lures the younger to a rock by the sea and pushes her in. She drowns, but her body, covered with gold and pearls, is recovered from the sea.

p. 129 *Allison Gross* (Child, 35)
An ugly witch has captured a young man and keeps him tied up in her tower. When he refuses to be her lover she turns him into a worm. Come Halloween, the queen rides by the tree where he is lying, strokes him three times and he is restored to his normal shape.

p. 130 *Fair Annie* (Child, 62E)
Fair Annie is a king's daughter who is kidnapped and sold to a nobleman, by whom she has seven sons. The nobleman decides he wants a wife of royal lineage and brings home a bride who is in fact Annie's sister. When the nobleman learns this, he sends the sister home and returns to Annie.

p. 132 *Fair Mary of Wallington* (Child, 91C)
All seven sisters of a family are destined to die of their first child. Five have already died and one of the remaining two, Mary, vows never to marry. The other marries a knight and in less than a year is going to give birth. She sends for her mother, but dies before she arrives. Mary refuses to marry, but her mother makes her, even although she knows it will mean her certain death..

p. 134 *Lamkin* (Child, 93A)
A mason, Lamkin, has built a castle for a lord who will not pay him. With the help of the lord's nurse he enters the castle and takes his revenge by killing the lord's baby.

p. 136 *The Hawthorn Green* (Crawfurd, 4)
This cautionary tale is about a young girl who is admiring a flourishing hawthorn tree when she asks the tree what would happen if she cut it down. The tree replies that it will blossom again, but that the girl, once she has lost her virginity, cannot do the same.

p. 136 *The Cruel Stepmother* (Crawfurd, 7)

A stepmother is jealous of her husband's only daughter and plots with the cook to have her murdered. The cook plans to kill her with his knife and serve her in a pie. The kitchen boy tries to save her, but he is threatened. When the father comes home, he asks where his daughter is and is told she has gone to a nunnery. But the kitchen boy tells him she is in the pie. The father has the stepmother burned at the stake, has the cook put in a pot of boiling lead, and makes the kitchen boy his heir.

p. 138 *The Bush of Broom* (Crawfurd, 27)

A young man meets a girl on the road from London to Newcastle and invites her to rest by a bush of broom. After he tempts her with money, she goes with him. Nine months later she has a child and the young man returns and marries her.

p. 139 *The Mason's Dochter* (Crawfurd, 39)

The beautiful daughter of a mason goes into service in a lady's household. There she meets the young steward who wants to marry her, but she dispassionately rejects him. One night he gets her drunk and goes to bed with her. Believing she is pregnant, he offers to marry her. Again, she rejects him. Afraid of what she might do to the child when it is born, he follows her and one night sees her throw something into the river. It is the child and he rescues it and cares for it. Two years later he takes her to meet the child and tells her how he saved it. But she murders the child and he is left broken hearted.

p. 142 *The Fraserburgh Meal Riot* (*Greig-Duncan*, 240A)

On 6 March 1813, a riot – in which fisherwomen played a prominent part – took place in Fraserburgh. The women were protesting the exporting of grain during a time of food shortage. They overturned a cart belonging to the grain dealers, Charles (of the poem) and George Simpson, and chased them through the town.

p. 142 *The Beauty of Buchan* (*Greig-Duncan*, 434)

The song refers to the disappearance of sheep from Buchan in the north-east of Scotland at the time the hills began to be cultivated. The poem is reputed to have been inspired by 'The Flowers of the Forest' and is often sung to that tune.

p. 144 *Hooly and Fairly* (*Greig-Duncan*, 584A)

p. 146 *Burke's Confession* (*Greig-Duncan*, 192D)

William Burke and his accomplice William Hare were the notorious murderers who supplied the Edinburgh anatomist Dr Robert Knox with bodies for dissection. When caught, Hare turned king's evidence and Burke was hanged.

p. 147 *Johnnie, my Man* (*Greig-Duncan*, 587K)

p. 148 *The Twa Brothers*

This is an example of a very old ballad (Child, 49) which was part of the repertoire of Jeannie Robertson, one of the great balladeers of modern

times. Two brothers are playing together at school, but decide to go up the hill and wrestle. As they fight, a knife falls out of one of the brother's pockets and mortally wounds the other.
(Song collected by Hamish Henderson and text printed by Herschel Gower and James Porter in *Scottish Studies*, Vol. 14, 1970, Part One.)

p. 149 *The Trooper and the Maid* (Hamish Henderson)
    Again, this is Jeannie Robertson's version of an old ballad (Child, 299). A trooper comes to the house of a girl in the evening and is kindly received. They spend the night together and in the morning are awakened by a trumpet. He must leave her and she begs him to come back and marry her. But he has no intention of returning.

p. 150 *The Hobo Song* (Hamish Henderson)

p. 151 *MacCrimmon's Lament* (Stephanie D. L. Smith, 'A Study of Lizzie Higgins as a Transitional Figure in the Development of the Oral Tradition in the North-East of Scotland', M. Litt. thesis, Edinburgh, 1975, p. 216)
    The MacCrimmon's were hereditary pipers to the MacLeods of Duevngan on Skye. The original is reputed to have been composed by MacCrimmon's sister on his departure with the men of MacLeod for Culloden.

p. 151 *Far over the Forth* (Smith, p. 221)

p. 152 *The Lassie Gathering Nuts* (Smith, p. 223)

p. 153 *The Silver Casket*. Mary Queen of Scots wrote the sonnets in French and 'Last Prayer' in Latin. The translations are from Clifford Bax's *The Silver Casket*.

p. 154 *Ane Godlie Dreame*
    Written during the Reformation, the poem is in the form of a dream vision and is vehemently anti-Catholic. Pinkerton notes that 'the dreadful and melancholy of this production are solely of the religious kind, and may have been deeply affecting to the enthusiastic at the period in which it was written' (quoted in *Select Scottish Ballads*, vol. 1, p. xxvii). That it was indeed popular is evident from the number of printed editions; the earliest edition of the work is 1603 (Edinburgh, Robert Charteris) and there were a further eight editions, the last in 1737.

p. 156 *My dear Brother, with courage beare the crosse*
    The sonnet is addressed to John Welch who, in 1605, was confined in the Castle of Blackness with other Presbyterian ministers on the charge of high treason.

p. 162 *The Flowers of the Forest*
    This lament was written for the Battle of Flodden (1513) in which the Scots were defeated by the English. The work was originally an old folksong and both versions given here are reworkings of the original.

p. 284 *At the Ring of Brodgar*
    The ring of Brodgar in Orkney is a circle of monoliths of prehistoric

date. The ring is 370 feet in diameter and at present there are twenty-seven stones (the original number seems to have been sixty).

p. 284 *In the Cathedral of St Magnus*

St Magnus, Earl of Orkney, was murdered on the island of Egilsay on 16 April 1117. He was honoured for his virtue and piety. He is buried in Kirkwall Cathedral which is dedicated to him.

Biographical Notes

Adam, Jean (1710–65) b. Crawfurdsdyke. Early in life she was a governess/housekeeper to a local minister, but later set up a day school for girls which in the end bankrupted her. She was a great admirer of Samuel Richardson and walked to London to meet him. She ended her life destitute and was admitted to the poorhouse in Glasgow where she died. *Miscellany Poems* (1734).

Anderson, Jessie Annie ('Patience') (1861–?) b. Ellon, Aberdeenshire. At the age of eleven she had an accident which left her paralysed. As a consequence she never attended school but was taught to read by her mother. *Across the Snow* (1894), *Songs in Season* (1901), *Songs of Hope and Courage* (1902), *Lyrics of Life and Love* (1903), *Old-World Sorrow* (1903), *Legends and Ballads of Women* (1904), *Lyrics of Childhood* (1905), *A Handful of Heather* (1906), *A Book of the Wonder Ways* (1907), *Flower Voices* (1908), *Dorothy's Dream of the Months* (1909), *Breaths from the Four Winds* (1911), *This is Nonsense* (1926), *A Singer's Year* (1928).

Angus, Marion (1866–1946) b. Aberdeen. She spent her childhood in Arbroath where her father was a minister. Like Violet Jacob, she is one of the poets of the vernacular revival whose work appeared in Hugh MacDiarmid's *Northern Numbers*. *The Lilt and other verses* (1922), *The Tinker's Road* (1924), *Sun and Candlelight* (1927), *The Singin' Lass* (1929), *The Turn of the Day* (1931), *Lost Country and other verses* (1937), *Selected Poems* (1950).

Baillie, (*née* Home) Lady Grizel of Jerviswood (1665–1746) Daughter of the Covenanter, Sir Patrick Home, Earl of Marchmont, she was reputed to have been involved in her father's intrigues against the government, adventures which later became the subject of *The Legend of Lady Grizel Baillie* by Joanna Baillie, who was a direct descendant (see next entry). Her work was published in Allan Ramsay's *Tea-Table Miscellany* (1724). See Countess Ashburnham, *Lady Grisell Baillie, a Sketch of her Life and Character* (1893) and R. Scott-Moncrieff (ed.) *The Household Book of Lady Grisell Baillie, 1692–1733* (1911).

Baillie, Joanna (1762–1851) b. Bothwell, Lanarkshire. Her first book of poems, *Fugitive Pieces*, was published anonymously in 1790. Her *Metrical Legends* (1821) are based on Scottish historical characters and her *Collection of Poems* (1823) shows her interest in Scottish landscape. She did not marry and made a considerable reputation for herself as a dramatist in London. See L. Longman (ed.) *The Dramatic and Poetical Works of Joanna Baillie* (1853) and Margaret S. Carhart, *The Life and Work of Joanna Baillie* (1923).

Bateman, Meg (1959–) b. Edinburgh. Studied at Aberdeen University and now teaches Gaelic in Edinburgh. Her work has appeared in *Chapman* and *Gairm. Oran Ghaoil* (Dublin, Coiscéim, 1990).

Begbie, Agnes Helen (n.d.) *The Rosebud Wall and other poems* (1906), *Christmas Songs and Carols* (1908).

349

Bell, Maria (d. 1899) *Songs of Two Homes* (1899).

Blackhall, Sheena (*née* Middleton) (1947–) Writes mainly about the north-east, often in Buchan dialect. She also writes short stories. *The Cyard's Kist and other poems* (1984),*The Spike o' the Lan' (1986), Hame Drauchtit* (1987).

Bone, Kate Y. A. *Thistle-bylaws* (1971).

Bulter, Rhoda (b. 1929) Writes in Shetland dialect. Her work has been anthologised in *A Nev Foo a Coarn: Shetland Poems* (1977) and *Linkstanes: Shetland Poems* (1980).

Burton, Ella (1845–?) b. Edinburgh. She was a prominent member of several educational and arts societies – The Ladies Educational Association, The Society of Arts, The Watt Institute – and gave lectures on such subjects as 'Women's Suffrage', 'Chaucer and his Contemporaries', 'The Heroines of Shakespeare', etc. She translated French and German poetry and published her work in a variety of newspapers.

Cailéin, Iseabail Ni Mheic (Isabel, Countess of Argyll) (*fl.* 1500). She was of the household of the Earl of Argyll, but may have been a daughter rather than the countess. Her work appears in various collections taken from *The Book of the Dean of Lismore*.

Caird, Janet (1913–) She also writes novels and chidren's stories. *Some Walk a Narrow Path* (1977) and *A Distant Urn* (1983).

Campbell, Anna (of Scalpay, Harris) (*fl.* 1773).

Campbell, Mary Maxwell (1818–86) Best known for 'The March of the Cameron Men' and 'The Lament for Glencoe', she also composed the music for them.

Carnegie, Mrs Lindsay (*née* Rait) (1844–?) b. Anniston. The daughter of a soldier, she married Henry Alexander Fulton Lindsay, one of the heroes of the Indian Mutiny. *Children of Today* (1896).

Cassady, Mary H. ('Vera') (n.d.) Her poetry was published mainly in local newspapers. *Sweet Vale of Orr, Lays and Lilts of Galloway* (1920).

Corcadail, Aithbhreac Inghean (*fl.* 1460) *Scottish Verse from the Book of the Dean of Lismore* (ed. William J. Watson) (1937).

Cortis-Stanford, Florence (n.d.) *Westering Winds* (1922).

Cousin, Anne Ross ('A.R.C.')(1824–1906) She was married to a minister of the Free Church of Scotland and wrote a number of hymns which became very popular. *Immanuel's Land and other poems* (1897).

Craig-Knox, Isabella (1831–1903) b. Edinburgh. The daughter of an Edinburgh hosier and glover, her poetry and essays were published regularly in *The Scotsman* under the name of 'Isa'. In 1859 she went to London where she became assistant secretary to the National Association of Social Science. She continued writing (mainly fiction) which was serialised in *The Quiver* and other magazines. *Poems by Isa* (1856), *Poems: an offering to*

Lancashire (1863) ('Printed and published for the Art exhibition for the relief of distress in the cotton districts'), *Duchess Agnes and other poems* (1864), *Songs of Consolation* (1874).

Cruickshank, Helen Burness (1886–1975) b. Hillside, Angus. She was educated at the village school and at Montrose Academy. Thereafter, she worked as a civil servant in Edinburgh for most of her life. She wrote mainly in the vernacular and was one of the early poets of the modern revival. A close friend of Hugh MacDiarmid, her correspondence with him shows that she was a mainstay of his family during the 1930s. In 1927 she founded the Scottish branch of PEN and remained secretary until 1934. Her *Octobiography* gives an interesting account of her life and much useful information about literary life in Scotland in the early modern period. *Up the Noran Water* (1934), *Sea Buckthorn* (1954), *The Ponnage Pool* (1968), *Selected Poems* (1950), *Collected Poems* (1976), *More Collected Poems* (1978).

Czerkawska, Catherine Lucy (1950–) b. Leeds. She now lives in Scotland and, in addition to her poetry, has published short stories and has written radio plays. *White Boats* (with Andrew Greig) (1973), *A Book of Men and other poems* (1976).

Elliot, Jean of Minto (1727–1805) Third daughter of Sir Gilbert Elliot of Minto, her only work to survive is her version of the 'The Flowers of the Forest'.

Evans, Sally *Poems and Rhymes*(1983), *Poems and Translations* (1983) and *Some Sunny Intervals* (1985).

Fell, Alison (1944–). In London in 1970 she worked with the Women's Street Theatre Group and *Spare Rib*. She has also established herself as a novelist with *Every Move you Make* (1984) and *The Bad Box* (1987). Poetry: *Bread and Roses* (1982), *Kisses for Mayakovsky* (1984), *Crystal Owl* (1988).

Fraser, Lydia Falconer (Miller) (d. 1876) She was the daughter of an Inverness merchant, but received part of her education in Edinburgh from George Thomson, Robert Burns's friend. She married Hugh Miller and was thought the intellectual equal of her famous husband; she edited several of his posthumous works.

Fraser, Olive (1909–77) b. Kincardineshire and lived in Redburn, Nairn. She graduated from Aberdeen University in 1927 with Honours English and an award for the most distinguished graduate in arts. She subsequently attended Girton College, Cambridge, where she was awarded the Chancellor's Gold Medal for poetry in 1935. She served with the W.R.N.S. during the war and after the war was librarian at the Bodleian Library. In 1956 she was diagnosed schizophrenic and spent many years in an asylum before being restored to health in 1961 by a woman doctor who correctly diagnosed her condition as hypothyroidism. *The Pure Account* (1981), *The Wrong Music: The Poems of Olive Fraser 1909–1977*, edited by Helena M. Shire (1989).

Frater, Anne, b. Lewis. She is currently studying Gaelic and French at Glasgow University. Her work has appeared in *Gairm*.

Garry, Flora (*née* Campbell) (1900) A graduate of Aberdeen University, she trained as a teacher and taught at Dumfries Academy and Strichen School. She married Robert Campbell Garry, Regius Professor of Physiology at the University of Glasgow. Although some of her work is in English, she is best known for her poems in the Buchan dialect. Her work was so popular in the North-East that her first collection of poems was sold out in a week. *Bennygoak and other poems* (1974).

Gillespie, Margaret (*née* Duncan, of Glasgow) See *The Greig-Duncan Folk Song Collection*, Vol. II.

Gillies-Brown, Margaret (n.d.) *Give me the Hill-Run Boys* (1978), *Hares on the Horizon* (1981), *The Voice in the Marshes* (1979), *No Promises* (1984).

Gillies, Valerie (1948–) b. Edmonton, Alberta. She spent her childhood in Edinburgh where she attended university. Later she lived in Mysore, South India, and that experience is reflected in her poetry. *Bed of Stones* (1981), *Each Bright Eye: Selected Poems 1971–1976* (1977).

Glover, Jean (1758–1801) b. Kilmarnock. A contemporary of Robert Burns, her work appears in *The Scots Musical Museum* (1792) where it is recorded that Burns described certain poems as 'the composition of Jean Glover'. She married a travelling player and was considered profligate. She died destitute.

Gordon, Anna (Mrs Brown of Falkland)(1747–1810) b. Aberdeen. Daughter of Thomas Gordon who held the Chair of Humanities at Kings College, Aberdeen, she married Revd Andrew Brown who had the church at Falkland. She learned her songs and stories from her mother, her aunt and family servants, and she is one of the richest sources of the ballads of the oral tradition. After her death her work was preserved in three manuscripts: the Jamieson Brown, the Tytler Brown and the Fraser Tytler Brown. The Tytler Brown manuscript was in Sir Walter Scott's possession in 1795 and 1800, that is, immediately prior to the publication of *Minstrelsy of the Scottish Border*. See David Buchan, *The Ballad and the Folk* (1972).

Grant, Anne of Laggan (*née* McVicar) (1755–1838) b. Glasgow. She spent most of her childhood in America where her father was an army officer. On returning to Scotland, she married a minister and they settled in the parish of Laggan in Inverness. She learned Gaelic and her interest in Highland culture is reflected in her work. After her husband's death, she went to live in Edinburgh and, noted for her wit and conversation, she made friends with Sir Walter Scott, Lord Jeffrey and Henry MacKenzie. *Poems on Various Subjects* (1803), *The Highlanders and other poems* (1808), *Eighteen Hundred and Thirteen: a poem in two parts* (1804). See *Memoir and Correspondence* (3 vols., 1844) edited by her son, John P. Grant.

Gray, Mary (1853–?) b. Huntley, Aberdeenshire. She spent part of her childhood in England and Germany and worked for a time as a telegraph clerk in Huntly. In 1876 she went back to Europe to continue her studies and to teach, but returned to Scotland in 1882 where she obtained an L.L.A. from St Andrews University. She is noted for her translations (sometimes into Scots) of Goethe, Schiller, Heine, Herder and Jacobi. *Lyrics and Epigrams after Goethe and other German Poets* (n.d.).

Gutteridge, Sue. She is a sociologist who has worked in adult education and is co-author (with Rebecca and Russell Dobash) of *The Imprisonment of Women* (1986). Her poetry has appeared in *Original Prints II* (Polygon).

Hamilton, Elizabeth (1758–1816) b. Ireland. She was brought up by her aunt in Stirlingshire. A friend of Joanna Baillie, she too lived in London for some time before she settled in Edinburgh. Her literary reputation rests mainly on her novel, *The Cottagers of Glenburnie* (1808), but she wrote on a wide range of subjects and published pamphlets on public education.

Hamilton, Janet (*née* Thomson)(1795–1873) b. Shotts, Lanarkshire. A spinner and weaver, she married in 1809 and had ten children. When she was young she taught herself to read, propping books on the spinning wheel so that she could read while she worked. She did not learn to write until she was fifty-four and at that time began publishing in Cassell's *Working Man's Friend*. *Poems and Prose Works of Janet Hamilton* (1885).

Higgins, Lizzie (1929–) b. Aberdeen. She is the daughter of Jeannie Robertson. She worked for many years as a fish-filleter in Aberdeen before becoming a professional folk singer. She was initially interested in pipe music and that interest is reflected in her songs. See Alie Munro, 'Lizzie Higgins and the oral transmission of ten Child ballads' in *Scottish Studies* Vol. 14, 1970, pp. 155–63.

Hunter, Anne (*née* Home) (1742–1821) She married the surgeon John Hunter in 1771 and published her work only after his death in 1793. She lived in London and befriended Joanna Baillie. Some of her poems were set to music by Haydn. *Songs and Poems* (1802).

Hutchison, Isobel Wylie (b. 1889) An author and horticulturalist she travelled to Alaska in the 1930s and published an account of her travels (with poems) in *North to the Rime-ringed Sun* (1934). *Lyrics from West Lothian* (n.d.), *The Northern Gate* (1927), *The Song of Bride* (1927), *Lyrics from Greenland* (1935).

Jacob, Violet (*née* Kennedy-Erskine) (1863–1946) b. Montrose. Daughter of the eighteenth Laird of Dun, she married an army officer and spent her early married life in India then returned to Scotland and settled in the north-east. Greatly interested in folklore, history and language, she published (in addition to her poetry) several historical novels and short stories. She is one of the earliest and most outstanding poets of the modern vernacular revival. *Verses* (1905), *Songs of Angus* (1915), *More Songs of An-*

gus and other poems (1918), *Bonnie Joan and other poems* (1921), *Two New Poems* (1924), *The Northern Lights and other poems* (1927), *The Scottish Poems of Violet Jacob* (1944).

Jamie, Kathleen (1962 –) b. Renfrewshire. She grew up in Midlothian and studied philosophy at Edinburgh University. In 1981 she received the Eric Gregory award for poetry and in 1982 a Scottish Arts Council Book Award for *Black Spiders*. *Black Spiders* (1982), *A Flame in your Heart* (1986) (with Andrew Greig), *The Way we Live* (1987).

Johnston, Ellen (*c.* 1835–73) b. Hamilton. She published poems on industrial life under the pseudonym of 'Factory Girl'. She is known to have received £50 from the Royal Bounty Fund, but died destitute at the Barony Poorhouse in Glasgow. Her work was published in *Bards of Angus and Mearns. Autobiography, Poems and Songs* (1867).

Kesson, Jessie (Jessie Grant Macdonald) (1916 –). b. Inverness. She lived in Elgin for a time with her mother but spent part of her childhood in an orphanage. Her early life later became the subject of the books on which her considerable reputation as a novelist now rests – *The White Bird Passes*, *Glitter of Mica* and *Another Time, Another Place*. After a chance meeting on a train, she became friends with Nan Shepherd who encouraged her to write. She subsequently produced novels, short stories, poems and scripted over ninety plays for the BBC. She now lives in London and is writing her autobiography.

Lindsay, Lady Anne (*née* Barnard, Countess of Balcarres) (1750–1825). She is reputed to have written 'Auld Robin Gray' when she was twenty-two. See *Lays of the Lindsays* (1824).

Lochhead, Liz (1947–) b. Motherwell. She attended the Glasgow School of Art and was an art teacher for eight years before becoming a full-time writer. She is also a dramatist and the folklore and faerytale themes of her poetry are carried over into her drama, *Blood and Ice* (1982), *Dracula* (1985). *Memo for Spring* (1972), *Dreaming Frankenstein and Collected Poems* (1984), *True Confessions and New Clichés* (1985).

Lochhead, Marion Cleland (1902–85) b. Wishaw, Lanarkshire. She was educated at Glasgow University but subsequently lived in Edinburgh most of her life. She also wrote novels, children's stories, biographies and popular histories. Her interest in traditional culture is reflected both in her creative work and in such studies as *The Scots Household in the Eighteenth Century*. She was one of the founder-members of the Scottish branch of PEN and was made a Fellow of the Royal Society of Literature in 1955. *Poems* (1928), *Fiddlers Bidding* (1939).

Lundie, Jane Catherine (1821–84) b. Kelso. She was married to a minister of the Free Church of Scotland and wrote mainly hymns.

Lyon, Mrs Angus (*née* L'Amy) (1762–1840) b. Dundee. She married the minister of Glamis where she lived most of her life. She left four books of poems in manuscript on her death and her work was published posthumously in *Bards of Angus and Mearns*.

Lyon, Anne (n.d.) *Poems* (1937).

Mabon, Agnes Stuart (of Jedburgh) (n.d.) *Homely Rhymes* (1887).

MacArthur, Bessie J. B. (1889–?). Her interest in Highland culture is reflected in her poetry and her drama. *The Starry Venture* (1930), *Scots Poems* (1938), *Last Leave* (1943), *From Daer Water* (1962), *And Time Moves On* (1972).

MacDonald, Ellie. Lives and works in Dundee. Her first collection of poems, *The Gangan Fruit*, is forthcoming.

MacKellar, Mary ('The Bardess of Clan Cameron', 1836–90) b. Fort William. *Poems and Songs in Gaelic and English* (1880).

MacKenzie, Hannah Brown (n.d.) b. Hamilton. She spent part of her early life in America and when she returned to Scotland she eventually settled in Glasgow. She worked as a reviewer for the *Glasgow Herald* and published her poems and stories in *The People's Friend, Highland Magazine, Scottish Reformer, Scottish Nights* and *The People's Journal*. *Worthy of Trust* (1885).

MacQueen, Mary (Mrs Storie)(1786–1854) Reputed to be of a travelling family, she married William Storie, a labourer, in Loch Winnoch on 25 August 1821. They emigrated to Canada in 1828 and settled in the township of MacNam by Hull in Upper Canada. Fourteen of her songs appear in *Andrew Crawfurd's Collection of Ballads and Songs, Vol. I.* (ed. Emily B. Lyle), Scottish Text Society, vol. 9.

Marshall, Agnes ('Marchbank')(1846–?) b. Edinburgh. A popular short story writer, her work was published mainly in *The People's Friend* and *The People's Journal*. *Songs of Labour* (1872), *Home and Country* (1892), *A Swatch of Hamespun* (1895).

Mary, Queen of Scots (1542–87) b. Linlithgow, the daughter of James V and Mary of Guise Lorraine. She spent most of her early life in France but returned to Scotland in 1561 to claim her throne. But her accession threatened Elizabeth I of England and Mary was imprisoned and forced to abdicate in favour of her son James VI. She was beheaded by Elizabeth on 8 February 1587 at Fotheringay Castle. Her sonnets formed part of the much disputed 'Casket Letters'. See *The Poems of Mary, Queen of Scots*, ed. Julian Sharman (1873), *The Silver Casket: Being the love letters and love poems attributed to Mary, Queen of Scots*, ed. Clifford Bax (n.d.), *Mary, Queen of Scots, An Anthology of Poetry*, ed. Antonia Fraser (1981).

McKay, Elise b. Kirkcaldy. She has published her work in *Aquarius, Words,* and *Outposts*. *Unravelling Knots* (1984).

McSeveney, Angela. She is a graduate of Edinburgh University and her work has appeared in *The Edinburgh Review, The London Magazine, Chapman* and *Original Prints II*.

Melville, Elizabeth (Lady Culross, the Younger, *fl.* 1599). Daughter of James Melville of Halhill, married John Colville (son of Alexander, commendator of Culross). She seems to have enjoyed a considerable reputation for her religious verse, but the two poems reprinted here are the only works which survive. The full version of *Ane Godlie Dream* is printed in *Early Scottish Metrical Tales*, ed. David Laing (London, 1889).

Mitchison, Naomi (*née* Haldane) (1897–) b. Edinburgh. Educated at the Dragon School, Oxford, she married the Labour politician G. Richard Mitchison (later Baron Mitchison). She lived in Africa in the 1960s and developed a special interest in the Bakgatha tribe of Botswana who adopted her as their adviser and Mmarona (mother). Better known for her novels than her poetry, her interest in classical mythology is reflected in her first book, *The Corn King and the Spring Queen*(1931). A prolific writer, her range includes biographies, children's stories and science fiction. *The Delicate Fire* (1933), *The Cleansing of the Knife* (1978).

Munro, Madeline *The Chant, A Highland Farm Childhood* (1983).

NicDhomhnaill, Mairi (Mary MacDonald) b. Grimsay, North Uist. She is a schoolteacher on Skye. *Mo Lorgan Fhin* (*My own Footprints*) (1985).

NicGilleain, Catriona (Catherine MacLean) (*fl.* 1680). She lived on the island of Coll and was composing verses in the latter part of the seventeenth century. See Derick Thomson, *An Introduction to Gaelic Poetry*.

NicGumaraid, Catriona (Catriona Montgomery) b. 1947, Skye. She and her sister, Morag, published their early poems in *A'Choille Chiar* (1974).

Nic a Phearsain, Mairi (Mary MacPherson) – Mairi Mhor Nan Oran ('Big Mary of the Songs')(1821–98). Born in Skye, she lived in Inverness and Glasgow. She was seventeen stone in weight and became something of a local legend because of her championship of social causes. She wrote and sang many songs on political issues and her 'Brosnachadh nan Gaidheal' ('Incitement to the Gaels') on the subject of land reform became popular and is reputed to have influenced the election of land-reform candidates in the Highlands between 1885 and 1886.

Nighean Alasdair Ruaidh, Mairi (Mary MacLeod)(*c*.1615–1706) b. Rodel on Harris. She was the daughter of Alexander MacLeod, a descendant of the chief of the clan. She was employed as a nurse in the chief's household but banished when she wrote songs which the chief disapproved of. She lived on Mull for many years, but returned to Harris upon agreeing not to write any more songs. *Gaelic Songs of Mary MacLeod*, ed. J. Carmichael Watson (1982).

Nighean Mhic Raghnaill, Sileas (Sheila MacDonald)(*c*.1660–1729). She was the daughter of Gilliesbuig, Chief of MacDonalds. She married Alexander Gordon of Camdell in 1685.

Ogilvy, Dorothea Maria of Clova (1823–95). Granddaughter of an Earl of Airlie, her work shows great sympathy for the plight of the poor. *My*

Thoughts: Poems (1870), *Poems* (1873), *Willie Webster's Wooing and Wedding on the Braes of Angus* (1868).

Oliphant, Carolina (the younger) (1807–31).

Oliphant, Carolina (Lady Nairne) (1766–1845). One of the most prolific songwriters of her day, she wrote upwards of eighty-seven songs to traditional airs, all of which appeared under her pseudonym 'Mrs Bogan of Bogan'. It was only after her death that her works were published in her own name. See Charles Rogers (ed.), *Life and Songs of the Baroness Nairne* (1869).

Pagan, Isobel ('Tibbie')(1741–1821). She lived in Muirkirk in Ayrshire. Born deformed, she is reputed to have lived an 'irregular' life. The hovel in which she lived was described as 'a favourite houf of the gentlemen of the neighbourhood, who, while they enjoyed her smuggled whiskey, made merry over her shafts of humour and wit, and took pleasure in hearing her sing'. For an account of her life see *The Ayrshire Contemporaries of Burns* (1840). *A Collection of Songs and Poems* (n.d.).

Paulin, Dorothy Margaret (1904 –?). She wrote mainly in the vernacular. *Country Gold and other Poems* (1936), *The Wan Water* (1939), *Solway Tide* (1957), *Springtime by Loch Ken and other Poems* (1963).

Quarrell, Christine. She was born and lives in Glasgow. Her work has appeared in *Original Prints II*.

Raine, Kathleen Jessie (1908–). Poet and scholar, her work deals mainly with the Scottish landscape, particularly of the Wester Ross area. She has published three volumes of her autobiography *Farewell Happy Fields* (1973), *The Land Unknown* (1975) and *The Lion's Mouth* (1977), and many critical works. *Stone and Flower* (1943), *Collected Poems* (1981).

Ransford, Tessa (1938–) b. India, educated in Scotland and lives in Edinburgh where she is director of the Scottish Poetry Library. *Poetry of Persons* (as Tessa Stiven) (1976), *While it is yet Day* (1977), *Light of the Mind* (1980), *Fools and Angels* (1984), *Shadows from the Greater Hill*(1988).

Reynolds, Margaret (1937–) *Original Prints II* (Polygon).

Rich, Vera, *Heritage of Dreams* (1964).

Richardson, Maimie A. (n.d.) *Moods and Dreams* (1926), *The Song of Gold* (1928), *Poems* (1931).

Robertson, Bell (of New Pitsligo, Aberdeenshire). A ballad singer of the north-east, she also wrote poetry (mainly religious verse) and modern versions of old ballad stories. See David Buchan, *The Ballad and the Folk* (1972) and *The Greig-Duncan Folk Song Collection*, Vol. II. *Lays of Buchan and other poems* (1906).

Robertson, Edith Anne (1883–1973), *Voices frae the City of Trees* (1955), *Collected Ballads and Poems in the Scots Tongue* (1967), *Translations into the Scots Tongue of Poems by Gerard Manley Hopkins* (1968), *Forest Voices* (1969).

Robertson, Jeannie (1908–75) b. Aberdeen. She was of a travelling family and was one of the most significant traditional singers of her day. She was first 'discovered' and recorded by Hamish Henderson in 1953 and her tapes are now in the archive of the School of Scottish Studies at Edinburgh University. For her services to folksong she was awarded the M.B.E. See Herschel Gower and James Porter, 'Jeannie Robertson: The Child Ballads', *Scottish Studies*, vol. 14, part one, 1970; 'Jeannie Robertson: The "Other Ballads"', *Scottish Studies*, vol. 16, part two, 1972; 'Jeannie Robertson: The Lyric Songs', *Scottish Studies*, vol. 21, 1977.

Robertson, Jenny. She has worked as a social worker in Glasgow and Liverpool. She spent a year at the University of Warsaw and spent one summer working with victims of concentration camps and ex-slave labourers. She has published a number of children's books and her play, *Aida of Leningrad*, was performed in Edinburgh in 1986. *Beyond the Border, Ghetto*.

Rose, Dilys (1954–). She was brought up in Glasgow and now lives in Edinburgh. She was awarded a Scottish Arts Council Bursary in 1985 and her work has appeared in *Chapman, Cencrastus, New Writing Scotland* and *Original Prints II*.

Rutherford, Alison (Mrs Cockburn) (1712–94) A distant cousin of Sir Walter Scott, she lived in Edinburgh after her husband's death and became part of the literati there. Noted more for her correspondence with David Hume, her most significant piece of poetry is this version of 'The Flowers of the Forest'.

Scott-Moncrieff, Ann (Agnes Shearer) (1914–43) b. Orkney. She worked as a journalist on *The Orcadian* but left Orkney when she was eighteen to work in London where she met and married the writer George Scott-Moncrieff. They returned to live in Scotland where she contributed regularly to BBC programmes. She also published children's stories – *Aboard the Bulger, The White Drake* and *Aunti Robbo* – and wrote short stories. Her poetry was published in *An Anthology of Orkney Verse*. She died at the early age of twenty-nine. See Edwin Muir's memorial poem, 'To Ann Scott-Moncrieff'.

Shepherd, Nan (1893–1981) Poet, novelist and critic, she was educated at Aberdeen University where she later received an honorary degree. For most of her life she worked as a lecturer in English at Aberdeen College of Education. She wrote three novels – *The Quarry Wood* (1928), *The Weatherhouse* (1930), *A Pass in the Grampians* (1933). *In the Cairngorms* (1934).

Shirer, Annie (of Kininmonth, Lonmay, Aberdeenshire) (n.d.) A dressmaker, she sent many songs to the collector Andrew Greig and in his articles in *The Buchan Observer* he acknowledged her contributions under the name 'A Kininmonth Lassie'. She also sent contributions for the *Rymour Club Miscellanea*. See *The Greig-Duncan Folk Song Collection*, vol. II.

Simpson, Margaret Winefride (n.d.). *Day's End: Poems in Scots and English* (1929), *The Amber Love: Poems from the French into Scots* (1932), *The Wind's Heart* (1934), *Keys of Morning* 1935), *Aisles of Song: Poems in Scots and English* (1937), *Heart's Country* (1945), *This Land of Moray* (1956).

Smith, Alison (1962–). She was born in Inverness and studied English at Aberdeen and Cambridge Universities. She now teaches at Strathclyde University. Her work has appeared in *The Scotsman*, *The New Statesman*, *New Writing Scotland* and *Original Prints II*.

Smith, Morelle (n.d.) *The Star Reader* (1979).

Spottiswoode, Alicia Anne (Lady John Scott) (1810–1900). A collector of traditional songs, she reworked many of them and also produced a great number of her own. See *Songs and Verses*, ed. E. David Douglas (1904).

Stuart, Alice V. (1899–?) b. Rangoon. Educated at St Hilda's School, Edinburgh and Somerville College, Oxford, she settled in Edinburgh and became a teacher. She was a founder-member of the Scottish Association for the Speaking of Verse. She also wrote a biography, *David Gray: The Poet of Luggie* (1961). *The Far Calling* (1944), *The Dark Tarn* (1953), *The Door Between* (1963), *The Unquiet Tide* (1971).

Swan, Annie Shepherd (1859–1943) b. Leith. She married James Burnett Smith and lived in London between 1896 and 1908. She published her first novel, *Aldersyde*, in 1883 and thereafter became a prolific, and popular, writer of romances. Her autobiography, *My Life*, was published in 1934.

Symon, Mary (1863–1938) *Deveron Days* (1933).

Taylor, Rachel Annand (1876–1960) b. Aberdeen and educated at Aberdeen University, she married and moved to Dundee and then to London. She wrote a number of prose works: *Aspects of the Italian Renaissance* (1923), *Leonardo the Florentine* (1923), *Dunbar the Poet and his Period* (1931). In 1943 she was given an Hon. LLD from Aberdeen University. *Poems* (1904), *Rose and Vine* (1909), *The Hours of Fiametta* (1910), *The End of Fiammetta* (1923).

Walker, Mrs (of Rayne, Aberdeenshire) (n.d.) See *The Greig-Duncan Folk Song Collection*, vol. II.

Walker, Meg (Mrs Margaret Caldwell of Lochwinnoch). A widow living at Bridgend in Lochwinnoch, she contributed to Andrew Crawfurd's collections. See *Andrew Crawford's Collection of Ballads and Songs* vol. I. (ed. Emily B. Lyle) Scottish Text Society, vol. 9.

Walton, Dorothy Seward (n.d.) *When Evening comes in the City* (1934).

Wells, Nannie K. b. Morayshire. Educated in Berlin, Paris, Aberdeen and St Andrews. She was a novelist, playwright and journalist. *Twentieth Century Mother and Other Poems* (1953).

Wood, Wendy (1892–1981) A noted champion of Scottish independence, she was also an artist and broadcaster ('Auntie Gwen' of BBC's *Children's Hour*). See *Astronauts and Tinkers*, ed. Joy Hendry (1985).

Acknowledgements

The royalties from this book will be donated to Shelter (The Scottish Campaign for the Homeless). This has been made possible through the generosity of the writers whose work appears in this collection. When I approached these women and asked them to contribute their work, I was impressed both by their generosity of spirit and by their wholehearted support for the project. To say 'thank you' in these circumstances seems inadequate, but is offered with all sincerity.

For permission to publish copyright material, acknowledgement is made to: Sheena Blackhall, Kate Y. A. Bone, Rhoda Bulter, Janet Caird, Catherine Czerkawska, Sally Evans, Alison Fell, Margaret Brown Gillies, Valerie Gillies, Sue Gutteridge, Lizzie Higgins, Kathleen Jamie, Jessie Kesson, Liz Lochhead, Ellie MacDonald, Elise McKay, Angela McSeveney, Naomi Mitchison, Madeline Munro, Christine Quarrell, Kathleen Raine, Tessa Ransford, Margaret Reynolds, Vera Rich, Jenny Robertson, Dilys Rose, Alison Smith and Morelle Smith.

The following holders of copyright are also acknowledged: Cora Cuthbert and Joy Hendry for the poetry of Wendy Wood; Sheila Clouston for the poetry of Nan Shepherd; Mrs Marjorie Lingen-Hutton for the poetry of Violet Jacob; Helena Shire for the poetry of Olive Fraser. Dr Emily Lyle and Professor John MacQueen of the Scottish Text Society are thanked for their permission to publish ballads from *Andrew Crawfurd's Collection of Ballads and Songs*, as are Michael C. Metson and the Aberdeen University Studies Committee for their permission to publish ballads from *The Greig-Duncan Folk Song Collection*. Hamish Henderson, Herschel Gower and James Porter are thanked for the text of Jeannie Robertson's ballads, and Stephanie D. L. Smith for the texts of Lizzie Higgins's ballads.

For permission to reprint from works listed, acknowledgment is made to the following publishing houses:

ABERDEEN UNIVERSITY PRESS: Flora Garry *Ten North-East Poets*; Olive Fraser *The Pure Account* and *The Wrong Music*; Edith Anne Robertson *Collected Poems and Ballads, The Greig-Duncan Folk Song Collection*. AKROS: Catherine Czerkawska *A Book of Men*; Flora Garry *Bennygoak and other poems*. ALLEN AND UNWIN: Kathleen Raine *Collected Poems, 1935-1980*. BLACKIE AND SON: Isobel Wylie Hutchison *North to the Rime-Ringed Sun*. BLIND SERPENT PRESS: Margaret Brown Gillies *Looking Towards Light*. CANONGATE: Valerie Gillies *Bed of Stone, Each Bright Eye;* Naomi Mitchison *The Cleansing of the Knife*. CASTLELAW PRESS: Kate Y. A. Bone *Thistle By-Laws*. RICHARD DREW: Naomi Mitchison *The Bull Calves*. ERUMWELL PRESS: Morelle Smith *The Star Reaper*. HERITAGE SOCIETY OF SCOTLAND: Wendy Wood *Astronauts and Tinkers*. L. ELKIN MATTHEWS: Rachel Annand Taylor

Poems. KIRKWALL PRESS: Vera Rich *Heritage of Dreams*. THE MORAY PRESS: Nan Shepherd *In the Cairngorms*. JOHN MURRAY: Violet Jacob *Songs of Angus*. OLIVER AND BOYD: Marion Lochhead *Fiddlers Bidding;* Jessie B. MacArthur, *Last Leave;* Mary Symon *A Scots Anthology*. OUTPOST PUBLICATIONS: Elise McKay *Unravelling Knots;* Margaret Brown Gillies, *Give me the Hill-Run Boys, Hares on the Horizon, The Voice on the Marshes*. POLYGON: Christine Cherry, Sue Gutteridge, Ellie MacDonald, Angela McSeveney, Christine Quarrell, Margaret Reynolds, Jenny Robertson, Dilys Rose, Alison Smith. *Original Prints II;* Liz Lochhead *Dreaming Frankenstein*. PORPOISE PRESS: Marion Angus *The Turn of the Day*. RAINBOW BOOKS: Sheena Blackhall *The Cyard's Kist*. RAMSAY HEAD PRESS: Janet Caird *A Distant Urn, Some Walk a Narrow Path;* Alice V. Stuart *The Unquiet Tide;* Tessa Ransford *Fools and Angels, Shadows from the Greater Hills*. REPROGRAPHIA: Liz Lochhead *Memo for Spring*. SERIF BOOKS: Helen B. Cruickshank *Selected Poems*. THULEPRINT: Rhoda Bulter *A Nev foo a Coarn*. VIRAGO: Alison Fell *Kisses for Mayakovsky*. YORICK BOOKS: Madeline Munro *The Chant*.

Acknowledgment is also due to the proprietors and editors of the following journals: *Cencrastus, Chapman, The Edinburgh Review, Gairm, Lines,* and *Scottish Studies*.

In the research for this collection many people have unstintingly offered their time, energy and knowledge, but very special thanks are due to the following: Tessa Ransford, Tom Hubbard and the Staff of the Scottish Poetry Library whose tireless efforts on behalf of Scottish poetry cannot be praised enough; Emily Lyle, editor of *The Greig-Duncan Folk Song Collection,* upon whose knowledge of the ballad and popular culture I have frequently drawn; the many colleagues, students and friends – male and female – in Edinburgh and Guelph whose interest and support sustained me in the difficult times. To the staff of Edinburgh University Library, the National Library of Scotland, the School of Scottish Studies and the library of the University of Guelph, I am indebted for the invaluable help they gave me in tracking down such of the lost or buried material which appears in this collection.

For their professional excellence and enthusiastic assistance I owe a great thanks to the staff of Edinburgh University Press. Also to Martin Spencer, the late Secretary to the Press, who gave me great encouragement with this project, and whose untimely death is a great blow to Scottish publishing.

In some cases it has been impossible to trace authors and executors, and so for the use of unauthorised insertions or for any omissions, forbearance is asked. If omissions or errors are forwarded to me, correction will be made in any subsequent reprint.

Catherine Kerrigan

I would like to thank the following:
Colm O Baoill for his editions of songs by Síleas na Ceapaich. Dòmhnall Meek for his editions of songs by Màiri Mhór nan Oran. J. L. Campbell for

ACNOWLEDGEMENTS

his editions of waulking songs. Màiri NicDhòmhnaill, Catriona Montgomery and Anne Frater for permission to include their own poems and English translations. Ronald Black, Dòmhnall Meek and John MacInnes for advice. Derick Thomson for his *Introduction to Gaelic Poetry* which was my starting point in making the selection. William Matheson, Flora MacNeill and others whose singing has brought these songs alive.

Meg Bateman

Index of First Lines

First lines of translations from the Gaelic are enclosed in square brackets.